GENE⟩ D0355773

HIS CAMPAIGNS IN VIRGINIA

1861-1865

WITH PERSONAL REMINISCENCES

BY

WALTER H. TAYLOR

ADJUTANT-GENERAL OF THE
ARMY OF NORTHERN VIRGINIA, C. S. A.

Introduction to the Bison Book Edition
by Gary W. Gallagher

University of Nebraska Press
Lincoln and London

Introduction copyright 1994 by the University of Nebraska Press
Manufactured in the United States of America

First Bison Book printing: 1994

⊗
The paper in this book meets the minimum requirements of American National Standard for Information Sciences—Permanence of Paper for Printed Library Materials, ANSI Z39.48–1984

Library of Congress Cataloging-in-Publication Data
Taylor, Walter Herron, 1838–1916.
General Lee, his campaigns in Virginia, 1861–1865: with personal reminiscences / by Walter H. Taylor; introd. to the Bison Book edition by Gary W. Gallagher.
p.   cm.
Previously published: c1906.
Includes bibliographical references.
ISBN 0-8032-9425-5
1. Virginia—History—Civil War, 1861–1865—Campaigns.
2. Lee, Robert E. (Robert Edward), 1807–1870.   3. United States—History—Civil War, 1861–1865—Campaigns.   4. Taylor, Walter Herron, 1838–1916.   I. Title.   II. Title: General Lee.
E470.2.T26   1994
973.7′3—dc20
94-27831   CIP

Originally published in 1906 by Nusbaum Books, Norfolk, Va. The maps have been redrawn for this Bison Book edition. The frontispiece photo has been added.

General Robert E. Lee flanked by his son, Custis (left), and the author, Walter Herron Taylor (right), in a photograph taken by Mathew Brady a week after Appomattox.

INTRODUCTION

by Gary W. Gallagher

Photographer Mathew Brady persuaded R. E. Lee to sit for a series of portraits at the general's residence in Richmond, Virginia, a week after Appomattox. In one of the images (see frontispiece), a seated Lee peers directly at the camera, his face betraying the immense strain of recent events. Standing at either side of Lee, each with one hand on the back of his chair, are the general's eldest son Custis and Walter Herron Taylor, former adjutant general of the Army of Northern Virginia. Both younger men gaze away from the probing lens, adding to the impact of Lee's intense visage. The three figures, all dressed in uniform, convey no sense of humiliation in this memorable study of soldiers in the immediate aftermath of an unsuccessful struggle for independence.

Walter H. Taylor had served Lee faithfully through virtually the entire conflict and surely belonged beside his chief in the days following Appomattox. The son of Walter Herron Taylor and Cornelia Wickham Cowdery Taylor, he was born on June 13, 1838, in Norfolk, Virginia. Reared in a family prominent among that city's business community, the young Taylor attended a private school run by Serena Holden for his initial instruction and later entered the Norfolk Academy, a respected educational institution founded in 1728. Giles B. Cooke, a longtime friend who also had been on Lee's staff, recalled late in life that as "a boy Walter Taylor entered into all our sports with spirit and zest and was among the foremost in his studies at school, being equally popular with boys and girls." Taylor compiled a good record at Norfolk Academy under the watchful eye of headmaster John Bowie Strange, an alumnus of the Virginia Military Institute who had added military science to the Academy's curriculum in 1845. Strange likely influenced Taylor's decision to seek admittance to VMI, recently founded in the Shenandoah Valley town of Lexington, where the young man embarked on a new phase of his studies in 1853.[1]

Circumstances prevented Taylor's completing a full career at VMI. Despite a brush with dismissal stemming from the overzealous hazing of a fellow cadet, he excelled academically during two years at the Institute. At the end of his third-class (sophomore) year in 1855, he ranked first in mathematics, second in Latin and drawing, tenth in composition and declamation, and first in general merit among the thirty-one members of his class. He also had earned the fewest demerits. Returning to Lexington for his second-class year in the fall of 1855, Taylor departed there upon learning his father had succumbed to yellow fever during an epidemic that swept through Norfolk. Colonel Francis H. Smith, superintendent of the Institute, sought to make it possible for Taylor to complete his schooling despite the tragedy, but the young man replied that his family needed him. He had examined his father's financial affairs closely and determined that he could, at age seventeen, take up the burden as head of the household. With the approval of his relatives, and the advantage of stock "amounting to $14,000 at [the] smallest possible calculation," Taylor concluded that pursuing a career in business "was the path of my future life pointed out by Providence."[2]

The next five years brought several changes. The Panic of 1857 and lingering effects from the yellow fever epidemic hampered Norfolk's economy, forcing the sale of the family's company in the winter of 1857. Taylor worked variously as a clerk with the Bank of Virginia, an auditor with the Norfolk and Petersburg Railroad, and, beginning in March 1859, first accountant for the Bank of Virginia.[3]

John Brown's raid on Harpers Ferry in October 1859 opened another chapter in Taylor's career. As with many other young Virginians, Taylor responded to events at Harpers Ferry by joining a volunteer militia company. Elected orderly sergeant of Norfolk's "Southern Guard," which soon became a company in Virginia's Fifty-fourth Regiment of Militia, he watched national events race toward the election of 1860 and its disruptive aftermath. In mid-April 1861, the firing on Fort Sumter and Abraham Lincoln's call for 75,000 volunteers to put down the rebellion prompted Virginia to join the seven Deep South states that had seceded during the winter of 1860–61. Taylor's company was mustered into state service on April 30 as Company G of the Sixth Virginia Infantry, with Walter holding a second lieutenant's commission. Shortly thereafter, R. L. Page, first cousin of R. E. Lee and Taylor's uncle by marriage, recommended his young kinsman for advancement. Taylor recounted his subsequent posting to Lee's staff in a reminiscence published in 1877: "On the 2nd day of May, 1861, in obedience to telegraphic orders from Governor Letcher, I repaired to Richmond, and was at once assigned to duty at the headquarters of the Army of Virginia."[4] A promotion to captain of Virginia forces on May 31, 1861, soon gave way to a first lieutenancy of infantry in the Confederate States Army to rank from July 16, 1861. Advanced to captain on December 10, 1861, to major of cavalry on April 21, 1862, and, finally, to lieutenant colonel on January 15, 1864, Taylor witnessed all the major campaigns associated with the Army of Northern Virginia from a position at the center of Confederate operations in the Eastern Theater.[5]

Service on Lee's staff involved an overwhelming burden of work, frequent frustration, and the privilege of working closely with a man whom Taylor came to respect deeply. Lee detested paperwork and quickly perceived that Taylor, the youngest member of his staff, possessed formidable bureaucratic gifts. A mounting tide of forms and other documents crossed Taylor's desk, as Lee increasingly relied on him to assure the efficient flow of paper at headquarters.[6] Loath to assemble a large staff, Lee ran the Army of Northern Virginia with a relative handful of officers, an element of his military personality that historians have criticized. Taylor sometimes bridled at the volume of work and his chief's refusal to enlarge the staff. In late summer 1864, for example, he confided to a friend after one tense exchange with Lee, "He is so unreasonable and provoking at times; I might serve under him for ten years to come and couldn't *love* him at the end of that period." Immediately after this flare-up the general gave Taylor a peach, prompting a somewhat wistful "Ah! but he is a queer old genius. I suppose it is so with all great men." Earlier Taylor had complained that other generals had "ten, twenty, and thirty Adjt. generals" on their staffs, while Lee had only himself. He labored long hours, hoping only to hear that "I please *my general*." He protested, "Everybody else makes me flattering speeches, but I want to satisfy *him*. They all say he appreciates my efforts but I don't believe it, you know how silly and sensitive I am."[7]

"The Tycoon," as Lee's staff sometimes called him, did appreciate Taylor. Douglas Southall Freeman, Lee's most famous biographer, observed that the youthful aide "soon made himself indispensable" after arriving in Richmond in May 1861. Because he expected each man to do his full duty, Lee exercised great restraint in singling out members of his staff for public praise. In January 1863, however, he spoke glowingly of Taylor in supporting his promotion to lieutenant colonel: "He is intelligent, industrious, and acquainted in the discharge of his duties, and his character irreproachable—I know of no better person for the appointment." G. Moxley Sorrel of James Longstreet's staff observed in his postwar reminiscence that while the commanding general had no real chief of staff the "officer practically nearest its duties was his extremely efficient adjutant, Walter Taylor." Certainly Lee would not have entrusted such responsibilities to a man whose abilities he questioned in the least.[8]

As with many ambitious and patriotic officers assigned to staff duty, Taylor longed to take a more active role on the battlefield. He may have looked to Lee as a model in this regard. During the war with Mexico, he surely knew, Lee had rendered remarkable service in the field while serving on Winfield Scott's staff. A few opportunities came Taylor's way. Late in the afternoon on May 10, 1864, word reached army headquarters that a Union assault had breached the western face of the Mule Shoe salient at Spotsylvania. Lee mounted to go to the point of danger, but Taylor and others held him back. "Then you must see to it that the ground is recovered," insisted the general, whereupon the staff spurred into action. Taylor hurried toward the fighting, where he took up a standard and joined other officers in directing a successful counterattack. Ten months later, along the White Oak Road outside Petersburg, Taylor again responded to a Federal threat with daring behavior under fire. A northern attack had just obtained possession of the road when "a fine looking young man, distinguished for his superb gallantry, rode up," recalled a witness to Taylor's appearance on the battlefield. "He galloped in front and between the lines, waved his hat, and shouted 'Come ahead boys! . . . .' The scene cannot be pictured and the enthusiasm cannot be imagined. With one redoubled and unceasing cheer, the line went forward and crushed everything in its path."[9]

Military affairs alone did not occupy Taylor's thoughts during the last days of the war. As the Army of Northern Virginia completed preparations for the evacuation of Richmond on April 2, 1865, he asked Lee's permission for a brief leave to marry his fiancé, Elizabeth Selden Saunders. Somewhat taken aback, the general nonetheless agreed, and the couple managed to be married shortly after midnight. They enjoyed a few bittersweet hours with friends before Taylor "[s]omewhere near four o'clock on the morning of the 3d of April . . . bade farewell to all my dear ones" and set out to rejoin Lee. A long life together lay ahead for the Taylors, during which they would rear a family of four daughters and four sons. Thoughts of the future likely mingled with awareness of a grim present as Taylor rode through Richmond toward the James River, taking in a scene of fires and smoke accompanied by a series of explosions near the Rocketts section of the city.[10]

Taylor returned to Norfolk after Appomattox and built an enviable reputation as a businessman. After declining an offer from Francis H. Smith in August 1865 to become treasurer at VMI, he co-founded Taylor, Martin and Company, a hardware concern that grew into Taylor, Elliot and Watters Company, the largest firm of its type in Norfolk by the early 1880s. In 1873 he helped establish and served as first president of the Seaboard Fire Insurance Company (it failed in 1880); that same year he joined other leading citizens of Norfolk in launching the *Norfolk Landmark,* a newspaper guided by editor James Barron Hope to a position of great influence in the late-nineteenth century. In 1877 he accepted the presidency of the Marine Bank of Norfolk. Taylor's energies for the rest of his professional life centered on the bank, and during his thirty-nine years as president it enjoyed substantial success. Beyond this role, Taylor figured in Norfolk's economic life as a director for thirty-five years on the board of the Norfolk and Western Railroad and for twenty years as French consular agent for the city.[11]

Blessed with abundant energy, Taylor also found time for politics and other public activities. He served in the state legislature between 1869 and 1873, joining a coalition of Democrats, former Whigs, and conservative Republicans to oppose Radical Republican forces. He participated in a range of veterans' activities, serving as the first corresponding secretary of the Association of the Army of Northern Virginia (founded in 1870 in Richmond with Jubal A. Early as its president) and later joining the United Confederate Veterans. A strong supporter of the Jamestown Tercentenary Exhibition, which Norfolk hosted over a seven-month period in 1907, Taylor considered it both a tribute to the first English settlement of his state and a testament to Norfolk's emergence as a major urban center on the South Atlantic coast. He maintained ties to VMI, serving on its Board of Visitors from 1870 to 1873 and again from 1914 until 1916. His philanthropies embraced the Norfolk symphony, a pair of homes for the aged, an orphanage, and St. Paul's Normal and Industrial School in Lawrenceville, Virginia, a trade school for African-Americans.[12]

Taylor's health failed markedly during the eighteen months preceding his death. Suffering from cancer, he "looked like a stick man" to one observer in January 1915. He took radium treatments in Baltimore but expressed scant hope that the regimen would prove successful. "Meanwhile, Thank God," he confided to a friend in early 1915, "I am not suffering any pain." His end came on March 1, 1916, in Norfolk, with burial in Elmwood Cemetery. He left an estate of $186,000 to his wife, who survived him by only a few months.[13] A piece in the *Richmond Times-Dispatch* indicated how closely Virginians and other former Confederates identified Taylor with his old chief: "Few men have been more honored in life than was Col. Walter H. Taylor, of Norfolk, and few are more honored in memory than he. . . . His books, his work in later years, his service to the community will live after him. But after those will live what may be carved on his tomb: 'He was the adjutant of Lee.'"[14]

The books mentioned by the *Times-Dispatch* constitute Taylor's principal legacy. He took an early interest in postwar discussions relating to the Army of Northern Virginia, corresponding with many former comrades and contributing articles to *The Southern Historical Society Papers* and the *Philadelphia Weekly Times*.[15] As one of those closest to Lee during the battle of Gettysburg, he was drawn into the acrimonious debate about James Longstreet's conduct during the 1863 Pennsylvania campaign. Although scarcely in agreement with Longstreet's Republican politics or his questioning of

Lee's generalship at Gettysburg, Taylor defended the former commander of the First Corps against charges leveled by Jubal A. Early and others that he had disobeyed an order from Lee to attack at dawn on July 2. Early pressed Taylor to take a more antagonistic stance toward "Old Pete," prompting a response marked by integrity and a touch of humor: "I properly appreciate the bantering manner after which you will persist in affecting to misunderstand what I have said to you in regard to 'my friend,' Longstreet," Taylor wrote Early in 1876. "I have never objected to a fair discussion amongst ourselves of the various events of the war and the part taken therein by those high in command." "What Genl Longstreet did or failed to do," added Taylor, "constitutes a legitimate subject of criticism; but it is unfair . . . to cast a doubt upon his fidelity to our cause." Willing to render a harsher verdict regarding Longstreet than a year earlier, Taylor thought "Old Pete" now "should be handled with ungloved hands"—but always with the understanding that he had served the Confederacy faithfully.[16]

In his writings through the 1870s, Taylor sought especially to establish the relative strengths of the Army of Northern Virginia and the Army of the Potomac. Many former comrades, including R. E. Lee, turned to him after Appomattox for information on this subject. This made sense, Douglas Southall Freeman observes, because "Taylor had been in general charge of the monthly returns of the Army and knew perhaps more than did any other man of the effective strength of Lee's forces from June 1, 1862, onward." Well-armed with figures, Taylor hoped to demonstrate that the Army of Northern Virginia had fought valiantly against long odds and deserved admiration for its efforts. He lavished attention on the 1863 campaign in Pennsylvania. At Gettysburg, he wrote Jubal Early in 1878, any fair method of counting would reveal that "the disparity in numbers must remain, in nearly every case startling. . . ."[17]

He presented his fullest reckoning of numbers in *Four*

Years with General Lee, a slim book that appeared in 1877. The preface states that Taylor's "humble task" in this work was to provide "a summary of the more prominent events in the career of the great Confederate leader, together with a comparative statement of the strength of the Confederate and Federal armies that were engaged in the operations in Virginia." *Four Years with General Lee* succeeded in offering a concise (though uninspired stylistically) overview of the war in the East, a few excellent vignettes of army headquarters, and some personal anecdotes about its author. Typical of the laudatory reaction among southern readers, one reviewer praised Taylor for setting the record straight about "the fearful odds against which we always fought" and ended with "the hope that this book will meet with such general favor as to induce the accomplished author to write a *full* history of the campaigns of the Army of Northern Virginia."[18]

Thirty years passed before Taylor presented his "full history" of Lee and his army in *General Lee, His Campaigns in Virginia, 1861–1865, with Personal Reminiscences.*[19] A substantial improvement over *Four Years with General Lee* and its often dry analysis of figures, Taylor's second book ranks as an essential title on the Army of Northern Virginia that offers a number of insights about its commander. Far from the austere "Marble Man" so often portrayed, Taylor's Lee exhibits humor, anger, and impatience as well as consideration for others, devotion to duty, and self-denial. The passages concerning Lee's day-to-day work at headquarters are particularly revealing. The general's intense dislike for bureaucratic drudgery warred with an equally strong work ethic demanding attention to every task—a combination that sometimes produced a foul humor. "He did not enjoy writing; indeed, he wrote with labor," observes Taylor, "and nothing seemed to tax his amiability so much as the necessity for writing a lengthy official communication." Not among those "men whose temper is never ruffled," Lee responded to one onerous bit of paperwork petulantly: "He was not in a very pleasant mood. Something irritated him, and he manifested his ill humor by a little nervous twist or jerk of the neck and head, peculiar to himself, accompanied by some harshness of manner." Taylor's subsequent assurance that Lee invariably "manifested a marked degree of affability" after such episodes does nothing to lessen the impression of Lee's volatility.[20]

Overall, Taylor expresses profound admiration for Lee and his army and fits comfortably into the Lost Cause school of interpretation. He characterizes Antietam as a tactical draw rather than as a strategic failure: "Neither side could claim a victory, although General Lee had repulsed the attacks of the enemy made upon his line, and that is all that can be said of the assault on the third day at Gettysburg by the divisions of Pickett and Pettigrew. It was repulsed. . . . We hear much of one, but little of the other." As for Gettysburg, he believes Ewell missed a potentially decisive opportunity on the afternoon of July 1, stresses that Longstreet moved far too slowly on July 2, and laments the failures of Stuart's cavalry. Although Taylor strives for fairness regarding Longstreet's larger service as a Confederate, he denounces that officer's "groundless, monstrous charge" that Lee pushed the offensive on July 1 until "enough blood was shed to appease him." Typical of Lost Cause writers, Taylor praises the loyal service of slaves during the war and deplores what he labels pernicious effects on black southerners of emancipation and the "vicious legislation" enacted during Reconstruction: "[T]heir conception of freedom is unbridled license, and their tendency to a life of idleness, immorality, and crime is truly sad and disheartening." Departing from many former Confederates in admitting that slavery "was the real issue at stake" during the secession crisis of 1860–61, Taylor nonetheless attributes the commencement of hostilities to northern aggression and Abraham Lincoln's call for 75,000 volunteers.[21]

Memorable passages about people and events enliven Taylor's narrative. Vignettes of Stonewall Jackson at VMI and as a Confederate general, of Henry A. Wise during the 1861 campaign in western Virginia, and of John Bankhead Magruder during the Peninsula campaign, as well as descriptions of Fredericksburg on December 13, 1862, and Richmond on April 2–3, 1865, compare favorably with any written by other Confederates. Characters and scenes appear against a backdrop of Lee's army resisting a more powerful foe until finally, in the face of unforgiving numerical reality, the end came at Appomattox: "Attrition had done its work—" states Taylor, "the career of the Army of Northern Virginia was closed and its banners furled; but the record of its achievements glows with undiminished splendor and constrains the admiration of the world."[22]

Available for the first time in paperback with maps prepared for this edition,[23] *General Lee* can instruct anyone interested in the war in Virginia. Taylor experienced the conflict from an enviable position, tried within the limits of one who venerated Lee and his army to render honest judgments, and produced a superior account. A striking counterpoise to recent literature critical of Lee, it will help readers understand why so many people have seen the Virginian as perhaps the greatest American captain.[24] The work of both admirers and critics should be consulted by diligent students, and Walter Taylor's book remains a necessary title for those hoping to make an informed judgment about Lee.

NOTES

1. Emanuel Meyer, "Walter Herron Taylor and His Era," unpublished M.A. thesis, Old Dominion University, 1984, pp. 1, 6–8, 12–14; Giles B. Cook[e], "Col. W. H. Taylor, A. A. G. Army of Northern Virginia: An Appreciation," in *Confederate Veteran* 34 (May 1916): 234.

2. Taylor's class rankings and other information relating to his career at the Institute may be found in his file in the VMI Archives, Preston Library, Virginia Military Institute, Lexington, Virginia [repository cited hereafter as VMIA]. His reasons for deciding not to

return to VMI are set forth in Walter H. Taylor to My Dear Friend [Francis H. Smith], September 24, 1855, VMIA.

3. Meyer, "Walter Herron Taylor," pp. 21, 24–25, 28.

4. Ibid., pp. 30, 32, 36; Walter H. Taylor, *Four Years with General Lee* (1877; reprint ed., Bloomington, Ind.: Indiana University Press, 1962), p. 11.

5. Walter Herron Taylor, Compiled Service Record, M331, Roll 243, National Archives, Washington, D.C. Taylor's promotion to major in the cavalry is an odd facet of his Confederate service about which the records offer no further details.

6. See Taylor, Compiled Service Record, for documents that suggest the scale of paperwork at headquarters. For example, a requisition dated September 22, 1863, requested six reams of letter paper, two thousand official envelopes, one thousand letter envelopes, and three boxes of pens. Taylor's justification for this order was a curt "supply exhausted."

7. Walter H. Taylor to B. Saunders, August 15, 1864 (first quotation), Taylor to Saunders, November 21, 1863 (second and third quotations), quoted in Meyer, "Walter Herron Taylor," pp. 48, 44. For a critique of Lee's inadequate staff by an officer who served as his chief of ordnance between June and September 1862, see Edward Porter Alexander, *Fighting for the Confederacy: The Personal Recollections of General Edward Porter Alexander,* ed. Gary W. Gallagher (Chapel Hill, N.C.: University of North Carolina Press, 1989), pp. 236, 273, 419.

8. Douglas Southall Freeman, *R. E. Lee: A Biography,* 4 vols. (New York: Charles Scribner's Sons, 1935–36), 1: 489; R. E. Lee to Confederate War Department, January 7, 1863, quoted in Meyer, "Walter Herron Taylor," p. 50; G. Moxley Sorrel, *Recollections of a Confederate Staff Officer* (1905; reprint ed., Wilmington, N.C.: Broadfoot Publishing Company, 1987), p. 69.

9. Freeman, *R. E. Lee,* 3: 313–14; Meyer, "Walter Herron Taylor," p. 54. For Lee's quotation to Taylor, see p. 240 of the text below.

10. For Taylor's quotation and account of his marriage, see pp. 277–78 of the text below.

11. Meyer, "Walter Herron Taylor," pp. 79, 93, 98, 101, 117, 155.

12. Ibid., 84, 87, 101, 104, 130, 152; J. William Jones and others, eds., *The Southern Historical Society Papers,* 52 vols. and three-vol. index (1876–1959; reprint ed., Wilmington, N.C.: Broadfoot Publishing Company, 1990–92), 2: 159 [set cited hereafter as *SHSP*]. On

the Jamestown Tercentenary Exposition, see Michael Kammen, *Mystic Chords of Memory: The Transformation of Tradition in American Culture* (New York: Alfred A. Knopf, 1991), pp. 130, 145, 267, 496.

13. Meyer, "Walter Herron Taylor," pp. 160–62 (Taylor's quotation is from a letter to L. E. Johnson, January 19, 1915).

14. Quoted in *Confederate Veteran* 24 (May 1916): 235.

15. For examples of Taylor's writings, see *SHSP* 4: 80–87, 124–39, 5: 239–46, and [Alexander K. McClure, ed.,] *The Annals of the War, Written by Leading Participants North and South* (Philadelphia: The Times Publishing Company, 1879), pp. 305–18. The piece in *Annals* first appeared in the *Philadelphia Weekly Times*, August 25, 1877.

16. Walter H. Taylor to Jubal A. Early, May 2, 1876, Jubal A. Early Papers, Library of Congress, Washington, D.C. Taylor's letter to Longstreet concerning the alleged "sunrise attack order" on the second day at Gettysburg is printed in *SHSP* 5: 75–76.

17. Douglas Southall Freeman, *The South to Posterity: An Introduction to the Writing of Confederate History* (1939; reprint ed., Wilmington, N.C.: Broadfoot's Bookmark, 1983), p. 64; Walter H. Taylor to Jubal A. Early, February 12, 1878, Jubal A. Early Papers, Library of Congress.

18. Taylor, *Four Years with General Lee*, p. [xiv]; *SHSP* 5: 96.

19. Printed by Braunworth Press of Brooklyn and distributed by the Nusbaum Book and News Company of Norfolk, the book carried an imprint date of 1906. Taylor had intended to publish with Doubleday-Page and Company of New York; however, demands that he revise his manuscript extensively, including a drastic reduction of the sections "which have to do wholly or chiefly with military affairs," prompted him to publish the book himself. Advertisements in *Confederate Veteran* magazine and elsewhere offered *General Lee* for $2.00 "postpaid to any address." I am indebted to Robert K. Krick, chief historian at Fredericksburg and Spotsylvania National Military Park, for information about Taylor's dealings with Doubleday-Page.

20. The quotations are on pages 25, 156, and 157 of the text below. Edward Porter Alexander also refers to Lee's habit of jerking his head when upset, calling it "that peculiar little shake of his head which he used when he was worried, & which we used to call snapping at his ear." Alexander, *Fighting for the Confederacy*, pp. 389–90.

21. The quotations are on pages 137, 195, 266–67, and 8 in the text

below. Taylor's overreliance on John B. Gordon's undependable post-war reminiscences underscore his Lost Cause approach. On the development of the myth of the Lost Cause, see Gaines M. Foster, *Ghosts of the Confederacy: Defeat, the Lost Cause, and the Emergence of the New South* (New York: Oxford University Press, 1987) and Thomas L. Connelly, *The Marble Man: Robert E. Lee and His Image in American Society* (New York: Alfred A. Knopf, 1977).

22. The quotation is on page 292 of the text below.

23. The four-color maps in the original edition, several of which folded out, could not be reproduced effectively.

24. Connelly's *Marble Man* and Alan T. Nolan's *Lee Considered: General Robert E. Lee and Civil War History* (Chapel Hill, N.C. University of North Carolina Press, 1991) are among the most influential works that question Lee's reputation as a superior military leader.

PREFACE

NEARLY thirty years ago I ventured to publish "Four Years with General Lee," in which my primary object was to assist in establishing the fact of the great numerical odds against which the army under General Lee had to contend in its encounters with the Federal armies opposed to it.

General Lee had expressed a purpose to do this, and after his death, before its accomplishment, the duty seemed logically to devolve upon me.

The preparation of that monograph necessitated the presentation of much purely statistical matter, and the scope of the work embraced, in most cases, mere mention only of the campaigns of General Lee in the war between the States of the Union. While I have not attempted herein to give a critical account of the several engagements in which the army under General Lee took part, such as the military student would ask, I have endeavored to present the salient features and to give a sufficiently comprehensive account of the troops engaged, and the results achieved, to enable the general reader to form a fair idea of each of the great battles fought.

These memoirs were not originally designed for publication; but I have been so frequently urged to write more in detail concerning the matters of which I have personal knowledge, and especially of General Lee, that I have concluded to publish them, in the hope that they may contribute in some degree to the clearer understanding of the events and operations in Virginia during that interesting period, and as an humble tribute to the noble character of the Great Commander who so often led the Confederate troops to victory.

"Four Years with General Lee" is out of print, and not to be had of the publishers. I have not hesitated, therefore, to introduce occasional excerpts here from that work that serve to illustrate some trait of General Lee's character, or that seemed to add to the smoothness of the narrative.

W. H. T.

CONTENTS

CHAPTER I

CHAPTER VIII

CHAPTER IX

CHAPTER X

CHAPTER XI

CHAPTER XII

CHAPTER XIII

CHAPTER XIV

CHAPTER XV

CHAPTER XVI

CHAPTER XVII

CHAPTER XVIII

CHAPTER XIX

CHAPTER XX

CHAPTER XXI

CHAPTER XXII

CHAPTER XXIII

CHAPTER XXIV

APPENDIX

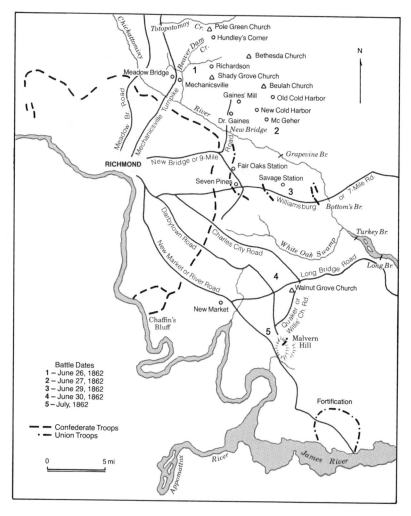

1. Battlegrounds in the Vicinity of Richmond, Va.

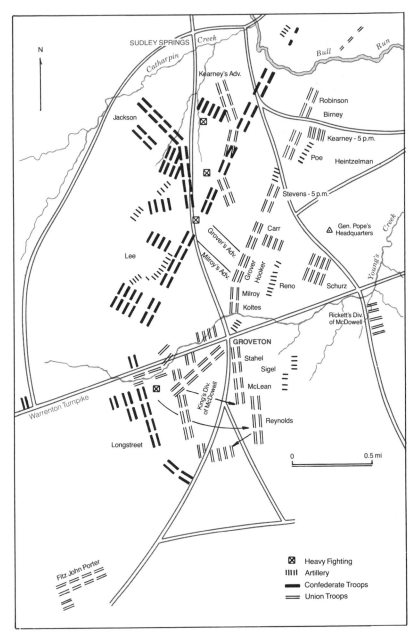

2. Battlefield of Manassas, Va., at close of the action August 29th, 1862

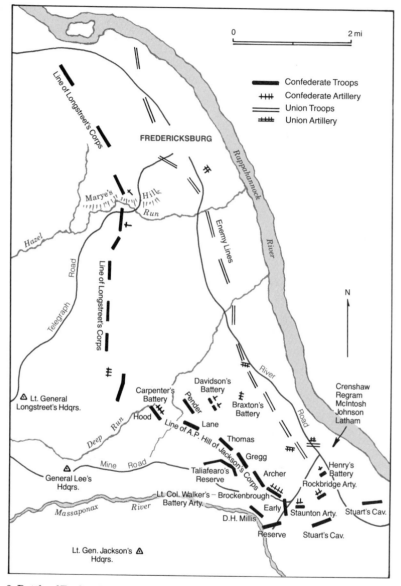

0   2 mi

Confederate Troops
Confederate Artillery
Union Troops
Union Artillery

Line of Longstreet's Corps

FREDERICKSBURG

Rappahannock

Marye's   Hill
          Run

Hazel

Enemy Lines

River

Line of Longstreet's Corps

Telegraph   Road

N

River

△ Lt. General
Longstreet's Hdqrs.

Davidson's
Battery

Crenshaw
Regram
McIntosh
Johnson
Latham

Carpenter's
Battery   Pender   Braxton's
                             Battery

Deep   Run

Hood   Line of A.P. Hill of Jackson's Corps   Lane

Thomas

Mine   Road

General Lee's △
Hdqrs.

Gregg

Road

Taliafearo's
Reserve   Archer

Henry's
Battery

Lt. Col. Walker's — Brockenbrough   Rockbridge Arty.
Battery Arty.

Massaponax   River

D.H. Millis

Early

Staunton Arty.   Stuart's Cav.

Reserve   Stuart's Cav.

Lt. Gen. Jackson's △
Hdqrs.

3. Battle of Fredericksburg, December 13th, 1862

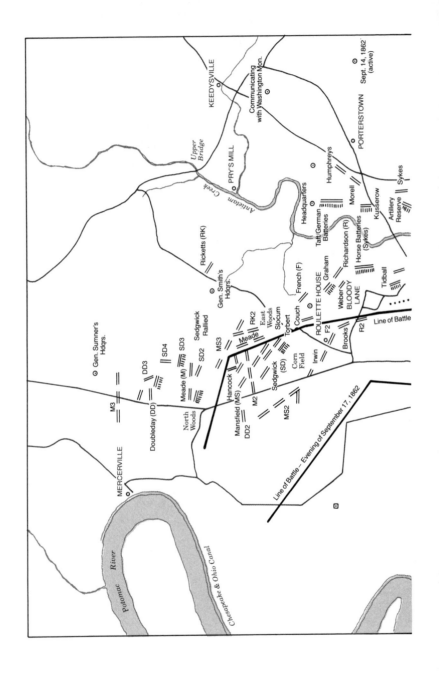

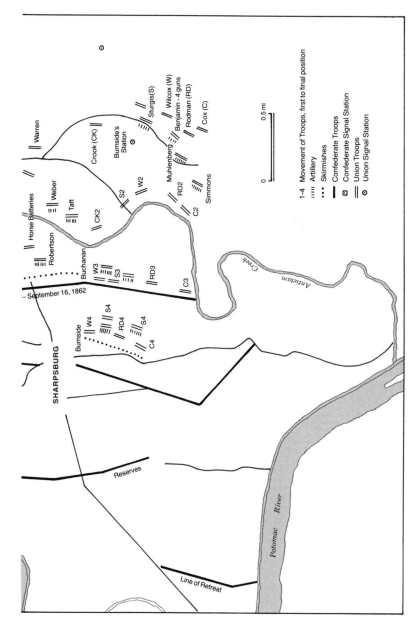

4. Battle of Antietam, September 16th and 17th, 1862

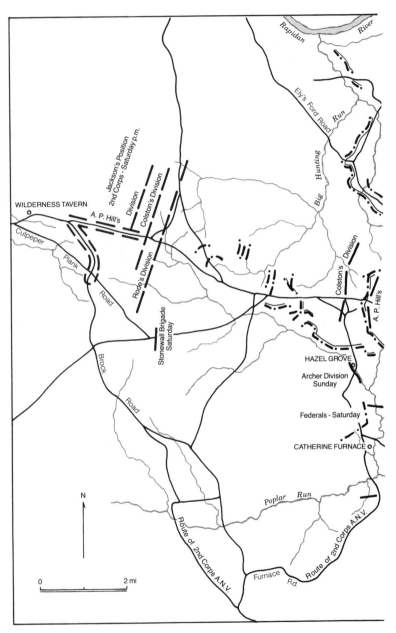

5. Battles of Chancellorsville, Salem Church, and Fredericksburg, May 2nd, 3rd, and 4th, 1863

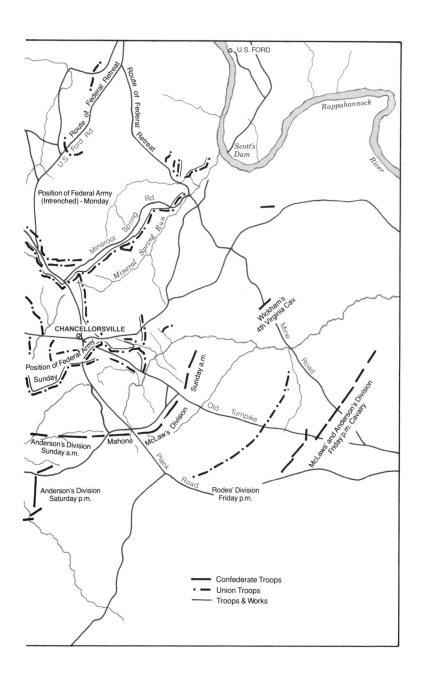

U.S. FORD

Rappahannock

River

Scott's
Dam

Route of Federal Retreat

Route of Federal Retreat

U.S. Ford Rd.

Position of Federal Army
(Intrenched) - Monday

Spring Rd.

Mineroot

Mineral Spring Run

Wickham's
4th Virginia Cav.

CHANCELLORSVILLE

Mine

Road

Position of Federal Army

Sunday

Sunday a.m.

Old Turnpike

Anderson's Division
Sunday a.m.

Mahone

McLaw's Division

Plank

Road

Rodes' Division
Friday p.m.

McLaws and Anderson's Division
Friday p.m. Cavalry

Anderson's Division
Saturday p.m.

Confederate Troops
Union Troops
Troops & Works

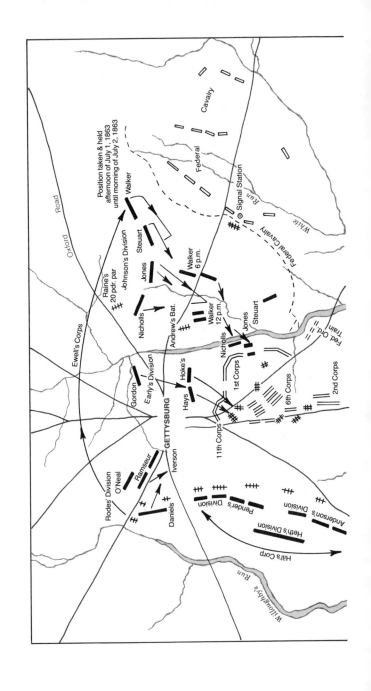

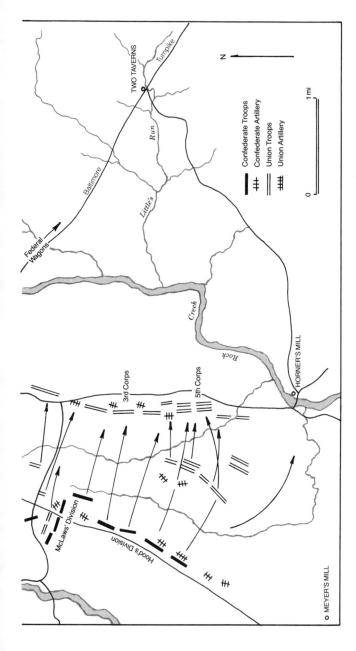

6. Battlefield of Gettysburg with position of troops, July 2nd, 1863

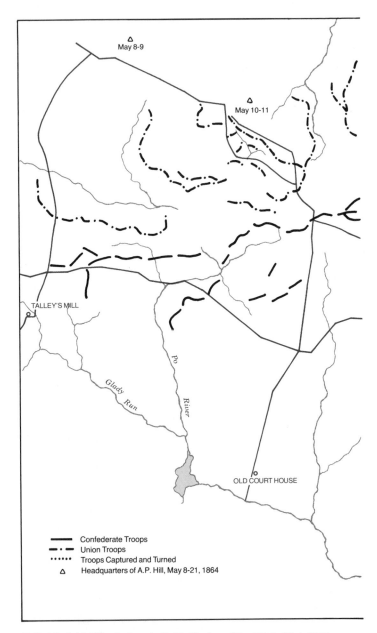

Δ
May 8-9

Δ
May 10-11

TALLEY'S MILL

Po

Glady Run

River

OLD COURT HOUSE

—— Confederate Troops
— · — Union Troops
•••••• Troops Captured and Turned
Δ   Headquarters of A.P. Hill, May 8-21, 1864

7. Battlefield of Spotsylvania C. H., Va. from May 8th to 21st, 1864

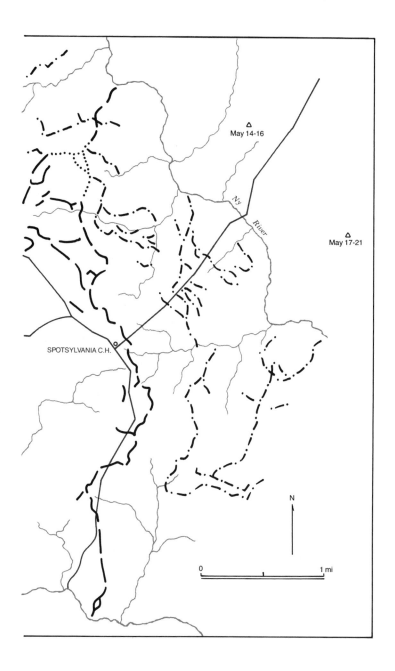

May 14-16

May 17-21

Ny River

SPOTSYLVANIA C.H.

N

0   1   1 mi

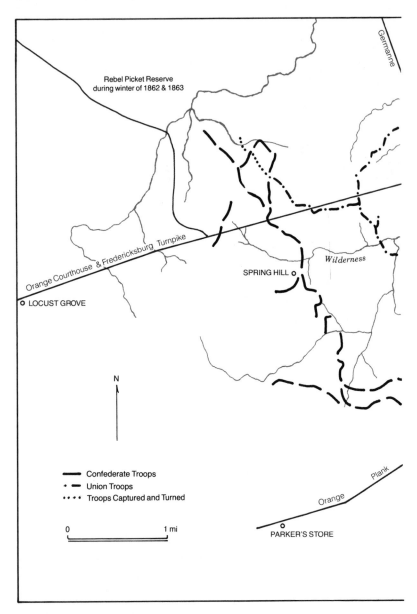

8. Battlefield of The Wilderness, Va., May 5th, 6th, and 7th, 1864

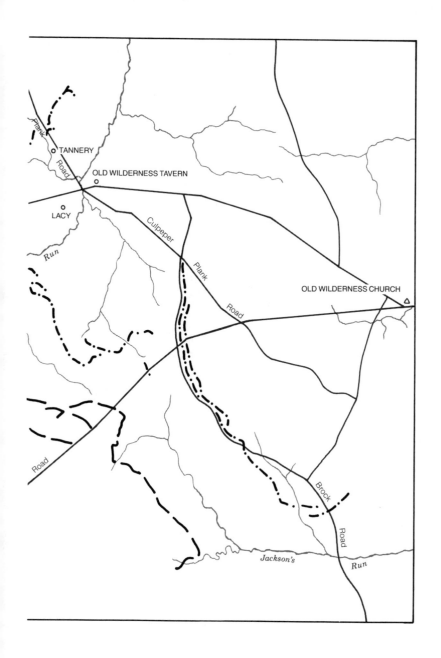

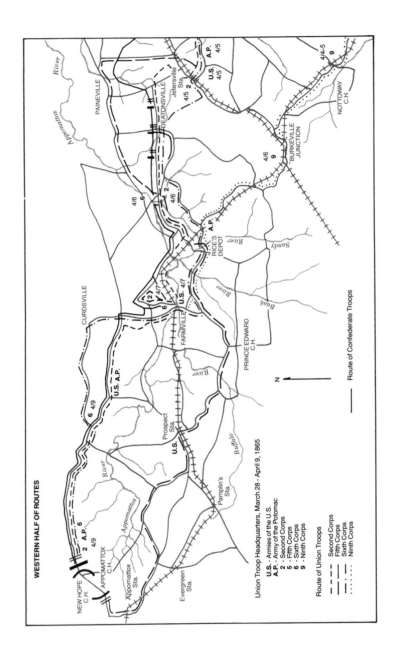

WESTERN HALF OF ROUTES

NEW HOPE C.H.

APPOMATTOX C.H.

2 A.P. 6
4/9

Appomattox Sta.

Evergreen Sta.

Appomattox River

6 4/9

U.S. A.P.

CURDSVILLE

Prospect Sta.

U.S.

Pamplin's Sta.

Buffalo

River

PAINEVILLE

Appomattox River

4/6 6

4/6 2

4/7
(2) 6
U.S. 4/7

FARMVILLE

PRINCE EDWARD C.H.

Bush River

RICE'S DEPOT

A.P.

Sandy River

DEATONSVILLE

Jetersville Sta.

4/5

U.S. A.P.
4/5 4/5

U.S.
4/5 2

4/6
9

BURKEVILLE JUNCTION

NOTTOWAY C.H.

4/4-5
9

N

Union Troop Headquarters, March 28 - April 9, 1865

U.S. - Armies of the U.S.
A.P. - Army of the Potomac
2 - Second Corps
5 - Fifth Corps
6 - Sixth Corps
9 - Ninth Corps

Route of Union Troops

- - - - - Second Corps
— — — Fifth Corps
·-·-·-· Sixth Corps
········· Ninth Corps

———— Route of Confederate Troops

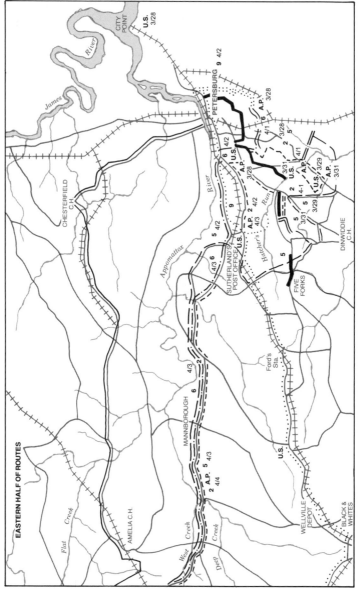

9. Operations of the Army of the Potomac under command of Maj. Gen. George G. Meade, from March 29th to April 9th, 1865. (This map, reading left to right or west to east, is continued below, which shows operations extending eastward to Petersburg.)

CHAPTER I

ALTHOUGH the claim of the right of a State to secede from the Union has been once and forever decided in the negative by the arbitrament of arms, in a long and bitterly contested war, it is, nevertheless, generally conceded by impartial students of history that when the original thirteen British colonies in America, which afterward became the United States, severed the ties that bound them to Great Britain and declared themselves free and independent States, the compact then formed for mutual protection and defense was not regarded as indissoluble. On the contrary, in after years, several States of the Union, in different sections and at different times, boldly avowed the right to leave the Confederation, and threatened to exercise it.

The question of the right of a State to secede is entirely distinct from the question of the wisdom, or the lack of wisdom, in so framing the Articles of Confederation, or the Constitution, as to permit the claim to such right to be made, by implication at least, or to leave the question open.

In considering such a matter, much depends upon the point of view. At this time and with our experience, very few, if any, can be found, North or South, who contend that there could be any stability or permanence in the government of a union of States of which one of

the fundamental principles was the right of any State
to dissolve the Union at will; but that does not affect
the question of such inherent right as claimed by the
founders of the Union, who were intensely jealous concerning the rights of the States, and who, time and
again, combated the idea that the United States was a
nation in the usual acceptation of the word, and who
resisted any attempted encroachment upon the rights
of the States not expressly delegated to the general
government. The State was sovereign; the Union was
an alliance between sovereigns. Nowhere was this
matter of State sovereignty more emphasized and more
jealously guarded than in the State of Virginia. The
young men of the State were early imbued with the
doctrine of States' rights, and while the people of Massachusetts, of New York, of the Carolinas, and of the
other States were their friends, their own people were
Virginians, and their country was Virginia.

The first suggestion of secession as a remedy for alleged grievances, and the first threat to exercise that
right, came from the New England States. In 1803 the
people of Massachusetts regarded unfavorably the acquisition of the territory of Louisiana, as in 1811 they
opposed the admission into the Union of the State of
Louisiana, and in 1843 the admission into the Union
of the State of Texas; and her public men spoke freely
of the right to secede from the Union, and clearly
intimated that circumstances might arise that would
cause Massachusetts to separate from the other States.
During the war between the United States and Great
Britain in 1812, the States of Massachusetts, Connecti-
cut, and Rhode Island opposed the war, refused to furnish troops, and threatened to secede from the Union
should certain conditions arise.

The attitude assumed by South Carolina in 1832, because of dissatisfaction with the revenue laws, again

threatened the integrity of the Union; it was then developed that there existed a pronounced difference of
opinion among the leading men in public life upon this
momentous question. The President was firm and obdurate in his determination to enforce the laws, and the
Governor of South Carolina was defiant in his purpose
to resist their enforcement. Wise counsels prevailed,
however, and, happily, this matter was adjusted without a rupture.

With the progress of time the advantages of the
Union became more and more apparent; and it is extremely doubtful if any attempt to dissolve it would
ever have been made had the institution of slavery not
existed.

Slavery existed in all of the colonies at the time of
the Declaration of Independence, and it continued to
exist in all the States for some time thereafter. The
labor of the slaves proved unprofitable, however, in the
more northern States, and this fact and the rigorous
character of the winter season in that section caused a
gradual deportation of all the slaves to the Southern
States, where they found a more congenial climate and
work for which they were better adapted. The enter-
prising citizens of the North sold their slaves to their
agricultural brethren of the South, neither having then
any qualms of conscience in the matter of "trading in
human chattels."

The question of slavery had not then assumed any
moral or political significance; and it is a cause for regret, from the ethical point of view, that the agitation
against the institution of slavery, on moral grounds, did
not occur before the slaves had all been segregated in
one section of the country, nor until after their former
owners in the North had received full payment in money
for all the slaves deported to the South.

In the early days in the history of the Republic there

were some of thoughtful mind and wise foresight who were opposed to slavery on philosophic grounds; but they differed widely in temper and in purpose from the abolitionists, whose attitude upon the question later found expression chiefly in anathemas against the owners of slaves. They looked with disfavor upon the trade in slaves and upon the introduction into this country of a horde of ignorant creatures of the black race, because they realized that in so doing labor in the lower walks of life would be degraded and made distasteful to the whites; they feared that it would be a hindrance rather than a help to the development of the material resources of the country; and they foresaw the dangers of any attempt to have these two races, between whom there could be no assimilation, live amicably together, side by side, without a recognition of the fact that in the natural order one is inferior, and, politically and socially, should be subordinate to the other. There is indisputable evidence of a strong sentiment in this direction having existed in the minds of leading men in Virginia, which State was the first to prohibit the importation of slaves, and this sentiment would have increased and continued to grow in that State had not the question been made one of party politics and arrayed the people of the Union into hostile factions on sectional lines. Our experience in the attempt made in the days of reconstruction to force the equality of the two races, by the enfranchisement of the blacks, proves the wisdom of their contention and brands that endeavor as the greatest political blunder of the nineteenth century.

At first the public utterances of men at the North in favor of the abolition of slavery were received most unfavorably, and in some cases led to mob violence, when those who lectured on this subject were interrupted and forced to desist. The number of these agitators increased, however, with the progress of time, and in the

year 1839 an attempt was made to organize the abolitionists into a political party.

A convention was then held for this purpose, and it
was declared "that every consideration of duty and ex-
pediency which ought to control the action of Christian
freemen requires the abolitionists of the United States
to organize a distinct and independent political party,
embracing all the necessary means for nominating candidates for office, and sustaining them by public suf-
frage."

The following year this question first assumed such a
degree of importance as to bring about the formation of
a political party, whose rallying-cry was the abolition
of slavery, with representatives from all the Northern
States called together in convention for the purpose of
nominating a candidate for the presidency of the United
States. Candidates for President and Vice-President
were put up, and in the ensuing election received 7059
of the popular vote cast. In 1844 candidates were again
placed before the people, and James G. Birney, a pronounced abolitionist, as the candidate for the presidency
of the National Liberty party, received 62,300 of the
popular vote cast. Meanwhile, the agitation of the
question of slavery became more and more intense, and
the hustings of the Northern States rang with passionate demands for its abolition. The two old parties,
Whig and Democratic, in the North, were divided on
this subject, each having an antislavery and a pro-
slavery wing.

In the Congress of the United States the debates upon
this question were frequent and showed much feeling.
The matter of slavery was forced to the front in the
discussion of nearly every political movement that then
engaged the attention of party leaders. In the creation
of new States, and in the acquisition of new territory,
there was always a contest in regard to it. The more

conservative leaders of the two old political parties, seeing the danger that threatened from its continued agitation, sought safety in compromise. The abolitionists outside of Congress opposed these compromise measures violently, denouncing them as " an agreement with hell and a covenant with death."

In 1848 the Free-soil or antislavery party was organized, and placed in nomination for the presidency Martin Van Buren, and for the vice-presidency Charles Francis Adams. In the ensuing election these candidates received nearly 300,000 of the popular vote cast. In 1856 the antislavery party, then known as the Republican party, nominated John C. Fremont for the presidency, and in the ensuing election he received 1,341,264 of the popular vote cast. The convention at which he was nominated adopted a plank denouncing " those twin relics of barbarism, slavery and polygamy." The cloud, at first no bigger than a man's hand, had now assumed mammoth proportions; the sky of one half of the Union was covered with dark and ominous clouds, from the deep recesses of which were heard constant rumblings, and from which there was an occasional flash and a peal that seemed to threaten the Republic with destruction. As is generally the case with attempts to bring about any great political or social revolution, so especially at this time many cranks and fanatics came to the front and appeared to lead in the movement for universal freedom. These fanatics, though filled with enthusiastic fervor for the advancement of a cause that, in the abstract, appealed strongly to the reason of thoughtful minds, were in all other respects uncertain, crooked, and dangerous.

In 1859 one of this execrable class became possessed of the idea that he was to be the deliverer of the colored race from slavery. With wicked intent, arson and murder being included in his line of assault, he invaded the State of Virginia with a small band of deluded followers, all armed, defied the legal authorities, called upon the slaves to revolt against their owners, and held out to them the promise of freedom and protection. There was a clash between this band of insurgents and the citizens and soldiers of the State, and blood was shed, many of the insurgents being killed. After indictment and trial, the leader of this terrible raid was hung by the authorities of the State as an insurrectionist. And yet, in after years, this man appeared a hero to many diseased minds, and his name was canonized by his fanatical sympathizers as a martyr.

President Buchanan, in his third annual message, December 19, 1859, in referring to this matter, wrote:

I shall not refer in detail to the recent sad and bloody occurrences at Harper's Ferry. Still, it is proper to observe that these events, however bad and cruel in themselves, derive their chief importance from the apprehension that they are but symptoms of an incurable disease in the public mind, which may break out in still more dangerous outrages and terminate at last in an open war by the North to abolish slavery in the South. Whilst for myself I entertain no such apprehension, they ought to afford a solemn warning to us all to beware of the approach of danger.

While the President then disavowed any personal apprehension of the terrible culmination of the efforts of the abolitionists into actual warfare, it must be admitted that matters had progressed very far in that direction to justify such language as this from the President to the Congress of the United States.

The two sections of the country were fast drifting toward the "irrepressible conflict" foreseen by Mr. Seward, then the most formidable opponent of Mr. Lincoln for nomination for the presidency by the Republican party. Mr. Lincoln received the nomination of his party in 1860, and was elected President in the fall of that year, receiving 1,866,352 of the popular vote, while his opponents in the aggregate received 2,810,501; his plurality, however, gave him the majority in the electoral college.

Although not an avowed abolitionist, in that he did not openly contend for the forcible abolition of slavery in the Southern States, Mr. Lincoln was what was called in the South a Black Republican, of pronounced type, thoroughly imbued with the ideas and teachings of the abolitionists, always on the antislavery side, restrained only by considerations of policy and by a shadow of respect for constitutional limitations, and, as events proved, only awaiting the presage of success to approve and decree the forcible freeing of the slaves of the South.

In the inauguration of the war that soon followed, the plausible pretext of the preservation of the Union was advanced in justification of the call to arms. There was a large element at the North opposed to interference with the internal affairs of the Southern States, that would never have approved of a resort to force to abolish slavery; nevertheless, that was the real issue at stake, and the mighty horde that claimed allegiance to a power higher than the Constitution swept everything to one side that tended to retard its movement, and ultimately demanded that the slaves be freed without regard to the private and public rights involved.

With such a party in power and such a man as President, the doubts and fears of the extreme Southern States were so intensely aroused by what they considered a serious menace to their peace and prosperity, that they determined to exercise their right of withdrawing from the Union. Seven Southern States seceded: South Carolina on December 20, 1860, Mississippi on January 9th, Florida on January 10th, Alabama on January 11th, Georgia on January 19th, Louisiana on

January 26th, and Texas on February 1, 1861. Here there was a halt; the tide appeared to have been checked; all eyes turned upon Virginia, whose people were assembled in convention to consider the crisis, and whose attitude was regarded with the keenest interest and anxiety. What would Virginia do?

In Virginia the sentiment was decidedly adverse to secession; the majority of her people were strongly opposed to the heroic measures adopted by the more southern States for the correction of their grievances; there was a sentimental and deep-rooted attachment to the Union, and a conviction that the fears entertained for the material and social welfare of the people of the South by reason of the inauguration of the administration of Mr. Lincoln, though not groundless, were much exaggerated.

On January 19, 1861, the General Assembly of Virginia resolved to send commissioners to Washington to unite with commissioners from such other States as would respond to her invitation to take part in an effort to adjust the unhappy controversies then existing. On February 4th this peace convention assembled, and delegates were present from fourteen free States and seven slave States. John Tyler of Virginia, ex-President of the United States, was chosen to preside over the conference; but no practical good attended its deliberations.

Meanwhile continued pressure was brought to bear upon the leading men of Virginia to induce them to join their friends farther South; by overtures from without and persuasive arguments from sympathizers within, it was endeavored to force Virginia to join the Southern Confederacy; but the convention was obdurate, and the State remained firm.

Soon after the inauguration of President Lincoln, Fort Sumter, in Charleston Harbor, became the center of the greatest interest. The State of South Carolina had demanded the surrender of that fort to its authorities, and it had been refused. The supply of provisions at the fort was nearly exhausted, and the officer in command had notified the authorities at Washington that unless supplies were furnished he would in a very short time have to abandon the fort. When this matter was first considered by Mr. Lincoln's cabinet, it was decided not to attempt to resupply the fort, as it would certainly precipitate a conflict; two weeks later the matter was again considered by the cabinet, and a majority decided that the attempt should be made. The Southern States that had seceded had organized themselves into a Confederacy, and Mr. Jefferson Davis had been chosen and inaugurated as President of the Confederate States of America. On March 1, 1861, the Confederate authorities had assumed control of military affairs at Charleston. On April 1st the Federal authorities, in response to a request for some assurance on this point, notified the Confederates that while the administration might desire to supply Fort Sumter, no attempt would be made to do this without previous notice to the Governor of South Carolina.

Meanwhile sentiment at the North was greatly divided; many of the leading men of that section favored inaction and opposed earnestly any attempt to coerce the Southern States back into the Union. Mr. Greeley, editor of the leading Republican paper, speaking of them as " erring sisters," admonished the people to "let them go in peace."

On April 8th the Federal government notified the Governor of South Carolina that it intended to send supplies to the garrison at Fort Sumter. On April 11th the Confederates again demanded the surrender of the fort, which demand was again refused. On April 12th the Confederates opened fire on the fort, and the fire was returned by the garrison, but no one was hurt. On April 14th, the supplies having been exhausted, the fort was surrendered. On April 15th the President of the United States issued a call upon the States in the Union for 75,000 men, for the purpose of coercing the States that had seceded. By this act Mr. Lincoln precipitated the war between the States.

It is true that South Carolina had ceded Fort Sumter to the United States for purposes of public defense, but it was of little value save for the defense of that State from attack by an alien foe. Many people at the North contended that the firing on the flag was a cause for war. It was a strained manifestation of offended pride; no such ebullition of temper had attended the first " insult to the flag," when on January 9th the *Star of the West*, with the flag of the Union at the peak, was fired on as she attempted to carry provisions to the garrison at Fort Sumter; but now the " irrepressible conflict" was to be inaugurated, and it was necessary to do everything possible to rouse the war-spirit of the people.

It is begging the whole question to treat the flag as the symbol of sovereignty or the ensign of a nation. The Union was not a nation; the United States was a confederation, not a kingdom. The flag was a composite banner in which every State had part and representation. At that time the Union was composed of thirty-three States, of which eighteen were free and fifteen slave. Seven of the Southern States had seceded; all the others, as well as the border States, were opposed both to the policy of secession and to the exercise of force to maintain the Union. Virginia, North Carolina, Tennessee, Kentucky, Arkansas, and Missouri refused to honor Mr. Lincoln's call for volunteers. Maryland was opposed to it, and suggested a truce and arbitration. Here were fourteen States to whom the flag belonged as much as to the other nineteen, and they saw no occasion for war. There was no question here of national pride or honor; no alien had done dishonor to the flag; no State had been invaded by hostile foe. Veil it as we may with the soothing reflection that the States that seceded are now reconciled and the Union happily reëstablished, the ugly fact stands out to view that in that epoch of the history of our country a rude shock was given to the maintenance of the principles of government for which we had successfully contended in the revolution against the rule of England. The fundamental idea, the basic principle of the Declaration of Independence was completely subverted; the assumption that all governments derive their just powers from the consent of the governed was conveniently relegated into deepest oblivion, and the growth of the principle that is the antithesis of this, which was then implanted, has been so insidious and so increasing that we have to-day the spectacle of a Republic of States embarked in the establishment of remote colonies, whose alien races are averse to our rule and who are kept in subjection by the force of arms, with only an occasional remonstrance from those prominent in the councils of the party in power. And, whereas, the safety and perpetuity of the Union were deemed by its founders to be involved in the rigid adherence to the lines then laid down concerning the rights reserved to the States and the limited powers delegated to the general government, in a strict maintenance of the dual system of government agreed on, that has been happily likened to the centripetal and the centrifugal forces that hold the earth to its dual revolution around its own axis and around its central sun, there was then inaugurated a movement tending to an enlargement of the powers of the general government and a dwarfing of the rights of the States that has continued to grow, and to-day finds expression and fruition in the bold usurpation of legislative powers by the Executive, and in a number of acts of Congress conferring upon the general government powers once considered inherent and exclusive in the States, tending toward a centralization of government and an obliteration of State lines. If it is contended that the changed conditions that confront us render it necessary to make corresponding changes in the form of government in order to secure a higher degree of security and happiness for the people, then it is time to cease to boast that the old and original form was the best ever known to the world.

The grievances that led to the revolt of the thirteen American colonies were no more serious than those that prompted the secession of the eleven Southern States from the Union. In the matters of population and material wealth, the latter were vastly superior to the former. The autonomy of the several States was universally admitted; complete systems of government existed in all the States, embracing the executive, legislative, and judicial departments; law and order prevailed throughout the southern half of the former confederation, and there was no thought or suggestion of any purpose to interfere in any way with the affairs of the Northern States. A very empire in extent of territory, the Southern States then had an aggregate of population of nearly ten millions, and to deny such a people the right of self-government was equivalent to a confession of error in the revolt against England, and the branding of the Declaration of Independence a subterfuge and a delusion.

Mr. Lincoln's call for troops was communicated to the authorities of Virginia, and on April 17th the convention assembled at Richmond passed the ordinance of secession, and the State withdrew from the Union. What other course was open to the people of Virginia, consistent with the conservation of her honor and good

name ? The traditions of the State and the honor of her
people made any other course impossible, and this will be
the verdict of the impartial critic, whatever may be his
predilections concerning the issues that led up to the war.

The people of our State had declared their love for the
Union and manifested an earnest desire to preserve peace
and to seek for a remedy for the grievances of the South
through the instrumentality of the votes of the people; in other words, to "fight it out within the Union,"
until a call was made by the President of the United
States upon the several States, Virginia included, for
their quota of soldiers, with which it was proposed
to coerce into submission the States that had seceded
from the Union; and then, and only then, when it was
inevitable that a fratricidal conflict was indeed upon us,
did our beloved commonwealth, always conservative,
yet ever influenced by the dictates of honor and of courage, sever the ties that bound her to the Union, resume
the position of a free and independent State, and declare
her purpose to resist the invasion of her territory by
the troops called into service to coerce her sister States
of the South.   Without abating one iota of their devotion to the Union, deprecating alike the extreme measures adopted by the States farther South for the adjustment of their grievances and the resort to arms inaugurated by the States of the North remaining in the Union,
the people of Virginia saw and considered but one
course as open to them.   Virginia had done all that was
possible with honor to avert the calamity; her efforts
to avoid a conflict had failed; war was already declared.
Her love, her sympathy, her interests, were with the
South.   Her sense of right and justice bade her array
herself against the Federal hosts, and, proudly erect and
defiant, she accepted the gage of battle and prepared to
receive the brunt of the shock of arms that was soon to
convulse a continent.

CHAPTER II

IN anticipation of trouble many volunteer companies had been previously organized in the different cities of the State, and these promptly offered their services, and were accepted. Several companies at Norfolk were organized into a battalion and became the nucleus of the army for the defense of that city.

Much interest centered at Norfolk because of the valuable navy-yard at that place, where a number of vessels of war were stationed, some out of commission and some armed, equipped, and ready for service; and because of the large quantity of ammunition stored at Fort Norfolk, of which the State had practically none. By direction of the governor, hulks were sunk in the channel below Fort Norfolk, in an attempt to prevent the passage out of the armed vessels of the Federals; these obstructions, in time, came to pester the Confederates, after the harbor came under their control, and when they needed channel room for the ironclad *Virginia* and other vessels of heavy draft.

The first service rendered by the soldiery was the taking forcible possession of the ordnance depot at Fort Norfolk. Two companies, under the command of Major William E. Taylor, were assigned to this duty. Although it was known that there was no garrison at the fort, but only a gunner in charge and a few men as caretakers, a certain thrill of excitement stirred the breasts of the young citizen soldiers as they marched to Fort Norfolk and took their first steps in the art of war. Skirmishers were thrown out at a low, dark spot on the road, and the major in command admonished caution as the men moved forward to flush the hidden foe. This was for the instruction of the young soldiers, as in reality there was no armed force of the Federals nearer than the navy-yard, a mile or so away; and that was on the defensive and preparing to get away. Another company, "The Greys," under the command of Captain R. C. Taylor, which had preceded by water, reached the fort first and quietly took possession. A formal demand for surrender was made upon Gunner Charles Oliver, United States Navy, in charge, who made some remonstrance, but who, recognizing the futility and folly of resistance, yielded up the place. He subsequently resigned from the service of the United States and gave his allegiance to the Confederate cause. The soldiers proceeded at once, in compliance with their orders, to remove the ordnance supplies to some place of safety away from the river-front, where they would be secure from seizure by the naval force of the enemy.

Plans were being devised for the seizure of the navy-yard, but not enough troops were yet available to attempt this by force of arms; indeed, with their vessels of war and the armed force at their disposal, the Federals there were absolutely safe from attack for weeks. It came as a surprise, therefore, when on the night of April 20th it was discovered that the Federals had set fire to the yard buildings and scuttled the ships in the stream not in commission, and that their armed fleet had quietly steamed down the Elizabeth River to Hampton Roads, conveying to that station all the officers and men on duty at the yard. The excitement in Norfolk was intense; as the soldiers hurried along the streets to their assembly-halls—for they had not yet gone into camp—women cried in an excited way from the windows of their homes, to ascertain what was burning that threw so intense a glare over the Southern heavens and caused the mad flames to leap to the zenith, with a fierce roaring and crackling that seemed to threaten the city and everything around it. In those days there were large ship-houses at the yard, within which the wooden vessels of largest class were constructed. In the stream was the old seventy-four *Pennsylvania*, and in one of the ship-houses another of the same class, the *New York*, that had never been launched; the *Merrimac*, afterward the Confederate ironclad *Virginia*, and other ships were made fast to the wharves. All these were burned or scuttled, and the next day the navy-yard presented a sad scene of destruction and desolation.

While these events were transpiring, Robert E. Lee of Virginia, colonel of the First Regiment of Cavalry, United States Army, then at Washington, regarded them with intensely painful interest and sorrowful emotions. A soldier by profession, he scorned the wily tactics of the political agitator and contemplated his actions with doubt and distrust. He had served in the army since his youth, and his heart thrilled with devotion to his chosen profession. He had served upon the staff of General Scott in the war with Mexico, and had been frequently mentioned for conspicuous gallantry and efficiency; he was regarded by General Scott as an officer of most distinguished ability, and was recommended by him for the command of the army in the field of the United States. He was warmly attached to the Union, with the formation of which his name was inseparably connected, by reason of the conspicuous service of his father and other members of the family, but he could not even contemplate drawing his sword against the people of his own State. In the abstract, he was no friend of the institution of slavery; he realized that slavery tended to degrade labor among the white people, and was not essential to the happiness or the material prosperity of his own State, where the conditions were very different from those that existed in the extreme South.

In commenting upon the annual message of President Pierce to Congress, in a letter dated December 27, 1856, General Lee wrote as follows:

I was much pleased with the President's message.* His views of the systematic and progressive efforts of certain people at the North to interfere with and change the domestic institutions of the South are truthfully and faithfully expressed. The consequences of their plans and purposes are also clearly set forth. These people must be aware that their object is both unlawful and foreign to them and to their duty, and that this institution, for which they are irresponsible and non-accountable, can only be changed by them through the agency of a civil and servile war. There are few, I believe, in this enlightened age, who will not acknowledge that slavery as an institution is a moral and political evil. It is idle to expatiate on its disadvantages. I think it is a greater evil to the white than to the colored race. While my feelings are strongly enlisted in behalf of the latter, my sympathies are more deeply engaged for the former. The blacks are immeasurably better off here than in Africa, morally, physically, and socially. The painful discipline they are undergoing is necessary for their further instruction as a race, and will prepare them, I hope, for better things. How long their servitude may be necessary is known and ordered by a merciful Providence. Their emancipation will sooner result from the mild and melting influences of Christianity than from the storm and tempest of fiery controversy. This influence, though slow, is sure. The doctrines and miracles of our Saviour have required nearly two thousand years to convert but a small portion of the

* See extract in Appendix.

human race, and even among Christian nations what gross errors still exist! While we see the course of the final abolition of human slavery is still onward, and give it the aid of our prayers, let us leave the progress as well as the results in the hands of Him who sees the end, who chooses to work by slow influences, and with whom a thousand years are but as a single day. Although the abolitionist must know this, must know that he has neither the right nor the power of operating, except by moral means; that to benefit the slave he must not excite angry feelings in the master; that, although he may not approve the mode by which Providence accomplishes its purpose, the results will be the same; and that the reason he gives for interference in matters he has no concern with, holds good for every kind of interference with our neighbor,—still, I fear he will persevere in his evil course. . . . Is it not strange that the descendants of those Pilgrim Fathers who crossed the Atlantic to preserve their own freedom have always proved the most intolerant of the spiritual liberty of others ?

While General Lee is thus seen to have deprecated the agitation at the North of the question of the forcible abolition of slavery in the South, he at the same time regretted as unwise and unnecessary the manifestations of a purpose to bring about the dissolution of the Union evidenced by the declarations and action of the leaders of political thought in the South; he was, in a word, in perfect accord with the line of conduct pursued by his native State, and when the issue of war was forced by Mr. Lincoln, he resigned his commission in the army of the United States, proceeded at once to Richmond upon the invitation of the Governor of Virginia, and accepted the position of Commander of the Provisional Army of Virginia, tendered him by the governor and State Convention.

It has been said that in reaching this conclusion General Lee had a struggle with himself in refusing the very alluring offer made to him by the Federal authorities of the command of the army to be put in the field under the President's call for troops; but those who knew him best understand that there was no struggle of this kind, although it was a serious trial to him to separate himself from a service to which he had devoted the best years of his life and all the ability he possessed. When it was intimated to him that the President would offer to him the command of the army that was to be brought into the field, he declined to entertain the proposition, stating to Mr. Lincoln's representative, candidly and conscientiously, that though opposed to secession and deprecating war, he could take no part in an invasion of the Southern States. In his account of this interview, General Lee says:

I went directly from the interview with Mr. Blair to the office of General Scott, told him of the proposition that had been made, and my decision. After reflection, upon returning home, I concluded that I ought no longer to retain any commission I held in the United States Army, and on the second morning thereafter I forwarded my resignation to General Scott. At the time I hoped that peace would have been preserved ; that some way would be found to save the country from the calamities of war ; and I then had no other intention than to pass the remainder of my life as a private citizen. Two days afterward, on the invitation of the Governor of Virginia, I repaired to Richmond, found that the Convention then in session had passed an ordinance withdrawing the State from the Union, and accepted the commission of commander of its forces which was tendered me.

At Richmond the machinery was already in motion for the creation of an army. The response to the governor's call for volunteers to resist the armed invasion of the State was prompt and general. Companies were being organized all over the State, except in the extreme northwestern or Panhandle district, where, by reason of the close contact and intimate commercial and social relations with the citizens of Ohio and Pennsylvania, a majority of the people were less imbued with the Virginia spirit and were rather sympathetic with the Northern side in the impending struggle. There was immediate need at headquarters for a few young men who had had some military education and experience, to carry on the details of the army work. General Francis H. Smith, superintendent of the Virginia Military Institute, and Captain Richard L. Page, of the Navy, military aids and advisers to the governor, were directed by him to make selections for this service. I was intimately known to General Smith, and closely connected by family ties to Captain Page, and so it happened that, with three or four others, I was designated for assignment to this duty. I was at that time a lieutenant of Company F of the light infantry, in the Third Battalion of Volunteers, of the Virginia militia, which company had offered its services, and had been enlisted for active service in the field. On May 2d I was directed by telegraph to proceed at once to Richmond and report to the governor for orders. On my arrival at Richmond I was commissioned first lieutenant in the Provisional Army of Virginia, and assigned to duty at General Lee's headquarters.

I had not previously known General Lee. I then saw him for the first time on the morning of my arrival at Richmond and before my assignment to duty. I was at breakfast at the Spotswood Hotel when he entered the room, and was at once attracted and greatly impressed by his appearance. He was then at the zenith of his physical beauty. Admirably proportioned, of graceful and dignified carriage, with strikingly handsome features, bright and penetrating eyes, his iron-gray hair closely cut, his face cleanly shaved except a mustache, he appeared every inch a soldier and a man born to command.

At that time Colonel Robert S. Garnett, holding a commission as adjutant-general of the State forces, the best informed and most capable man in military detail that I ever met, was General Lee's right-hand man in organizing and marshaling the troops that were to constitute the Army of Virginia. My first service was under his immediate supervision, and to him I was greatly indebted for the experience then gained in all matters of detail in active military service.

General Lee anticipated a severe struggle. There were many prominent men on each side of the controversy who contended that the war would be of short duration; with them there was a disposition to underrate the steadfastness of purpose and the endurance of the other side; and they pretended to expect a sharp, short, and decisive contest. The first call of Mr. Lincoln for volunteers was for three months' service, and the leaders on both sides contended that the war would not last ninety days. General Lee took an entirely different view of the case. He seemed to realize the magnitude of the impending conflict; he gaged correctly the indomitable will, the untiring energy, the fertile resources, the pride of opinion, that characterized the people of the North; and he knew full well that there would be no holiday affair in a conflict between the two sections of the United States, each animated by a traditional devotion to cherished institutions, each boasting the proud lineage of the Anglo-Saxon, each determined to win or die, and each confident of success.

He looked upon the vaporific declamations of those on each side who proposed to wipe their adversaries from the face of the earth in ninety days as bombastic and foolish. Notwithstanding his views, so freely expressed, and his recommendation that the volunteers be enlisted for the war, the Virginia troops, as also most of those of the other Southern States, were enlisted for twelve months. The civil authorities could not bring themselves to believe that there could possibly be any need for an armed force beyond that time.

In the South troops were being sent to Virginia as fast as organized by the several States, and in the North a large army was being collected for the defense of Washington and for the invasion of Virginia. On April 19th the passage of the Sixth Massachusetts Regiment through the city of Baltimore created a riot. A delegation from that city visited Washington the next day and informed the President that Federal troops would not be allowed to pass through that city without fighting their way. In view of these facts, it was suggested that troops destined for Washington should go by rail as far as Perryville, thence by water to Annapolis, and thence by rail to Washington. The people of Maryland, however, unprepared for war, were soon overawed; an armed Federal force occupied the city of Baltimore, and troops were freely moved across the State and through the city of Baltimore without molestation.

Events now followed one another in rapid succession. Virginia formally joined the Southern Confederacy; the seat of government of the new Republic was moved from Montgomery to Richmond; the organization of the Army of Virginia was complete; formal transfer of the Virginia troops was made to the Confederacy, and the War Department assumed the conduct of military affairs at Richmond.

General Garnett, relieved of his duties as adjutant-general of the Virginia forces, was available for other service, and was sent by General Lee to the northwestern part of the State to take command of the troops operating in that section. All commissions in the several staff departments of the Provisional Army of Virginia, of those not attached to troops serving in the field, were declared void. I held at that time such a commission as assistant adjutant-general, with the rank of captain, which ceased to be effective after the transfer of the Virginia troops to the Confederacy. I was continued on duty by General Lee, however, who obtained for me a commission as first lieutenant in the infantry of the regular army of the Confederate States, with orders to report to him for duty as aide-de-camp; this was followed later by an appointment as captain in the adjutant-general's department of the Provisional Army of the Confederate States.

The Provisional Army of Virginia having ceased to exist as an organization by reason of its having been merged into the Provisional Army of the Confederate States, the position of General Lee as commander of the Virginia forces was purely nominal, and his authority and functions as commander-in-chief terminated. He was appointed one of five generals provided for by an act of Congress in the Army of the Confederate States. The headquarters of the Provisional Army of Virginia were discontinued after two months of active work; but during that time ties of friendship were formed that would be as enduring as the everlasting hills.

I had excellent opportunities at that time to observe General Lee as a worker, and I can say that I have never known a man more thorough and painstaking in all that he undertook. Early at his office, punctual in meeting all engagements, methodical to an extreme in his way of despatching business, giving close attention to details,—but not, as is sometimes the concomitant, if not the result of this trait, neglectful of the more important matters dependent upon his decision,— he seemed to address himself to the accomplishment of

every task that devolved upon him in a conscientious
and deliberate way, as if he himself was directly ac-
countable to some higher power for the manner in which
he performed his duty. I then discovered, too, that
characteristic of him that always marked his intercourse and relations with his fellow-men—scrupulous
consideration for the feelings and interests of others;
the more humble the station of one from whom he received appeal or request, the more he appeared to desire
to meet the demand, if possible, or, if impracticable, to
make denial in the most considerate way, as if done
with reluctance and regret. His correspondence, necessarily heavy, was constantly a source of worry and
annoyance to him. He did not enjoy writing; indeed, he
wrote with labor, and nothing seemed to tax his amiability so much as the necessity for writing a lengthy
official communication; but he was not satisfied unless
at the close of his office hours every matter requiring
prompt attention had been disposed of. After a day's
work at his office he would enjoy above all things a ride
on horseback. Accompanied by one or two of his military household, he would visit some point of interest
around Richmond, making the ride one of duty as well
as pleasure; and no sculptor or artist can ever repro-
duce in marble or bronze the picture of manly grace and
beauty that became in those days so familiar to the
people in and around Richmond in the person of General
Lee on his favorite horse. After his return from such
excursions, in the closing hours of the day, he would
take the greatest pleasure in having the little girls of
the neighborhood gather around him, when he would
talk and joke with them in the most loving and familiar
way. I am quite sure that many of Richmond's handsome matrons of to-day recall with emotions of pride
and pleasure the occasions when, as happy, careless
girls, they were petted and caressed by the greatest sol-

dier and the purest man of his day and generation. As may be inferred from what has already been said, the life then led by General Lee was one of great simplicity and without parade or ostentation; neither then nor later, when in active service with the army, did he care for display of any kind.

CHAPTER III

A T this period President Davis became very anxious about the condition of affairs in the western portion of Virginia. Our forces, under General Garnett, had been defeated by the Federals under General McClellan; Colonel Pegram, with about six hundred troops of Garnett's army, had been compelled to surrender; and the main army, under General Garnett, had been defeated at Laurel Hill on July 9th, forced to retire, overtaken and vigorously assailed on July 13th at Carrick's Ford, where, in rallying his men, the brave Garnett was killed. General Loring had been assigned to the command of that army and had fallen back and taken a defensive position at Valley Mountain. Mr. Davis wished to send General Lee to that section to restore confidence to the troops and check the Federal advance. There was, moreover, a lack of harmony between generals Floyd and Wise, who were operating separate commands in the Kanawha district, and it was hoped that the presence of General Lee would tend to harmonize their differences.

The President held his wish in abeyance until after the battle of Manassas, and in the latter days of July General Lee left Richmond for his new field of duty. He was accompanied by his two aides, Colonel John A. Washington and myself. The journey was made as far as Staunton by rail, and from thence the party proceeded on horseback to Monterey, in Highland County. The ride through the country was most enjoyable; that section abounds in lovely scenery, and the mountain air was most invigorating and a delightful change from the heated atmosphere of the crowded city. On arriving at Monterey the delights of a ride on horseback were very seriously impaired by the setting in of a rainy season, and to the same cause is to be attributed the appalling degree of sickness that then prevailed among the troops, as also the great difficulty experienced in getting supplies to the front for the army. Writing from Huntersville on August 4, 1861, General Lee says:

I reached here yesterday to visit this portion of the army. . . . The soldiers everywhere are sick. The measles are prevalent throughout the whole army. You know that disease leaves unpleasant results and attacks the lungs, especially in camp, where the accommodations for the sick are poor. I traveled from Staunton on horseback. A part of the road I traveled over in the summer of 1840, on my return to St. Louis. If any one had told me that the next time I traveled that road would have been my present errand, I should have supposed him insane. I enjoyed the mountains as I rode along. The views were magnificent. The valleys so peaceful, the scenery so beautiful! What a glorious world Almighty God has given us! How thankless and ungrateful we are!

And a few days later he wrote from Valley Mountain:

I have been three days coming from Monterey to Huntersville. The mountains are beautiful, fertile to the tops, covered with the richest sward of blue grass and white clover. The inclosed fields wave with a natural growth of timothy. This is a magnificent grazing country, and all it wants is labor to clear the mountain-sides of timber. It has rained, I believe, some portion of every day since I left Staunton; now it is pouring.

Colonel Washington, Captain Taylor, and myself are in one tent, which, as yet, protects us.

There is much of interest and pathos to me in the recollection of the time when that little military family of three, with one wagon for our equipage and provisions, and two servants, constituted the headquarters of the general-in-chief. As I recall the events of my first campaign, at Valley Mountain, my heart is filled with emotions in which sadness and thankfulness are strangely commingled. To my youthful mind there was much to inspire respect, admiration, and affection in the contemplation of the character of two such men as General Lee and Colonel Washington; the advantage to result to a young person of impressionable age by an intimate association with two such noble spirits cannot be too highly esteemed. Short though my acquaintance was with Colonel Washington, for he was among the earliest of the chivalry of Virginia slain on the field of battle, the incidents of our camp life are indelibly impressed upon my mind and make a picture of sweet and tender memories that delight in the contemplation and yet evoke the sigh of regret at the loss of two such noble men. A spirit of devotion to the Giver of all good and of love for all His works pervaded that camp in the mountains that was in striking contrast to the spirit of passion and hate that animated the men who had precipitated trouble and arrayed in hostile ranks the two sections of our country. The daily morning and evening prayer of my elder associate on the staff; the Bible that claimed his constant perusal and that served as a depository in which to press the lovely wild flowers that he gathered and thus prepared with loving heart and hands for transmission to his daughters, of whom he spoke with the tenderest affection and solicitude; the converse around our camp table, in which there was so much of courtesy and refinement; the deferential treatment of these two Virginia gentlemen each for the other—are all vividly recalled by me after these many years as the sweetest odor of lovely flowers long since faded and fallen away, but the remembrance of whose fragrance is a perennial delight.

General Lee's son (afterward major-general), W. H. F. Lee, was in command of a battalion of cavalry of the army, under General Loring. He was ordered by General Lee to make a reconnoissance on a certain road, and General Lee allowed Colonel Washington, at his own request, to accompany the reconnoitering party. The force had not advanced very far before it rode into an ambuscade of the enemy; there was a volley of musketry, and Colonel Washington was killed. The next day his body was sent into our lines under a flag of truce. I was greatly shocked in the contemplation of my noble companion and friend cold in death; and as I looked upon his inanimate form as it lay there on the side of Valley Mountain, I thought of that other valley, of the shadow of death, through which he had just passed, never to return; I thought of those dear little girls of his and of the utter desolation that had so suddenly come to their happy home; and I began to realize something of the horrors of war. And then I asked myself why it was so,—why were these people, so lately friends, arrayed in hostile ranks with such deadly purpose? And as I reasoned, it seemed to me that one side was acting clearly on the defensive; its country was being invaded, its homes and its firesides threatened; all that it asked was to be let alone and to be permitted to enjoy the fruit of the victory it had won jointly with the other from England, in the establishment and the maintenance of the principle that all governments derived their just powers from the consent of the governed. But what motive impelled the other side? Was it the lust of power? Was it the distorted view of the idealist of his duty to force his theories upon his neighbor? Or was it the development into action of the implacable hatred that had long slumbered in the heart of the abolitionist against the so-called aristocracy of the South? As these questions forced themselves upon me, I became embittered; resentment took possession of my heart, and the man on the other side became my enemy. A fratricidal war! How sad it was!

After an unsuccessful attempt to surprise the Federal forces at Cheat Mountain and on Valley River, the Confederates reoccupied their fortified position at Valley Mountain. Heavy rains continued, the roads were in dreadful condition, and it did not appear likely that there would be any active movement in that section for some time. About the 18th or 19th of September General Lee left Valley Mountain, and proceeded to the Kanawha district. With only a young subaltern as companion, he made the journey on horseback. Passing through White Sulphur Springs, the journey was continued to Meadow Bluff, to which point General Floyd had fallen back with his little army. General Wise was several miles in advance at Sewell Mountain, confronting Rosecrans's army, with his Legion, having refused to obey General Floyd's order to fall back.

We had now reached the fall of the year, and the nights were already very cold. As before stated, our camp equipage was exceedingly limited, as were our supplies of all kinds. One very cold night, as we drew close to our camp fire, General Lee suggested that it was advisable to make one bed, put our blankets together in order to have sufficient covering to make us comfortable, and so it happened that it was vouchsafed to me to occupy very close relations with my old commander, and to be able to testify to his self-denial and his simplicity of life in those days of trial for all. Indeed, when one contemplates the evenly rounded character of General Lee, no trait of his appears to greater advantage or impresses one more profoundly than his utter self-abnegation. He always seemed anxious to keep himself in the background, to suppress all consideration of himself, to prevent any notice of himself. A more modest man did not live. He was painfully embarrassed by the slightest evidence of admiration, and absolutely opposed to any plan or proposition looking to the enhancement of his comfort or to doing honor to himself. Whenever he received intimation of any such purpose, he would endeavor to prevent such action, and never failed to advance the suggestion that inasmuch as the men in the ranks of the army were upon scant rations and deprived of many comforts, it devolved upon all to do what was possible for them, adding that it would bring no happiness or enjoyment to him to have more than was absolutely necessary for his own comfort and efficiency, when he realized the trials and deprivations to which his soldiers were subjected. He preferred to share discomfort with his men. Actuated by this desire, he would never consent, until toward the close of the war, to occupy a house or establish his headquarters about a homestead; but when on the march, would send one of his staff ahead to select a good spot for a small camp, and few would recognize in this modest array of tents and equipage the headquarters of the army.

I have already alluded to his great regard and respect for the feelings and interests of others; those who came in contact with him could not fail to discover that he acted under strong conviction of duty and in hearty sympathy with all who were engaged in the same cause with himself. Such a combination tended in a marked degree to qualify him for the rôle of peacemaker, an umpire in differences, quite aside from the authority that he exercised as a commander. As an illustration of this, I would cite his consummate tact in rescuing our little army in southwestern Virginia from a most embarrassing condition, that had its origin in the divergent views and strong personal antagonism that existed between generals Floyd and Wise, who were, as has been stated, operating with separate commands. Although General Floyd was senior in rank to General Wise, he failed to secure his subordination or even his coöperation in matters wherein there was a difference of opinion between them. At Sewell Mountain a council of war was held, at which it was determined to make a stand and give battle in the position then occupied. At the time both concurred in this line of action; but from some cause that developed soon thereafter, General Floyd decided to fall back and ordered General Wise to do the same with his troops. The messenger who bore this order to General Wise, it was said, carried back the message: "Tell General Floyd I will 'do no such thing; I propose to stay here and fight until doomsday," or words to that effect. I cannot vouch for the literal accuracy of this defiant and insubordinate declaration of a most heroic purpose; but it was told to me as I have related, and was generally believed in the army.

I recall another incident of the gallant stand then made by Wise's command, which, although when viewed in one way it appears very absurd, will no doubt strike all old soldiers as illustrating the possession by the general of what is called good horse-sense. The enemy had driven in the skirmishers and were advancing in force upon the main line held by our men. The firing of small arms was heavy along the line, and matters began to look serious, for we had an insignificant force, when General Wise rode up to a young lieutenant, who commanded a section of artillery, and ordered him to open fire with his guns. A dense forest prevented the lieutenant from seeing any of the enemy, and he stated as much to General Wise, adding that if he opened fire he would "do no execution." The incessant fusillade of rifles and the whistling of minnies seemed to emphasize the wisdom of the general's reply, "D—n the execution, sir, it's the *noise* that we want." Any veteran of the infantry who has crossed the open field, or struggled through thickets and undergrowth, when advancing in line of battle, or who has lain behind intrenchments expecting an assault, will recognize at once the force of General Wise's suggestion, and recall the satisfaction and support he has derived under such circumstances from the noise of the heavy guns just in his rear.

Of course the presence of General Lee reconciled for a time the discordant elements of that army. He promptly advanced General Floyd's command to the position held by General Wise, and so united the army; but to secure discipline and render the force effective, it was necessary to have the two commands combined under one commander; and the President, acting upon General Lee's suggestion, sent to General Wise an order relieving him from duty in that department, which, however, contained no reflection upon him. It was only by the tact and good management of General Lee that General Wise was induced to comply with the President's command; and I remember that he told General Lee that he wished him to understand that he left the field and repaired to Richmond in deference to *his* judgment and counsel, rather than in compliance with the orders from the department. He was a grand old man, heroic in his courage and of inflexible will, knowing little of subordination, but ever ready to fight and steadfast to the last.

CHAPTER IV

AFTER the campaign in western Virginia, General Lee returned to Richmond, where he remained but a short time, however, and on the 6th of November, 1861, proceeded to the Department of the South Atlantic, for the purpose of designing and supervising the construction of a line of defense along the coasts of South Carolina, Georgia, and Florida. For this work he was admirably fitted and equipped, having had great experience in the engineer corps of the army, and having gained for himself great distinction during the war with Mexico, under General Scott, where he served in that branch of the service. His experienced eye at once detected the weak as well as the strong points of this extended coast-line, and under his direction a system of defensive works was constructed that constituted a monument to his skill as an engineer.

There was a marked contrast between the character of the service and the condition of the troops in eastern Virginia, South Carolina, and Georgia, and that of those left behind us in western Virginia. The men who served in western Virginia were subjected to unusual trials and deprivations. The season was a most unfavorable one; it rained almost without intermission during the time of our stay in that department, sickness prevailed in the army to an alarming extent, rations were

short, clothing insufficient, and, altogether, great discomfort characterized that campaign; whereas, when I
visited Norfolk I found a soldiery well dressed, well fed,
and abundantly supplied in all respects, the fortifications were strong and elaborate, the camps were in excellent condition, and guard duty and company and
battalion drill seemed to constitute the only demands
made upon the time and patriotism of the men.

I well recall the impression made upon me by the sight
of a number of volunteers passing through the streets
of the city in handsome uniforms, with nicely starched
collars and cuffs, in all respects appearing as if "on parade" in time of peace; and it looked to me as if the
soldiers there were enjoying a holiday, so striking was
the contrast between these men and the poor ill-fed,
shivering fellows I had served with in western Virginia.
The day of trial, however, came also to these, later on
in the progress of the war; and they proved in every
respect equal to the strain, for whether on the march,
in the bivouac, or in the advancing line of battle, none
manifested greater powers of endurance, nor gave more
convincing proof of daring courage and unquenchable
spirit than the pet volunteer companies of the cities,
carrying upon their rolls the very flower of the Southern
youth, that were first in the field in response to the call
of their States, and of which was composed in great part
the force that occupied Norfolk and its vicinity.

A similar state of affairs existed in the Southern Department of South Carolina, Georgia, and Florida, but
there the contrast was even more noticeable in the
climate and the generally favorable conditions of the
service. Autumn was now well advanced, but instead
of the muddy roads, the barren rocky hills, and the cold
winds that swept down from the mountain-sides in
western Virginia, causing the men to huddle about the
fires in their bleak and comfortless camps, we had ex-

cellent quarters, a genial climate, the greatest profusion of lovely flowers, roses of many varieties, and camellias blooming in the open air and gently swayed by softest Southern breezes, all nature decked in holiday attire, and the bright uniforms and glittering arms of the soldiers only adding to the beauty of the scene.

Our stay in that department was as a peaceful rest after a period of constant trial and of great hardship; it was not, however, without its quota of exciting incidents. It was then that occurred the unequal but gallant contest in Port Royal Sound between the Confederate mosquito fleet, under the command of Commodore Tatnall, and the formidable Federal squadron, under Admiral Du Pont. It is difficult to exaggerate the great advantage to the Northern side in the war between the States in having absolute control of the water. Not only had the Federals a navy of fair proportions, judged by the standards of that period, but they also had facilities for constructing formidable vessels of war of the largest size. The Confederates had not a single man-of-war, nor was there a yard in the South that had the facilities for building ships. The hull of the old *Merrimac*, partially destroyed by order of Commodore Paulding when the Federals left the Norfolk navy-yard, furnished to the Confederates their single opportunity in the East of constructing a floating engine of war worthy of the name; and the decisive victory of the ironclad *Virginia* over the Federal fleet in Hampton Roads marked an epoch in naval warfare, and demonstrated what the Confederate naval officers were capable of accomplishing when the opportunity was given them of a test of strength with their adversaries.

The Confederate naval force, under Commodore Tatnall, consisted of the side-wheel steamer *Savannah*, carrying his flag, the paddle gun-vessel *Resolute*, and the small steamers *Sampson* and *Lady Davis*. An eye-witness, writing under date of November 12, 1861, described this fleet as " one frail river steam-boat the *Savannah*, with two or three tugs improvised into men-of-war." The United States squadron, under Admiral Du Pont, embraced the frigates *Wabash* and *Susquehanna*, the sloops *Mohican, Seminole*, and *Pawnee*, the sailing sloop *Vandalia*, and eight gunboats.

The main purpose of the Federals was to capture or silence the land batteries at the entrance to Port Royal Sound. On the morning of November 4th Commodore Tatnall observed several of the enemy's vessels engaged in taking soundings near the bar, at the entrance to the harbor, and he proceeded at once to give them battle. The little cockle-shells steamed to within a mile and a half of the most advanced vessels of the formidable Federal fleet and opened fire upon them; the firing was kept up for nearly an hour, when the little fleet retired within the harbor. The next day the enemy was again engaged, and for over an hour the gallant Tatnall defied his powerful antagonists, with but little damage to his fleet. Two days later the Federal squadron forced the issue and steamed into the harbor, their whole attention being given to the batteries at Fort Walker and Fort Beauregard on either side of the entrance. Commodore Tatnall then advanced to within range and opened fire upon the leading frigate of the Federal squadron; of course this contest was of short duration, and when the formidable men-of-war took serious notice of the Confederate punts, these latter, to avoid being blown out of the water, made good their retreat to the shoal creeks, beyond reach of the Federal ships.

Brigadier-General T. F. Drayton, in his report of the engagement on November 7th between the Federal fleet, numbering fifteen war steamers and gunboats, and forts Walker and Beauregard, at the entrance of Port Royal Sound, says:

To Commodore Tatnall, flag-officer, Confederate States Navy, and the officers and men of his little fleet, I cannot too highly express my admiration of their intrepidity and hardihood in attacking the enemy's gunboats on the 4th and 5th instant. These encounters, by interrupting their soundings and the location of their buoys, no doubt prevented our being attacked on Tuesday, the 5th instant, before our reinforcements reached us. I must also acknowledge the assistance extended to us by the gallant commodore, with his boats, on the night of our retreat from the island.

In these operations Captain Richard L. Page, Confederate States Navy, was a most efficient second in command to Commodore Tatnall. In a report of the engagement published in the *Savannah Republican* November 12, 1861, he is thus spoken of:

Early in the evening of this day (5th) we were all much gratified by the arrival of Captain Page, Confederate States Navy, of Virginia, the second in command to flag-officer Tatnall. This accomplished officer, whose reputation in the old service, to which he had long been a bright ornament, is well known, was a most valuable addition to our force, and, as events proved, to the army also, which is somewhat indebted to his personal exertions for the satisfactory retreat made by it.

Captain Page was afterward transferred to the army and commissioned brigadier-general; he won imperishable renown, later in the war, by his heroic defense of Fort Morgan, in Mobile Bay, against the attack of the powerful Federal fleet, under Admiral Farragut. He was cousin to General Robert E. Lee; was strikingly like him in person, and cherished the same lofty ideals of man's duty to his God and to his fellow-man.

In the fight at Port Royal Sound there was a striking illustration of the unnatural character of the war then being waged. General Thos. F. Drayton, Confederate States Army, was in command of the Confederate land

forces that defended forts Walker and Beauregard;
and his brother, Commander Percival Drayton, United
States Navy, was in command of the Federal steamer
Pocohontas that took part in the attack upon these
forts. Brother against brother!

General Lee and his staff were present in Charleston
at the time of the great fire that nearly destroyed that
beautiful city on December 11, 1861. While crossing
the Ashley River in an open row-boat, as we approached
the city we observed the light of the fire, but did not
attach much importance to it; we proceeded to the hotel known as the Mills House and repaired to the dining-
room. While seated at the table partaking of our meal
in a leisurely way, we became aware of great excitement prevailing outside, manifested by the rapid rush
of people and the noise of passing engines and vehicles.
When we left the room and went to the front of the
house, we were amazed at the rapid progress of the fire
and realized that a great calamity had befallen that
proud and beautiful city. To obtain a better view of
the conflagration, General Lee, with his staff, repaired
to the roof of the hotel, from which point we had an
unobstructed view of the grand and awfully sublime
spectacle of a city in flames. The progress of the fire
had been exceedingly rapid, and all around us appeared
a roaring, seething sea of fire. Men, women, and children rushed frantically about the streets, for the most
part apparently dazed and without aim or purpose, except to save themselves, while others struggled along
under a load of household effects, seeking to place the
same in some position of safety. And now the fire had
reached the opposite side of the street from us, and the
flames from the burning buildings almost lapped our
position; the heat had become intolerable, and we hastened to descend to the lower floor of the hotel. There we
found everything in confusion. Soldiers and firemen

were trying to save the building by putting blankets
thoroughly saturated with water around the casings of
the windows and wherever any wood was exposed.   The
inmates of the house hastily gathered together such of
their effects as could be removed, and left; our party
proceeded to the private residence of Mr. Charles Alston,
on the Battery, out of the line of danger and kindly
offered for General Lee's use.

The hotel was saved after great exertion on the part
of the firemen and soldiers.   The next morning revealed
a scene of desolation rarely witnessed: hundreds of
buildings, among them some of the most imposing in
the city, were smoldering in ruins, and thousands of
people were without shelter or the means of providing
for their wants; stores, dwellings, churches, and public
buildings had been destroyed, and after having cut a
wide swath through the city, from the Cooper to the
Ashley River, the flames finally died away for lack of
material upon which to feed.

CHAPTER V

IN March, 1862, General Lee returned to Richmond, and was assigned on the 13th, under the direction of the President, to the command of all the armies of the Confederacy. This position was created by special act of Congress, and under its provisions General Lee was allowed a personal staff of a military secretary, with the rank of colonel, and four aides-de-camp, with the rank of major. Of the staff that General Lee had in the Southern Department, none accompanied him to Richmond except myself. Colonel A. L. Long, who had been his chief of artillery in that department, was offered the position of military secretary and accepted it. The general very kindly offered me the choice between remaining in the adjutant-general's department of the service or an appointment as major and aide-de-camp under the new law. I told him my only choice was to serve where he might assign me; but upon being pressed by him to declare my personal preference, I told him I would rather be an aide. My principal reason for this choice was that I would be spared much confinement about headquarters and the annoyance and trouble of attending to papers and routine work, and be more on the field. One of the positions of major and aide-de-camp was therefore given to me; and the three others appointed were Major T. M. R. Talcott, Major Charles Marshall, and Major Charles S. Venable.

Very little was known and very little has since been made public of the character of the service then rendered by General Lee. The duties that devolved upon the President of the Confederate States were exceedingly onerous. Called upon to exercise the functions of the chief magistracy of a government created as it were in a day, and involving the welfare of ten millions of people and the destiny of eleven States, constituting a Republic of imposing size and character, it was beyond the limit of human power for him to direct the affairs of state in all the civil departments, and at the same time to give proper attention to the demands made upon him as commander-in-chief of the Confederate forces, under the provisions of the Constitution. The recognition of the necessity for relief in this direction led to the passing of the act of Congress before alluded to, creating the position of military adviser to the President. From the very nature of the case, however, the position was not one calculated to bring renown or special honor to him who occupied it. In all cases where there is dual authority, absolute accord in purpose and in the employment of means and agencies for carrying out that purpose, congeniality of temperament, and deference for the views of another, are essential to a smooth working of the machinery; and wherever this accord is lacking, and especially if there is any difference in rank or station, either friction and confusion are likely to result, or else one suppresses his own opinions, defers to those of the other and practically becomes his mouthpiece. We have seen something of this in the occasional conflict between the Secretary of War and the general in command of the army of the United States. Nevertheless, the services of General Lee as military adviser to the President and as commanding general of all the armies in the field were most valuable. Unfortunately, the record of that service was destroyed; but I have one rough draft of a letter from General Lee to General Jackson, dated April 29, 1862, which will show something of the character of the service then rendered. General Jackson had written to General Lee requesting that five thousand men be detached from the army in front of Richmond and sent to him, that he might overthrow the armies of generals Milroy and Banks that were opposing him in the Valley of Virginia. The answer to this letter was written by me in accordance with instructions received from General Lee; but he wished to alter the phraseology in one or two places, and interlined it in his own handwriting, so I prepared a fresh, clear copy for his signature, which was sent to General Jackson. It reads as follows:

> HEADQUARTERS, RICHMOND, VA.,
> April 29, 1862.

MAJOR-GENERAL T. J. JACKSON,
   Commanding, etc., Swift Run Gap, Va.

GENERAL:

I have had the honor to receive your letter of yesterday's date. From the reports that reach me that are entitled to credit, the force of the enemy opposite Fredericksburg is represented as too large to admit of any diminution whatever of our army in that vicinity at present, as it might not only invite an attack on Richmond, but jeopard the safety of the army in the Peninsula. I regret, therefore, that your request to have five thousand men sent from that army to reinforce you cannot be complied with. Can you draw enough from the command of General Edward Johnson to warrant you in attacking Banks? The last return received from that army shows a present force of upward of thirty-five hundred, which, it is hoped, has been since increased by recruits and returned furloughs. He does not appear to be pressed; it is suggested that a portion of his force might be temporarily removed from its present position and made available for the movement in question. A decisive and successful blow at Banks's column would be fraught with the happiest results, and I deeply regret my inability to send you the reinforcements you ask. If, however, you think the combined forces of General Edward Johnson, with your own, inadequate for the move, General Ewell might, with the assistance of General Anderson's army, near Fredericksburg, strike at McDowell's army, between that city and Acquia, with much promise of success; provided you feel sufficiently strong alone to hold Banks in check.

Very truly yours,

R. E. LEE.

It will be well understood by those who knew General Jackson that such a suggestion as that here made by General Lee came to him as an inspiration and a command. Without detracting in the least from the credit due to General Jackson, it may be claimed that he took the suggestion of General Lee into immediate consideration, and proceeded to carry it into effect.

Within ten days after the date of General Lee's letter, that is, on May 8th, General Jackson formed a junction between his command and that of General Edward Johnson, attacked General Milroy at McDowell, and defeated him; and on May 25th, having united his command and that of General Ewell, by authority of General Lee, he attacked and defeated General Banks.

Occasionally we hear mention in some quarter of a comparison of the relative merit, as soldiers, of generals Lee and Jackson. I always discourage such comparison, preferring to think of each as peerless of his kind. Each excelled in his own sphere of action: for quickness of perception, boldness in planning, and skill in directing, General Lee had no superior; for celerity in his movements, audacity in the execution of bold designs, and impetuosity in attacking, General Jackson had not his peer.

As another has expressed it, "If Lee was the Jove of the war, Stonewall Jackson was his thunderbolt. For the execution of the hazardous plans of Lee, just such a lieutenant was indispensable."

During this period of service of General Lee, the admirable line of earthworks for the defense of the city of Richmond was constructed in accordance with his designs; and every preparation was made to resist the army under General McClellan that was then advancing upon the Confederate capital by way of the Peninsula.

At this time I was thrown very much with President Davis, and not only learned to admire him greatly, but also to entertain for him a warm personal affection. Of all the prominent men in civil life from the South with whose names and service I was familiar, he came nearer than any to the ideal that I had set up as a standard for those leaders of the people. His knowledge of constitutional law and familiarity with the principles of representative government are generally acknowledged to have been unexcelled by any of his contemporaries; his capacity for work was extraordinary for one of his physique; his quick perception and the readiness with which he dealt with difficult situations were in constant demand in overcoming the friction incidental to the establishment of a new government; and his personal manner was cordial and attractive. In my intercourse with him he would often lead the conversation into channels of especial interest to a young man, and I was naturally drawn toward one who, though of high station, came down to a lower plane, invited my confidence and manifested an interest in my affairs. It was said of Mr. Davis that he was always true to his friends, and that through good report and ill report he stood by them. As was almost inevitable, it sometimes happened that his appointments to office were not of the happiest kind; and his reluctance to see the inefficiency of a friend no doubt caused a certain amount of criticism by those who demanded a sacrifice of all such private considerations where the good of the service was involved. Then, again, it may be claimed that he was too much influenced by political pressure and a desire to placate party leaders, whose chief aim was to strengthen themselves at home; but after this is said, he was still, in my judgment, by far the best qualified man of his time available for the onerous duties that devolved upon the chief executive of the new Confederacy.

In the year 1878 I received a letter from Mr. Davis, dated January 31st, in which he requested certain information concerning the operations at Cheat Mountain, in the western part of Virginia, in the fall of 1861, from which I make the following extract:

General Lee gave me orally a full account of the movement to surprise the enemy in the valley; but time and intervening circumstances do not allow me confidently to rely upon my memory. Were you with General Lee when with a portion of his command he made a night ascent of one of the peaks, and under cover of the fog reconnoitered the camp of the enemy? Can you tell me what troops were with him, and why he was not seconded in his proposition to make the attack, notwithstanding the failure of the signal agreed upon for the joint attack by the three divisions of his force? General Lee was severely and unjustly criticized for that campaign, and you may recollect that the blame was thrown jointly upon him and myself; but he magnanimously declined to make an official report which would have exonerated himself by throwing the responsibility of the failure upon others. His oral report to me was confidential, and I, therefore, wish to obtain facts otherwise. In the *New York Evening Post* of the 24th of January I find a review of your "Four Years with General Lee," in which the reviewer assumes that some remarks of yours are suggestive of the blunders by me which prevented General Lee from executing his own wise pur-

poses, and that you have from a delicate consideration forborne
plainly to expose those blunders on my part. I have not yet
read your book, and hope the reviewer has made a mistake in en-
rolling you in the large army of my assailants, which, since the
war, has been liberally reinforced from the South.

The passage in "Four Years with General Lee" here
referred to reads as follows:

It is a very simple matter to trace through the dates here
given the steady progress toward the inevitable doom which,
sooner or later, awaited the Confederates in their inflexible purpose to hold the city of Richmond.   General Lee was opposed to
that policy which designated certain points as indispensable to
be held, except so far and so long as they possessed strategic value
to the armies operating in the field.   He maintained that the determination to retain possession of such under all circumstances
and at any cost caused a fallacious value to attach to success
in such endeavor, and, in event of failure, entailed a moral loss
on us and assured an elation to the enemy altogether dispropor-
tionate to the material benefit to be derived from continued possession; not that he would not have made an earnest effort to
save such points as Vicksburg and Richmond from falling into
the hands of the enemy, but when it came to a siege, to settle
down behind intrenchments and permit the gradual and complete
circumvallation of the place besieged, by an adversary with unlimited resources of men and material, he preferred to move out,
to maneuver, to concentrate, and to fight.

His policy at Petersburg would have been to unite the greater
portion of his army, before it wasted away from incessant battle
and from desertion, with that under General Johnston, and to
fall upon General Sherman with the hope of destroying him, and
then, with the united armies, to return to confront General
Grant.   Having the interior line, he could move to accomplish
such purpose much more quickly than his adversary could to
thwart it.   Such a policy involved the giving up of Richmond,
it is true; but that which was pursued involved the same thing

with a certainty more absolute, and left Sherman to overwhelm Johnston and at the same time to destroy the granaries of the Confederacy, from which Lee's army was supplied.   In my opinion, as a general rule, the administration was in perfect accord with General Lee in all his designs, and gave a hearty co-operation in all his movements ; but I think the exception was furnished in the persistent effort to hold Richmond and Petersburg, after it became evident that it could be but a question of time, and would probably involve the complete exhaustion of the principal army of the Confederacy.

This was a plain statement of fact without denunciatory comment, and could not be considered an attack on Mr. Davis.   In my reply to his letter I said that I could not be responsible for inferences drawn from what I had written by the critics who wrote for the newspapers; and that I preferred not to make any reply to the intimation or suggestion in his letter until he had read what I had said.   As we exchanged letters after that, and as he freely quoted from my book in his "Rise and Fall of the Confederacy," I indulged the hope that he was satisfied that I was still his warm admirer and friend, and that my name was not to be enrolled among his traducers.

CHAPTER VI

THE Confederate forces occupying the Peninsula between James and York rivers, at that time were under the command of General J. B. Magruder. A line of defense had been established from Yorktown across the Peninsula to the Warwick and James rivers. General Magruder had under his command about eleven thousand men. General McClellan, then in command of the Federal Army of the Potomac, had abandoned the old route by way of Manassas and transferred his army to the Peninsula with the purpose of advancing upon Richmond by that route, with his base of supplies on York River. He advanced his army up the Peninsula from Fortress Monroe, and on the 4th of April appeared in front of the line occupied by the Confederates. This line of defense was a very strong one, but General Magruder, who knew of McClellan's change of base, when he realized the presence of the enemy in such overwhelming numbers, called lustily for reinforcements. The defense put up by General Magruder before he was reinforced was one of the most heroic of the war. In his report of this siege he says:

From the 4th of April till the 3d of May this army served almost without relief in the trenches. Many companies of artillery were never relieved during this long period. It rained almost incessantly; the trenches were filled with water. No fires could be allowed. The artillery and infantry of the enemy played upon our men almost continuously, day and night. The army had neither coffee, sugar, nor hard bread, but subsisted on flour and salt meats, and these in reduced quantities, and yet no murmurs were heard. The best drilled regulars the world has ever seen would have mutinied under a continuous service of twenty-nine days in the trenches, exposed every moment to musketry and shells, in water to their knees, without fire, sugar, or coffee, without stimulants, and with an inadequate supply of cooked flour and salt meats. I speak this in honor of those brave men whose patriotism made them indifferent to suffering, to disease, to danger, and to death.

And General Magruder knew of what he spoke; he had seen real service in the army of the United States, and was fully qualified to speak of the powers and the spirit of the men of the regular army. He was a typical soldier, the most picturesque that I ever saw. It was a real treat to see General Magruder in full military costume. Of commanding presence, very florid complexion, military whiskers, and much color in his uniform, his was a most impressive and attractive figure, a typical West Point soldier; and then there was in his manner and deportment a great fascination for those about him. Tradition links many interesting incidents with his name. I recall one or two worthy of mention. Some years before the war he was stationed at some post on the Canadian border, opposite or near to which was an English post. The officers of the two commands exchanged civilities. The English entertained the Americans at dinner, at which the display of silver was unusual. Magruder was the caterer of the mess when the time came for the Americans to give a return of civilities. Invitations were formally issued, and Magruder went to work to eclipse the Englishmen. It is said that the display of plate excelled anything ever seen under similar circumstances. The menu was a study in the art of the *cuisine* and the intricacies of the French language; the *entrées* and the wine were simply appalling in their profusion; and Magruder's reputation as a caterer was established. In the conversation between him and his English neighbor at table, he was asked what the annual pay was of an officer of his grade. He replied, with his lisp, " Weally, I don't know; we turn our pay over to our thervants." Of course the silver was hired, but, nevertheless, the mess was bankrupt, and it required a long time to recover its normal financial condition.

Another incident occurred at Yorktown. General Magruder took his meals in the house of a citizen, whose family very kindly looked after his comfort; and, no doubt, his bill of fare was a little better than that he described as his soldiers' in the report just now quoted. At any rate, it may be relied upon that he made the best of what he had, and his fine manners never forsook him. One day he had a visit from an officer of high rank, and he wished to do the best thing possible in the matter of entertaining him. He ordered dinner to be prepared at a certain hour, and directed that everything be served in first-class style. There was much excitement around the kitchen, and that attracted the attention of one of those old fellows whose home was in the trenches, and who longed for a change of diet and was foraging around for something in that line. The odor from the cooking viands took possession of his senses entirely. He was an earnest observer of every movement of the servants, and when he saw that dinner was ready, he quietly moved into the dining-room and secured his seat. In a moment the folding-doors were thrown open, and General Magruder appeared, accompanied by his honored guest and followed by his numerous staff. The unabashed veteran in search of a change of diet held his ground quietly and firmly, but Magruder was paralyzed. What did it mean, this uninvited guest who had not on a wedding-garment ? He halted. Turning sternly to the veteran, he asked, " Who are you, thir?" The soldier promptly gave his name and command. "Well, thir, what are you doing here, thir?" The soldier replied that it was his purpose to get something to eat. "Well, thir, and do you know with whom you propose to dine?" Promptly came the reply, "No, and I don't care a d—n either. I used to be particular in such matters before the war, but it don't make a d—d bit of diffeérence now." Magruder was thunderstruck. Lost in admiration, and extending both arms toward the veteran, he exclaimed with his inimitable lisp, "Your impudenth ith thublime, thir; keep your theat, thir," and the dinner proceeded.

As soon as the purpose of the Federal commander to advance by way of the Peninsula was fully disclosed, General Johnston, then in command of the Army of Northern Virginia, was directed to move all his available troops to the support of General Magruder, and to proceed thither himself and take command of the forces thus united. His military department was extended to include the city of Norfolk, and all the troops stationed there were placed under his command. Soon after General McClellan arrived in front of the lines occupied by General Magruder he made one ineffectual attempt to carry them by storm; failing in this, he settled down for a regular siege.

General Johnston assumed command on the 17th of April. General McClellan continued the work of preparation for the bombardment of the Confederate position for several weeks. On the night of May 3d, in anticipation of an attack from the heavy guns of the enemy, General Johnston evacuated his lines and began his retreat up the Peninsula. The rear-guard of his army was vigorously assailed at Williamsburg, but such was the character of the resistance made that the ardor of the pursuing army was checked, and he was permitted to continue his retreat, without further molestation, toward Richmond. Meanwhile he had directed the evacuation of Norfolk, and ordered General Huger, with the troops under his command thus relieved, to join him in front of Richmond.

General McClellan continued his advance and was soon at the Chickahominy River. In the latter part of May he moved two of his army corps to the south side of the river to a point known as Seven Pines. On May 31st General Johnston determined to attack this force, hoping to overwhelm it before it could be reinforced from the other side of the river. In the battle that followed General Johnston was wounded and disabled. General G. W. Smith was the next to him in rank, and temporarily assumed command of the army. The enemy during the night reinforced the corps on the south side, and there was no serious fighting on the next day.

On June 1st General Lee assumed personal command of the army in the following order:

SPECIAL ORDERS, HEADQUARTERS, RICHMOND, VA.,
  No. 22.   June 1, 1862.

In pursuance of the orders of the President, General R. E. Lee assumes command of the armies of eastern Virginia and North Carolina. The unfortunate casualty that has deprived the army in front of Richmond of the valuable services of its able general is not more deeply deplored by any member of the command than by its present commander. He hopes his absence will be but temporary, and while he will endeavor to the best of his ability to perform his duties, he feels he will be totally inadequate to the task unless he shall receive the cordial support of every officer and man.

    By order of General Lee.
      W. H. TAYLOR, A. A. G.

CHAPTER VII

OF General Johnston's staff, Colonel Thomas Jordan, his adjutant-general, and his aides accompanied him in his retirement. Captain A. P. Mason, assistant adjutant-general, remained at army headquarters. Colonel R. H. Chilton of the regular army was assigned to duty with General Lee about the middle of June. The personal staff of General Lee embraced then the following officers: Colonel R. H. Chilton, assistant adjutant-general; Colonel A. L. Long, military secretary; majors Walter H. Taylor, T. M. R. Talcott, Charles Marshall, and Charles S. Venable, aides-de-camp; and Captain A. P. Mason, assistant adjutant-general.

To one not experienced in such matters, no just conception can be formed of the voluminous character of official papers that find their way to army headquarters whenever a halt is called in active operations and an opportunity is offered the men to present in writing their petitions and grievances. Sometimes it would seem as if every man in the army had some matter to submit for the consideration of the commanding general. Some of these cases were unimportant, some were of more importance as affecting the discipline and efficiency of the army, and some were of a serious character, requiring both skill and tact in the proper disposition to be made of them. The general in command of an army in the field has his mind so occupied in the consideration of matters of greater importance than these as to be unable to consider them all, or to give to them any considerable portion of his time and attention. The theory is that he is served by an officer who speaks by his authority and in his name, who is supposed to be so well informed as to his chief's views and purposes, and so familiar with army regulations, as to be able to lay down definite principles and lines of action for guidance in determining all matters of army detail that would meet his approval, and to make all decisions of the questions presented to conform to these established principles. In times of peace, with a limited command, no doubt every such communication could be made to receive the personal attention of the officer in command; but not so with a large army in the presence of the enemy. General Lee could not bear to be annoyed with the consideration of these matters of routine. When the staff was first organized a large batch of these papers was submitted to him every morning, and it was his habit to have the members of his staff arranged around him in a semicircle, and as each paper was submitted to him he would pass it to one of the staff, in regular order, with instructions as to how it should be disposed of. This went on for a short time, and then he called me to him and said that he would have to put me back in the office. I knew what he meant, and I acted accordingly. He wished relief from such annoyances; he had real work to do and wished to be rid of these matters of detail. It was truly a knotty and difficult case that reached him after that, unless it involved an officer of very high rank. I had charge of the adjutant-general's department from that time to the end at Appomattox. Colonel Chilton had charge of the inspector-general's department until December, 1863, when he was made brigadier-general and assigned to duty in the office of the adjutant-general of the army at Richmond. Colonel Long was made brigadier-general of artillery and assigned as chief of that service with the second corps in September, 1863. Major Talcott was transferred to the engineers in the summer of 1863, and Captain Mason rejoined General Johnston when he recovered from his wound and resumed active duty. This left the general with one adjutant-general and two aides, and thereafter that constituted his personal staff to the end of the war. The chiefs of the several departments of the service attached to his staff moved, camped, and messed apart from him, though always within call and reporting to him daily for orders.

On assuming command of the army General Lee ordered the troops that had taken part in the battle of Seven Pines back to their former positions, and proceeded to strengthen his lines by the erection of additional earthworks and to bring his army to the highest possible state of efficiency. The decided check given to the Federal army by General Johnston's attack at Seven Pines gave ample time for the accomplishment of these objects, and very soon conditions were such as to impart to the Confederates a feeling of confidence in their ability to hold their position, and to cause General McClellan to hesitate a long time before making any attempt to carry these lines by a direct assault. In rear of these lines, nearer to Richmond, very formidable defensive works had been erected, and the knowledge of this fact gave additional confidence to the defending army in front. General Lee, however, soon ceased giving consideration to these excellent arrangements for defense; they had served their purpose in restoring confidence to his men and in giving him time to take in the situation. Already his active mind was engaged in studying the position of his adversary and in discovering the best way, under existing conditions, of taking the offensive.   The brilliant campaign of General Jackson in the Valley of Virginia had greatly alarmed the Federal authorities at Washington; it created fears for the safety of that city and tended to relieve the pressure upon the army under General Lee.   General McDowell, who had been at Fredericksburg, and so threatened General Lee in any aggressive movement he might undertake, had been recalled to Washington for its defense and to aid in the overthrow of General Jackson. The time seemed propitious to General Lee for taking aggressive action.   If a blow was to be struck, then was the time.

The army of General McClellan, over one hundred thousand strong, confronted General Lee; its right rested near Meadow Bridge, on the north side of the Chickahominy River, and its line extended southward to Golding's Crossing, where it crossed to the south side and continued to White Oak Swamp.   Porter's corps constituted its right wing and occupied the line on the north side of the river; the corps of Franklin, Sumner, and Heintzelman held the line on the south side of the river, and Keyes's corps was in reserve at Bottom's Bridge.   Formidable earthworks had been constructed along the entire line, and it was deemed out of the question by General Lee to attempt to make a direct assault.   It was necessary, then, to make the attack on the right or left flank, and steps had to be taken to ascertain which held out the greater promise of success.

In order that he might be more accurately informed of the character of the ground covering the approaches to the two flanks of the Federal army, and of the feasibility of turning either one or the other, General Lee ordered General J. E. B. Stuart, with about twelve hundred cavalry and a battery of artillery, to move to the right and rear of the Federal army and be guided by circumstances, in an endeavor to get this information, as to how far he should go and by what route he should return. Never was an order more perfectly carried out; never a purpose more successfully accomplished. The raid of General Stuart completely around the army of General McClellan has passed into history as one of the most brilliant exploits of that arm of the service.

General Lee's purpose was now fully determined: he would make the attack on the enemy's right flank. There has been some foolish talk about credit being due to another for this plan of attack. General Early was made very indignant some time after the close of the war because of the claim advanced that General Lee was indebted to another for this suggestion, and in a letter to me dated April 29, 1876, after speaking in rather strong language of those who thus sought to lessen the credit due to General Lee, he puts the matter very clearly thus:

It may be very true that, in speaking about the proper mode of attacking the enemy, Longstreet may have thought it was best to attack on the enemy's right flank, while Hill (D. H.) may have thought it best to attack the other. The attack had to be made on the one or the other, as there was no chance to attack in the center, and men would of course have some opinion as to which was the right one to attack.

General Lee then developed his plans to the authorities in Richmond, which may be briefly stated here, and which met with the approval of President Davis and the War Department. He was very anxious to have General Jackson deliver another stunning blow to his adversaries operating in the Valley of Virginia; and then, before they had time to recover, to come by the quickest possible route, with all his available force, to join him in an attack on the Federal army under General McClellan. To carry out this design and to make sure against any miscarriage as to General Jackson's success,

large reinforcements were to be sent to him, the effect
of which would be, not only to make assurance doubly
sure with Jackson, but to deceive the enemy as to General Lee's ultimate purpose.

Reinforcements were forwarded to General Jackson;
but the element of time became so important, in General
Lee's opinion, that he decided not to wait until Jackson
could carry out his plan to attack in the valley, but to
bring him down at once with his whole force, including
the reinforcements just sent, leaving only a small corps
of observation, and to attack McClellan's army without
further delay. Orders to this effect were sent to General
Jackson, and on the 18th of June his army started to
join General Lee; on the 22d it had reached Frederick's Hall. General Jackson left his army there during the night of the 22d, and proceeded on horseback to
General Lee's headquarters for the purpose of having a
personal conference about the plan of attack.

I had not seen General Jackson since I left the Virginia Military Institute, where I had been under his
tutelage as a cadet. In personal appearance and manners he was the same "Old Jack" that I had then
known. It seems odd to me at this day to contrast the
estimate in which he is now universally regarded with
the reputation that he had when he was a professor of
natural philosophy at Virginia's military school. Austerity of manner and silence were then his chief char-
acteristics, although when once the outer shell was
pierced he was always genially warm in manner and
sympathetic at heart. He was certainly regarded in
those days by the people of Lexington and by the
cadets as a most eccentric character. It was said of
him that although he had all his text-books well at his
command, he never deviated from the text to the
right or left. He was a thoroughgoing Presbyterian,
with a strong leaning to fatalism, and I have often

thought that to this trait and his unquestioning faith in the efficacy of prayer, however irreconcilable the two may appear to some, was due much of his success in battle. While regarded by the cadets as odd and peculiar, he possessed a degree of manliness and a disposition to waive all question of rank in smoothing out a personal disagreement that attracted and won the esteem of young men. In addition to his duties as professor of physics, he was instructor of the corps of cadets in artillery tactics. It was here that the cadets took especial pleasure in making his performance of duty a severe trial to him. He was made the butt of their jokes, and it afforded them the greatest pleasure to bring about confusion by removing the linch-pins from the guns or caissons, and so overturning them; or by rushing the guns or caissons down the incline of the campus with such an impetus as to make it impossible to "halt" before there was a collision with the fence that then inclosed the drill-ground.

There was something indescribably droll in the manner in which he sang out his orders with a nasal twang peculiar to himself. I seem to hear him now as he followed out the stereotyped maneuvers, always terminating with a prolonged "Quick, trot, march!" As there were no horses used, the cadets did the pulling of the guns and caissons, and so were constructively horses. I recall an occasion when one of the cadets had hurt the feelings of his "off horse" by treading on his toes, or barking his shin, and the wounded one made the air sulphurous with his vigorous but unparliamentary use of his mother tongue, and that in such a tone as to be heard all over the campus. Quietly and solemnly "Old Jack" stepped up to the sergeant of the detachment, and pointing to the angry cadet, said, "Report that *horse* for profanity."

On another occasion a cadet who was rather slow of

movement, in truth a little lazy, when the command was given, "Limbers and caissons, pass your pieces, Q-u-i-c-k, t-r-o-t, m-a-r-c-h !" sauntered along, and was left behind, rejoining his piece on the return movement. The next day a report was made out against him for his refusal to obey orders, and he handed in an excuse that read something like this: " Report, not *trotting* at artillery drill. Excuse, I am a natural *pacer.*"

But to return to the conference with General Lee on the afternoon of the 23d of June. General Jackson reported the progress already made by his troops, and indicated the time necessary to enable them to reach the point of the proposed attack. The plan of battle was discussed, all of the division commanders being present. The conference over, General Jackson went at once to rejoin his troops. General Lee now felt that his army was sufficiently well in hand to justify him in issuing the order of attack.

The army under General Lee embraced the divisions of Longstreet, A. P. Hill, D. H. Hill, Magruder, Huger, Holmes, and the troops under Jackson, consisting of his own and Ewell's divisions, and the reinforcements recently sent him, to wit, Whiting's division and Lawton's brigade—in all about eighty thousand men.

The order of attack, dated June 24th, contemplated that by the 25th the command under General Jackson would be in position at Ashland on the Richmond, Fredericksburg, and Potomac Railroad, a point about fifteen miles north of Richmond; and it was ordered to proceed on that day toward Slash Church and to encamp at a convenient point west of the Central (Chesapeake and Ohio) Railroad. At three o'clock on Thursday morning, June 26th, General Jackson was to advance on the road leading to Pole Green Church, communicating his march to General Branch, whose brigade had been in the neighborhood of Hanover Court House, who was then to cross the Chickahominy and take the road leading to Mechanicsville and rejoin his division under A. P. Hill. As soon as the movements of these columns were discovered, General A. P. Hill, whose command constituted the left of General Lee's army, was ordered to cross the Chickahominy at Meadow Bridge and move directly upon Mechanicsville. To aid General Hill in his attack, the heavy batteries on the Chickahominy were ordered to open on the Federal batteries at Mechanicsville. The enemy being driven from Mechanicsville, and the way made open over the bridge near that point, General Longstreet with his division was to cross the Chickahominy to the support of General A. P. Hill; and General D. H. Hill was to cross with his division to the support of General Jackson. These four commands were ordered to keep in communication with each other, to move in *echélon*, and, if practicable, on separate roads, General Jackson in advance, and to endeavor to drive the enemy from his position above New Bridge, General Jackson bearing well to the left, turning Beaver Dam Creek and taking the direction of Cold Harbor. This having been accomplished, the assaulting columns were to press the enemy toward the York River Railroad, closing upon his rear and forcing him down the Chickahominy. The commands of generals Magruder and Huger were to hold the Confederate lines on the south side of the Chickahominy, watch closely the result of the movements on the north side, and to make such demonstrations against the enemy in their front as to discover what he was about, and if favorable opportunity offered, to convert the feint into a real attack; and should the enemy abandon his intrenchments, to pursue him closely. General Stuart with the bulk of the cavalry force was to cross the Chickahominy and take position on the left of General Jackson.

CHAPTER VIII

MECHANICSVILLE

THE time for the commencement of the movement had been determined after a careful consideration of the time necessary to enable General Jackson's command to get into position, and no miscarriage was looked for in this direction. Thursday, the 26th, arrived, and General A. P. Hill, who was to open the battle, had everything in readiness, and only awaited the arrival of General Jackson. General McClellan, with two thirds of his army on the south side of the Chickahominy, was confronted by but twenty-five thousand Confederates. Unless attacked, he might assail this force and attempt to capture Richmond. Indecision on the part of the Confederates under these conditions would have invited disaster. After waiting until three o'clock in the afternoon, without any sign of Jackson's troops, and presuming that by the time he crossed the Chickahominy and got into position General Jackson would connect with his left, General A. P. Hill crossed over Meadow Bridge with his division. He drove the enemy out of Mechanicsville and was soon in front of the strongly fortified position along Beaver Dam Creek, constituting the right of the Federal line and held by the command of General Fitz John Porter. General A. P. Hill promptly deployed his troops and made dispositions to assault that line. In addition to his own division, he was reinforced by Ripley's brigade of D. H. Hill's division. He had every reason to rely upon the coöperation of General Jackson, who was to attack the enemy's right flank and rear, but as yet no sign of the approach of Jackson's troops. What had become of them? Why this unexpected delay? Those were anxious moments to Hill and to all. Colonel Allan, chief ordnance officer of Jackson's command, in his book "The Army of Northern Virginia," thus explains this delay:

Jackson, who was to have passed Ashland on the 25th and camp in the vicinity of the Virginia Central Railroad, was only able to reach Ashland on that day. . . . The long forced march of Jackson to Ashland had consumed half a day more than was expected. He had consequently reached the Central Railroad, his arrival at which point was to be the signal for the movement of the other divisions, five or six hours late; and his march all day, though vigorously pressed, had been impeded to some extent by the enemy's scouting parties, but far more by the unknown character of the country, which was all new to him. He had therefore not reached Beaver Dam Creek in time to dislodge, or in conjunction with A. P. Hill to overwhelm, McCall.

It was a remarkable fact that in all these movements of the Seven Days' Battles around Richmond the Confederates were operating to the greatest disadvantage because of their ignorance of the country and the lack of accurate maps showing its topography and the location of the roads. One would have supposed that in the time which had elapsed since the commencement of the war accurate surveys and maps would have been made of the country for miles around the city of Richmond, and of every approach to that city likely to be attempted by the enemy; but neither generals nor officers of the staff had any such information, and, as a rule, the country people who were relied on as guides seemed to have no knowledge of such matters beyond the immediate vicinity of their homes.

Hill's troops advanced in gallant style until they reached Beaver Dam Creek, which was practically impassable in the face of a determined foe. Several attempts were made to reach the Federal line, but as there was no simultaneous attack upon its flank and rear, they were repulsed with heavy loss. The firing continued until about 9 P.M., when the engagement ceased.

General Lee ordered the battle to be renewed at dawn on the 27th, when Jackson, whose command was now up, would be in position to coöperate, and to carry out the original plan of attack. This, however, would be attended with very different conditions. General McClellan was now fully aware of the purpose of General Lee, and had time to strengthen and reinforce the threatened flank. The spirited advance made by the troops of A. P. Hill and the approach of Jackson, now fully disclosed, made it evident to the Federal commander that, although a strong line for defense against direct attack, the position along Beaver Dam Creek would be untenable when turned by Jackson; so during the night the Federals retired from that line and took up their second line, extending from the Chickahominy along Powhite Creek, by Gaines's Mill to Cold Harbor— naturally a strong line, and greatly strengthened by the erection of breastworks and the construction of abatis.

GAINES'S MILL AND COLD HARBOR

On the morning of the 27th the attack was renewed as originally contemplated in General Lee's order of battle. A. P. Hill's division was in the center; Longstreet's division was in reserve, in the rear and to the right of A. P. Hill; and the commands of D. H. Hill

and Jackson were on the left. Again the troops of
A. P. Hill were the first to become engaged. The fighting soon became fast and furious. Hill seemed to be
contending alone against the whole Federal right wing,
as Jackson's movements were again unaccountably
slow; and as no attack was being made on the enemy's
right, he was enabled to concentrate in his resistance
to the assault of A. P. Hill. General Jackson, in his
report of the battle, thus explains his attitude at that
time:

Soon after General A. P. Hill became engaged, and being
unacquainted with the ground, and apprehensive, from what
appeared to me to be the respective positions of the Confederate
and Federal forces engaged, that if I then pressed forward our
troops would be mistaken for the enemy and fired into, and hoping that generals A. P. Hill and Longstreet would soon drive
the Federals toward me, I directed General D. H. Hill to move
his division to the left of the road, so as to leave between him
and the woods on the right of the road an open space, across
which I hoped the enemy would be driven.

To aid General A. P. Hill in his endeavor to force the
lines of the enemy, General Lee directed General Longstreet to advance some of his brigades against the Federal left, with the hope that this would have the effect
of drawing off troops from the enemy's right, prevent
any strengthening of the force in A. P. Hill's front, and
by weakening the right of the Federal line afford a better opportunity to generals Jackson and D. H. Hill for
making a lodgment there. General Longstreet, in
speaking of the movement, says:

Three brigades were sent to open fire and threaten their left
from the forest edge, with orders not to cross the open. These
brigades engaged steadily, and parts of them essayed to pass the
field in front, as their blood grew hot, but were recalled, with

orders repeated to engage steadily, only threatening assault, the army all the while engaged in efforts to find a point that could be forced.

Meanwhile, General Jackson had discovered from the direction and sound of the firing that General A. P. Hill was having heavy work, and so he ordered a general advance of his entire command, which commenced with D. H. Hill upon the left, and extended to the right through Ewell's, Jackson's, and Whiting's divisions in the order named. In some way General Whiting with his division, consisting of his own and General Hood's brigades, found his way to our right, and reporting to General Longstreet, asked that he be put into battle.

General Lee now ordered a simultaneous advance of his whole line. General Longstreet, who up to this time had only threatened assault, now pushed his troops forward, the two brigades of Whiting and Hood advancing with the brigades of Longstreet's division. These troops advanced with great impetuosity against the Federal left; they assaulted the enemy's position at Gaines's Mill with a determination and courage that insured success. Forcing their way through abatis, they scaled the heights, carrying several intrenched lines, and finally driving the Federals in confusion across the plateau in rear of the heights so stubbornly defended and so gallantly captured.

Simultaneously with the advance of the brigades of Longstreet's division the whole Confederate line moved forward. The troops of Jackson and D. H. Hill had then gotten into position, and attacked the enemy's right flank and center with great impetuosity. The success of General Longstreet's division, supported by General Whiting, in piercing the enemy's lines, and the heavy assault made by the troops of Jackson and D. H. Hill on the right flank of the enemy, caused their whole line to give way, and the right wing of the Federal army retreated upon the main body, pursued by the successful Confederates.

No more creditable performance can be found in the history of the Army of Northern Virginia than the capture of the Federal position near Gaines's Mill by the brigades of Longstreet's and Whiting's divisions, and better soldiers never fought. There was some question at the time as to what troops first pierced the Federal lines, but General McClellan in his report says that the Confederates "threw fresh troops against General Porter with their greatest fury, and finally gained the woods held by our left. This reverse, aided by the confusion that followed an unsuccessful charge by five companies of the Fifth Cavalry, and followed as it was by more determined assault on the remainder of our lines, now outflanked, caused a general retreat from our position to the hill in rear, overlooking the bridge." And General Jackson in his report says: "The Fourth Texas, under the lead of General Hood, was the first to pierce these strongholds and seize the guns." This clearly proves that the part of the Federal line that was the first to give way was their left, where the brigades under Longstreet made their attack, and accords with my own impressions formed at the time.

As in this battle the Confederates were acting on the aggressive, assaulting intrenched lines, their losses were very heavy. The losses on the Federal side were also very heavy. This was especially noticeable where Hood's brigade made its assault. In riding over the field at that point, I recall that I had to exercise great care in guiding my horse not to strike a dead or wounded Federal soldier.

On the morning of the 28th, when the Confederate skirmishers were advanced, it was ascertained that the enemy had retired to the south side of the Chickahominy, where McClellan's whole army was then con-

centrated. The York River Railroad, the artery by
which General McClellan's army had received its supplies, was seized by General Stuart with his cavalry,
and the Federal commander was forced to select a new
base of supplies. He had to choose between the Peninsula and James River, and he determined to go to James
River, where he would have the protection of gunboats.

General McClellan had conceived the most exaggerated ideas concerning the strength of General Lee's army.
It is difficult to understand how he was so greatly de-
ceived: he had, or should have had, pretty accurate information concerning the Confederate forces that had
been operating on the Peninsula; he had been in contact with Johnston's army at Williamsburg and at Seven
Pines; he knew General Johnston well enough to understand that he would not have retreated before him
had he not been outnumbered. He had under his command about one hundred and five thousand effective
men, excluding the troops at Fortress Monroe.

Previous to the attack of General Lee almost daily
appeals were sent by General McClellan to the authorities at Washington for reinforcements, in which he represented that he was greatly outnumbered, and, at the
same time, expressed again and again his purpose to
take aggressive action. On June 2d he telegraphed to
Washington: "Our left is within four miles of Richmond. I only wait for the river to fall to cross with the
rest of the force and make a general attack. The morale
of my troops is now such that I can venture much. I
do not fear for odds against me." On June 7th he telegraphed: "I shall be in perfect readiness to move forward to take Richmond the moment that McCall reaches
here and the ground will admit the passage of artillery."
On June 11th he reported: "McCall's troops have commenced arriving at the White House. . . . Weather
good to-day. Give me a little good weather, and I shall

have progress to report here." On June 14th he said: "Weather now very favorable. I shall advance as soon as the bridges are completed and the ground fit for artillery to move." On June 18th: "After to-morrow we shall fight the Rebel army as soon as Providence will permit." On June 25th he sent up a wail over his lack of men: "The Rebel force is stated at two hundred thousand, including Jackson and Beauregard. I shall have to contend against vastly superior odds, if these reports be true; but this army will do all in the power of men to hold their position and repulse any attack. I regret my great inferiority of numbers, but feel that I am in no way responsible for it, as I have not failed to represent repeatedly the necessity of reinforcements. . . . I will do all that a general can do with the splendid army I have the honor to command, and if it is destroyed by overwhelming numbers, can at least die with it and share its fate; but if the result of the action which will probably occur to-morrow or within a short time is a disaster, the responsibility cannot be thrown on my shoulders. I feel there is no use in my again asking for reinforcements."

On June 2d General McClellan did not fear for the odds against him. On June 25th he seemed to have suffered from a dreadful nightmare, and to have been in mortal terror of the innumerable hosts about to overwhelm him. He gave too great credence, no doubt, to the reports of his secret-service corps. In a memorandum of "General Estimates of the Rebel Forces in Virginia" made by the secret-service men, and published with his report, will be found the following:

One hundred and eighty thousand troops at Richmond prior to reinforcements from Charleston. Rebel troops in the Seven Days' Battles, including Jackson's whole force, estimated at two hundred and twenty thousand to two hundred and sixty thousand.

Now that the smoke of battle has cleared away and time has permitted a winnowing of fancy from fact, the truth stands revealed that the strength of General Lee's army in the Seven Days' Battles was under eighty-one thousand men. In the battles of Gaines's Mill and Cold Harbor the Confederates engaged numbered about fifty thousand, and the Federals opposing them numbered about thirty-five thousand; but it should be borne in mind that these latter were acting on the defensive and fighting behind fortifications. Later in the war there was another encounter about this same spot, Cold Harbor; then the positions were reversed: General Lee was on the defensive and General Grant made the assault. There has never been any question as to which side then had the most men. The Confederates on the defensive made impregnable the position they had captured in the Seven Days' Battles; the Federals, after heroic and most courageous but vain efforts to capture the position they had once lost, sullenly refused to move when again ordered forward to assault it.

The troops constituting the right wing of the Federal army that were defeated at Gaines's Mill and Cold Harbor, in their retreat had destroyed the bridges over the Chickahominy in their rear; and it was not practicable for the Confederates to reconstruct them in the presence of the enemy, whose artillery completely commanded the river and its banks. The army of General McClellan held all the bridges on the lower Chickahominy, and the way was open for it to retreat by way of the Peninsula, or by a direct route to James River, as might be deemed most advantageous. If the retreat should be down the Peninsula, then General Lee would need his troops, where the recently engaged force already was, on the north side of the Chickahominy; it was necessary to wait until the purpose of General McClellan was fully discerned. General Lee, therefore, was inactive on the

28th, as it was not ascertained until late in the evening of that day that General McClellan was retreating to James River.

SAVAGE STATION

On the next day the pursuit of the retreating army began. General Lee ordered Longstreet and A. P. Hill to recross the Chickahominy at New Bridge and to take direction of the army in retreat. Meanwhile it was discovered that the enemy had abandoned their line in front of generals Huger and Magruder, and they were ordered to pursue the Federal army. General Jackson was ordered to cross the Chickahominy at Grapevine Bridge and take up the line of pursuit. In all the movements of the Confederates in the pursuit of General Mc-Clellan's army, they were greatly hindered and delayed by the character of the country, abounding there in small streams and extensive swamps, and by the ignorance of the general staff concerning the roads. General Jackson was delayed on the 29th by the necessity of repairing the Grapevine Bridge, which the Federals had partially destroyed. This delay on the part of Jackson's troops was not anticipated, and from it some confusion resulted. General Magruder, who was advancing by the Williamsburg road, was the first to come up with the enemy, and promptly engaged his rear-guard. General Jackson, who was expected to cross the river at Grapevine Bridge, would have thus been in position to co-operate with General Magruder, and he had orders to this effect. General Jackson, in his official report of these battles, says that he was delayed all day by the necessity of reconstructing the bridge by which he was to cross to the south side of the Chickahominy.

The military student will naturally seek some explanation of the fact that no more decisive blow was given by the Confederates to the retreating Federal army. He will discover that the history of that pursuit is but a record of lost opportunities, and he will ascertain that the failure to accomplish more was due, in great part, to unlooked-for impediments encountered by the division commanders in moving over a section of country unknown to them and admirably adapted to defense, which delayed their own movements and deprived others of the coöperation expected of them. The delay of Jackson in crossing the Chickahominy deprived Magruder of the coöperation he looked for at Savage Station, and naturally caused him much anxiety. It was reported to him by General D. R. Jones, who commanded the brigade on the left of Magruder's line, and who appears to have been in communication with General Jackson, that in response to a request from him to know if he could rely on his coöperation, he had received reply from General Jackson to the effect that he "had other important duties to perform." It was this, perhaps, that led General Magruder to fear that he was not to have Jackson's support.

I cannot explain to what General Jackson referred in his reply to General Jones; but certainly there is no room for misunderstanding as to his orders. General Lee, on being told of the apprehension concerning Jackson's support entertained by General Magruder, sent him a message, quoted in Vol. XI, Part II, page 675, of War Records as follows:

I learn from Major Taylor that you are under the impression that General Jackson has been ordered not to support you. On the contrary, he has been directed to do so, and to push the pursuit vigorously.

As it was, while those of Magruder's brigades that were put into action at Savage Station did splendid service, a considerable portion of his force did not become engaged, and night put an end to a conflict without decisive results. General Lee says in his report:

> Late in the afternoon Magruder attacked the enemy with one of his divisions and two regiments of another. A severe action ensued and continued about two hours, when it was terminated by night. The troops displayed great gallantry and inflicted heavy loss upon the enemy, but, owing to the lateness of the hour and the small force employed, the result was not decisive, and the enemy continued his retreat under cover of darkness, leaving several hundred prisoners, with his dead and wounded, in our hands. But the time gained enabled the retreating column to cross White Oak Swamp without interruption and destroy the bridge.

FRAZIER'S FARM

General Jackson reached Savage Station on the 30th. He was directed to continue the pursuit. In his advance he captured so many prisoners and small arms that he was compelled to detach two regiments to guard them. His advance was checked at White Oak Swamp: the bridge had been destroyed. The enemy occupied the opposite side of the swamp and so commanded the banks as to prevent the rebuilding of the bridge. Generals Longstreet and A. P. Hill continued their advance and in the afternoon came upon the enemy at Frazier's Farm. From the position occupied by General Huger on the right, his coöperation was looked for on that flank. Having no knowledge of the cause of General Jackson's delay, his coöperation was looked for on the left.

Meanwhile, General Holmes, who with a part of his division had crossed from the south side of James River on the 29th, had moved down the river road, and on the 30th encountered the retreating army near Malvern Hill. He opened upon the enemy with artillery, but soon discovered that the batteries opposed to him greatly outnumbered his own, and also that the fire of the gun-boats from James River guarded this part of their line. General Magruder was ordered to support General Holmes, but, being at a greater distance than had been supposed, he did not reach the position of the latter in time to assist in an attack.

General Huger reported that his progress was ob-structed; soon, however, firing was heard on the right of Longstreet, which was supposed to be by the troops of General Huger, and General Longstreet opened with his artillery to give notice of his presence. This devel-oped the fact that the enemy was present in great force, and an engagement was brought on at once, although is was not designed that this should be until the troops of General Huger were in position to attack.

General Longstreet threw troops forward as rapidly as possible to the support of the attacking columns. Again, however, owing to the nature of the ground, the desired coöperation of commands failed. Only the divi-sions of Longstreet and A. P. Hill were engaged. The enemy was in position and numerically exceeded the attacking columns. General Longstreet says in his re-port: "The enemy, however, was driven back slowly and steadily. Contesting the ground inch by inch, he succeeded in getting some of his batteries off the field, and, by holding his last position until dark, in with-drawing his forces under cover of the night." General Jackson was delayed by the difficulties attending his effort to force the passage of White Oak Swamp. Gen-eral Lee, in his report, said: "The battle raged furiously until 9 P.M. By that time the enemy had been driven with great slaughter from every position but one, which he maintained until he was enabled to withdraw under cover of darkness."

Major-general McCall was taken a prisoner in this battle. To illustrate the character of the fighting on both sides, as seen by him, the following extract is given from his official report:

Soon after this a most determined charge was made on Randol's battery by a full brigade advancing in wedge shape, without order, but in perfect recklessness. Somewhat similar charges had been previously made on Cooper's and Kern's batteries by single regiments without success, they having recoiled before the storm of canister hurled against them. A like result was anticipated in Randol's battery, and the Fourth Regiment was requested not to fire until the battery had done with them. Its gallant commander did not doubt his ability to repel the attack, and his guns did indeed mow down the advancing host, but still the gaps were closed and the enemy came in on a run to the very muzzle of his guns. It was a perfect torrent of men, and they were in his battery before the guns could be removed, and the enemy, rushing past, drove the greater part of the Fourth Regiment before them. I had ridden into the regiment and endeavored to check them, but with only partial success. It was here my fortune to witness one of the fiercest bayonet fights that perhaps ever occurred on this continent. Bayonet wounds, mortal or slight, were given and received. I saw skulls crushed by the butts of muskets, and every effort made by either party in this life-or-death struggle, proving indeed that here Greek had met Greek.

MALVERN HILL

General Jackson reached the scene of the battle at Frazier's Farm early on July 1st, and was ordered to continue the pursuit by the Willis Church road. His advancing column was soon fired upon by the enemy, who nevertheless continued to fall back until he reached Malvern Hill, where he was found in force, most advantageously placed, with a large number of batteries on the crest of the hill, supported by masses of infantry partially protected by earthworks.

A great part of the day was consumed in reconnoitering the position of the enemy and in getting the different commands in position for attack. The position of the Federals on Malvern Hill was indeed formidable; it could hardly have been stronger. In its entire front the ground was open for some distance, and every approach was commanded by the numerous guns that poured from its crest. To reach this position the Confederates had to advance through a broken country, traversed throughout its whole extent by a swamp that very greatly interfered with the movements of the troops. It was late in the day before any advance was made. Jackson was on the left, with the divisions of Whiting and D. H. Hill and one of the brigades of Ewell's division in front, Jackson's own division and the balance of Ewell's being in reserve. Two brigades of Huger's division were on Jackson's right, and Magruder's division and one of Huger's brigades constituted the right of the line. Orders were issued for a general advance at a signal to be given, but, as General Lee says in his report, concert of action by the troops was prevented by the causes referred to. General D. H. Hill was the first to become engaged. His troops advanced gallantly and drove back the first line of the enemy, but the fire from the Federal batteries was terrific, and he was forced to relinquish most of the ground he had gained, after suffering heavily and inflicting great loss upon the enemy. General Hill complained bitterly of the failure of the other divisions to support him. He says in his report:

The front line of the enemy was twice broken and in full retreat when fresh troops came up to its support. At such critical juncture the general advance of the division on my right and left must have been decisive. Some half an hour after my division had ceased to struggle against odds of more than ten to one and had fallen back, McLaws's division advanced, but to share a similar fate.

On the right the divisions of Huger and Magruder attacked in the same gallant style, but with the same ultimate result. Some of the brigades advanced bravely across the open field and attempted to carry the hill by assault, driving back the infantry and compelling the most advanced batteries to retire to escape capture; but owing to a lack of coöperation among the assaulting columns, the enemy was enabled to concentrate and so to strengthen the threatened part of their line with reinforcements as to compel the Confederates to yield the positions gained. The fighting continued late into the night, but all efforts to pierce the enemy's line failed. The Federals retired during the night, leaving their dead unburied and their wounded as they fell. They abandoned three pieces of artillery and thousands of small arms. As expressed by General D. H. Hill, "None of their previous retreats exhibited such unmistakable signs of rout and demoralization. The wheatfields about Shirley were all trampled down by the fugitives, too impatient to follow the road. Arms, accouterments, knapsacks, and overcoats were strewn on the roadside and in the field."

The cavalry under General Stuart that had seized the York River Railroad on June 28th had proceeded, under the orders of the commanding general, down that railroad, to ascertain if there was any movement of the enemy in that direction. General Stuart reached the vicinity of the White House on June 29th without serious opposition. At his approach the enemy destroyed an immense quantity of stores accumulated at that point, and retreated toward Fort Monroe. General Stuart then proceeded with the main portion of the cavalry, in compliance with his orders, to guard the lower bridges of the Chickahominy. On the 30th of June he was directed to recross the river and to move to coöperate with General Jackson, and reached the scene of operations, at Malvern Hill, at the close of the engagement at 9 P.M. on July 1st.

On the morning of July 2d it was discovered that the enemy had retired during the night, leaving his dead and wounded on the field, and other unmistakable evidence of demoralization and haste. Pursuit was ordered immediately. The cavalry under General Stuart being in advance, General Stuart put his column in motion for Haxall's, hoping to intercept the enemy there. His advance soon reached the river road in rear of Turkey Creek, where many prisoners were captured, and a small body of his men reached the vicinity of Haxall's and became satisfied that the enemy was not there. He then endeavored to gain the fork of the roads near Shirley, but found that position well defended by the enemy's infantry, but, from what was learned from the prisoners captured, it was evident that the retreating army had gone below that point. Meanwhile, a part of his force was engaged in harassing the enemy's rear, and in collecting prisoners and small arms abandoned by the retreating Federals. That night a squadron of cavalry with a howitzer, under Captain Pelham, was sent toward Westover, with orders to reach the immediate vicinity of the river road below, so as to shell it, if the enemy attempted to retreat that night.

During the night Captain Pelham reported to General Stuart that the enemy had taken position between Shirley and Westover, and indicated the advantage to be gained by occupying Evelington Heights, a plateau from which the enemy's camps could be completely commanded.

In his report General Stuart says:

I found Evelington Heights easily gained. A squadron in possession vacated without much hesitation, retreating up the road, the only route by which it could reach Westover, owing to the impassability of Herring's Creek below Roland's Mill. Colonel Martin was sent around farther to the left, and the howitzer brought into action in the river road, to fire upon the enemy's camp. Judging from the great commotion and excitement caused below, it must have had considerable effect. We soon had prisoners from various corps and divisions, and from their statements, as well as those of citizens, I learned that the enemy's main body was there, but much reduced and demoralized. I kept the commanding general apprised of my movements, and I soon learned from him that Longstreet and Jackson were en route to my support. I held the ground from about 9 A.M. until 2 P.M., when the enemy had contrived to get one battery in position on this side the creek. The fire, however, was kept up until a body of infantry was found approaching by our right flank. I had no apprehension, however, as I felt sure Longstreet was near-by; and although Pelham reported but two rounds of ammunition left, I held out, knowing how important it was to hold the ground until Longstreet arrived. The enemy's infantry advanced, and the battery kept up its fire. I just then learned that Longstreet had taken the wrong road, and was at Nance's Shop, six or seven miles off. Pelham fired his last round, and the sharpshooters, strongly posted in the skirt of wood bordering the plateau, exhausted every cartridge, and had at last to retire.

The progress of the infantry, meanwhile, had been greatly retarded by a heavy storm, and by obstacles placed in the roads by the retreating enemy. Longstreet was further delayed by the necessity for countermarching his command, having been misled by his guide, and did not reach the point occupied by Stuart until late in the afternoon of the 3d. Jackson, who was following, reached the scene early on the morning of the 4th, and drove in the pickets of the enemy. General Stuart then pointed out the position of the enemy, now occupying, apparently in force, the plateau from which he had shelled their camps the day before, and suggested a route by which the plateau could be reached. Generals Longstreet and Jackson conferred together concerning the advisability of attack, and determined to await the arrival of General Lee.

After having thoroughly examined the ground, General Lee concluded that the natural strength of the position occupied by McClellan's army, and the protection further given it by the Federal gunboats, made it unadvisable to attempt to carry it by assault, and the men of his army were permitted to enjoy some days of inactivity, that they might rest and recuperate.

In the Report* of the Committee of Congress of the United States on the Conduct of the War, it is said:

The retreat of the army from Malvern Hill to Harrison's Bar was very precipitate. The troops, upon their arrival there, were huddled together in great confusion, the entire army being collected within a space of about three miles along the river. No orders were given the first day for occupying the heights which commanded the position, nor were the troops so placed as to be able to resist an attack in force by the enemy; and nothing but a heavy rain, thereby preventing the enemy from bringing up their artillery, saved the army there from destruction. The enemy did succeed in bringing up some of their artillery, and threw some shells into the camp, before any preparations for defense had been made. On the 3d of July the heights were taken possession of by our troops, and works of defense commenced, and then, and not until then, was our army secure in that position.

General Casey testified before the same committee as follows:

* Report of the Committee on the Conduct of the War, Part I, page 27.

The enemy had come down with some artillery upon our army massed together on the river, the heights commanding the position not being in our possession.   Had the enemy come down and taken possession of those heights with a force of twenty or thirty thousand men, they would, in my opinion, have taken the whole of our army, except that small portion of it that might have got off on the transports.   I felt very much alarmed for the army until we had got possession of those heights and fortified them.   After that it was a strong position.

The firing of the little howitzer was a mistake. Every effort should have been made to hasten the march of the infantry and the field-artillery; and in the meantime only a squadron or two of cavalry for the purpose of observation should have occupied Evelington Heights.   General Stuart retired from the heights at 2 P.M., and some of Longstreet's divisions came up late that evening.   The testimony is abundant to prove the fact that no attempt was made by the enemy to take possession of Evelington Heights until after their camp had been fired upon by the horse-artillery.   Only a few hours more and the infantry, with field-batteries, would have been up, and would have made sure of the plateau commanding the position held by the enemy.   This, however, is rather a narrative of facts than a lament; and the reader will be left to draw his own inferences and make his own conjectures of what might have been, taking the cue from the testimony of General Casey given above.

The retreat of General McClellan's army to Malvern Hill was admirably conducted.   There appears to have been considerable demoralization after that.

In considering the causes that contributed to prevent a more complete victory to the army under General Lee, after all that has been said, we cannot emphasize too strongly the fact that more was not accomplished be-

cause of the character and personality of the men behind the guns on the Federal side. The army under
General McClellan was made up largely of the flower
of the manhood of the Northern and Eastern States, and
his lieutenants were men and soldiers of a very high
type. The system of bounties and substitutes that subsequently prevailed in the recruiting of the ranks of the
Federals had not then begun to operate, and under the
generally acknowledged and remarkable administrative
powers of General McClellan his army had been raised
to the highest degree of efficiency. Nothing less than
an army of the finest material, most excellently officered,
could have so well resisted the terrible blows delivered
by the Confederates under General Lee.

General Lee in his report says:

Under ordinary circumstances, the Federal army should have
been destroyed. Its escape was due to the causes already stated.
Prominent among these is the want of correct and timely information. This fact, attributable chiefly to the character of the
country, enabled General McClellan skilfully to conceal his retreat, and to add much to the obstructions with which nature
had beset the way of our pursuing columns; but regret that
more was not accomplished gives way to gratitude to the Sovereign Ruler of the universe for the results achieved. The
siege of Richmond was raised, and the object of a campaign,
which had been prosecuted after months of preparation at an
enormous expenditure of men and money, completely frustrated.
More than ten thousand prisoners, including officers of rank,
fifty-two pieces of artillery, and upward of thirty-five thousand
stands of small arms were captured. The stores and supplies of
every description which fell into our hands were great in amount
and volume, but small in comparison with those destroyed by
the enemy.

CHAPTER IX

GENERAL LEE MANEUVERS TO DRAW GENERAL McCLELLAN AWAY FROM RICHMOND

THE army under General McClellan had been defeated, but it was still a formidable force. In his testimony before the Committee on the Conduct of the War, the Federal commander gave the strength of his army at Harrison's Landing as between eighty-five and ninety thousand men. The position occupied by it could not be assailed with any promise of success. Its proximity to the Confederate capital, its practically unassailable position, its ability to cross the river without opposition and move upon Richmond from the south side, combined to make the situation one of profound solicitude, and called for the exercise of prompt and heroic measures on the part of the Confederate commander.

Quietly to assume the defensive and thus afford General McClellan the time and opportunity that he desired to recruit and strengthen his shattered divisions, and to swell his army to its original strength by the addition of heavy reinforcements, of which he had been positively assured by the Federal authorities, would be equivalent to a surrender of all the advantages resulting to the Confederates from their dearly bought victories in the Seven Days' Battles, and would again reduce the city of Richmond to a state of siege.

It was necessary to devise some plan of campaign that

would compel the withdrawal of the hostile army from its position of constant menace. The disaster that had overtaken the army under General McClellan had greatly excited the fears of the Federal authorities for the safety of Washington, and General Lee realized fully the importance of playing upon that fear, and of carrying it, if possible, to a frenzy, by such a determined move against the capital as would cause a public demand for the immediate removal of the army under General McClellan from its position on the James River to the defense of Washington.

But was it safe for General Lee to attempt such a movement with the troops at his command? It required great confidence in his own judgment to carry out a campaign apparently so bold and fraught with such possibilities to the enemy, should events prove that the estimate put upon their sagacity was at fault. It required, also, great confidence in his lieutenants and in his troops to place them where the odds would be greatly against them, and where courage and endurance of the highest order would be required to assure success.

On the Federal side, General Pope had been assigned to the command of the troops in and about Washington, and of the army in its front. The strength of the army in the field, as given by General Pope, was about forty-three thousand, and embraced the forces under generals Fremont, Banks, and McDowell.

General Pope had gained some prominence in his former field of service in the West, and came to his new command with the waving of banners and the blare of trumpets, and evidently with a very poor estimate of the Confederate soldier. He had much to learn; and, " as pride goes before a fall," so his bombastic proclamations to his army formed a fitting prelude to the disaster that was soon to overtake and overwhelm him. He announced to his troops, by way of a suitable introduction of himself: "I have come to you from the West, where we have always seen the backs of our enemies, from an army whose business it has been to seek the adversary and beat him when found, whose policy has been attack, not defense. I presume I have been called here to pursue the same system, and to lead you against the enemy." Well might General Lee and Stonewall Jackson hesitate about getting within gunshot of this redoubtable warrior, but they do not appear to have heard him.

The army under General Pope was then occupying the line of the Rappahannock River, and seriously threatened the line of railroad from Richmond to Gordonsville. The purpose of General Pope, as related by him before the Committee on the Conduct of the War, was to have marched upon Gordonsville and Charlottesville, destroying the railroad, and then to move upon Richmond from the west.

It was imperative, then, for General Lee to check the advance of General Pope's army. The Confederate commander, with the small force at his command, was surely beset with difficulties at this time. One adversary with ninety thousand men was but a day's march from the Confederate capital, safely intrenched, and ready to take advantage of any invitation to attack, or any false step of his opponent. Another adversary with forty-three thousand men, unopposed, threatened to move upon his unprotected communications, and advance upon the capital from the west. To oppose the two, he had an army of about sixty-five thousand men available for operations in the field.

After allowing his army to enjoy a rest of about ten days, General Lee detached General Jackson, with the troops of his command, embracing his old division of four brigades and Ewell's division of three brigades, with orders to proceed toward Gordonsville, which point he reached on July 19th, and to move against Gen-

eral Pope. General A. P. Hill was soon ordered to follow with his division, and to join General Jackson.
While these movements were being made, General Lee
covered the city of Richmond with his remaining divisions.

On the 9th of August General Jackson attacked and
defeated a part of the army of General Pope at Cedar
Run.   In this battle General Jackson had engaged the
brigades of Early, Taliaferro, Garnett, Winder, Thomas,
Branch, Archer, and Pender, making together between
eleven and twelve thousand men.   On the Federal side
the force engaged consisted of Banks's corps, about eight
or ten thousand strong.   Banks was driven from the
field, and the Confederate pursuit continued for over a
mile.   Rickett's division of McDowell's corps reached
the scene of action late in the day, and served to check
the Confederate advance.   During the night General
Pope was further reinforced by the arrival of Sigel's
corps, so that on the morning of the 10th General Jackson was confronted by the greater part of Pope's army,
and the other part was but a short distance away and
hurrying to his support.   Two days of inactivity followed.   On the 11th General Pope, under a flag of truce,
asked permission to bury his dead.   Under the existing
conditions General Jackson could not resume the offensive. He had accomplished all that he dared to undertake with the force under his command: he had attacked
a portion of the army under General Pope, routed it
before it could be reinforced, greatly alarmed the authorities at Washington, and given to them a final argument, if one was needed, in favor of the withdrawal
of the army under General McClellan from its position
on James River to the support of the army in front of
Washington.   General Jackson therefore decided to retire on the night of the 11th toward Gordonsville.

Already the strategy of General Lee had accomplished

the desired results. On the 4th of August General McClellan received orders to withdraw his army from the Peninsula, and on the 6th General Halleck, the Federal commander-in-chief, wrote to General McClellan:

You and your officers at our interview estimated the enemy's forces in and around Richmond at two hundred thousand men. Since then you and others report that they have received and are receiving large reinforcements from the South. General Pope's army covering Washington is only about forty thousand. Your effective force is only about ninety thousand. You are thirty miles from Richmond and General Pope eighty or ninety, with the enemy directly between you, ready to fall with his superior numbers upon one or the other as he may elect. Neither can reinforce the other in case of such an attack.

On the day of the battle of Cedar Run General Halleck wired General McClellan to begin at once the transfer of his army from the James River to Acquia Creek. The defeat of Banks's corps at Cedar Run greatly excited the fears of the Federals for the safety of Washington, and additional and urgent orders were sent to General McClellan to hasten the abandonment of the position at Harrison's Landing and the removal of his army to the front of Washington, to avert the threatened attack upon that city.

Meanwhile, all of General Pope's troops had joined him, including those under General King at Fredericksburg. He had also been reinforced by the divisions of Reno and Stevens, of Burnside's corps, that had been brought up from North Carolina, and, disembarking at Aquia Creek, had moved to Fredericksburg, and thence, by orders from Washington, to reinforce General Pope.

General Lee had now become pretty well convinced, from the reports that reached him, of the proposed withdrawal of McClellan's army from its position on James River.

The alternative was presented to him of following that army down the Peninsula, with the view of harassing it, and, if opportunity offered, of dealing it a decisive blow; or of reinforcing General Jackson with all of his available force, and moving against General Pope before the troops from the Peninsula could reach him.

General Lee reasoned, as appears from his report, that although the victory at Cedar Run had temporarily checked the advance of Pope's army, that army was being rapidly reinforced and would soon resume aggressive operations. Burnside's corps from North Carolina had already joined Pope, and a part of McClellan's army was believed to have left Westover for the same purpose. It therefore appeared that active operations on the James River were no longer contemplated by the Federals, and that the most effectual way to relieve Richmond from any danger of attack from that quarter would be to reinforce General Jackson and advance upon General Pope.

Accordingly, on the 13th of August General Longstreet was ordered to proceed to Gordonsville with his division and two brigades under General Hood. General Stuart was directed to move with the main body of his cavalry to that point, and General R. H. Anderson was directed to leave his position on James River with his division and to follow General Longstreet. These forces having assembled in the neighborhood of Gordonsville, General Lee determined to advance against the enemy at once. The army under General Pope, fifty thousand strong, occupied the line of the Rapidan, his right being at Locust Dale and Robertson's River, and his left at Raccoon Ford on the Rapidan.

On August 19th General Lee issued the following order:

General Longstreet's command, constituting the right wing of the army, will cross the Rapidan at Raccoon Ford and move in the direction of Culpeper Court House. General Jackson's command, constituting the left wing, will cross at Somerville Ford and move in the same direction, keeping on the left of General Longstreet. General Anderson's division will cross at Somerville Ford, follow the route of General Jackson, and act in reserve. The battalion of light artillery under Colonel S. D. Lee will take the same route. The cavalry under General Stuart will cross at Morton's Ford, pursue the route by Stevensburg to Rappahannock Station, destroy the railroad bridge, cut the enemy's communication, and, operating toward Culpeper Court House, will take position on General Longstreet's right.

In his report General Lee says that the movements contemplated in his order were to have been commenced on the 18th of August, but the necessary preparations not having been completed, the execution of the order was postponed to the 20th. In the interval the enemy became apprised of his design and retired beyond the Rappahannock.

A day or so previous to the date given above General Stuart had ordered his cavalry to move in the direction of Raccoon Ford. He expected that General Fitzhugh Lee with his brigade would be in the neighborhood of Verdierville, on the plank road to Fredericksburg, on the 17th of August; and on the evening of that day he rode with his staff to that point to meet his troops. Finding that Lee's brigade was not there, and being unable to learn anything about it from the people of the vicinity, he sent Major Fitzhugh, of his staff, on the road on which he had expected Lee to move, to look for him. General Stuart remained at Verdierville. At an early hour next morning he was aroused by the noise of moving horses and wagons, and on going to the road he

ascertained that they were coming along the route that
he had expected General Fitzhugh Lee to take. He
took the approaching troops for his own men, but sent
out two officers to ascertain the facts. He was soon
undeceived, as these officers were fired upon, turned
about hurriedly, and were pursued. General Stuart,
bareheaded and without his cloak, ran for his horse,
mounted, rode rapidly to the rear, jumped a high fence,
and, with several of his staff, sought shelter in a neigh-
boring body of woods. Stuart was not the man, however, to go very far unnecessarily. He says in his report:
"Having stopped at the nearest woods, I observed the
party approach and leave in great haste, but not without my hat and the cloak which had formed my bed.
Major Fitzhugh in his search for Fitz. Lee was caught
by this party and borne off as a prisoner of war." This
misadventure of General Stuart was the subject of many
a joke at his expense, but none laughed more heartily
over the recollection of his hasty departure from Verdierville than he did. What a splendid fellow Stuart was!
Of fine physique, possessing great powers of endurance,
courageous to an exalted degree, of sanguine temperament, prompt to act, always ready for fight—he was the
ideal cavalryman. How genial he was! There was no
room for "the blues" around his headquarters; the hes-
itating and desponding found no congenial atmosphere
at his camp; good will, jollity, and even hilarity, reigned
there. The banjoist was almost as indispensable an ad-
junct to the headquarters of the cavalry as was the
adjutant-general. Songs and laughter often revealed
Stuart's bivouac when other signs failed in the darkness of night. And what happiness was his if circumstances caused his tent to be pitched within calling distance of lovely women! How many happy hours were
passed by him and his staff at the beautiful "Bower"
in the Valley of Virginia! It was a refreshing sight to

see him as he moved off from camp followed by his staff, and to catch the merry glance of his eye as he pointed with pride to a garland of flowers, or autumn leaves, decorating his horse's neck, the work of sweet woman's hand! Let it not be supposed, however, that there was no sober nor serious side to the character of this gallant soldier. Behind and underlying all this freedom from care and light-heartedness there was a vein of earnest conviction and of deep devotion to principle, a recognition of man's dependence upon his Maker, and an abounding faith in the promises of his Redeemer, as proclaimed in the gospel of peace. While no soldier was ever more ready than he for the fray, none ever realized more fully the personal danger it involved, nor faced more courageously the issue of life or death that attended his every movement in response to the call of duty.

The capture of Major Fitzhugh revealed General Lee's plans to General Pope. The latter says in his report:

The cavalry expedition sent out on the 16th, in the direction of Louisa Court House, captured the adjutant-general of General Stuart, and was very near capturing that officer himself. Among the papers taken was an autograph letter of General Robert E. Lee to General Stuart, dated Gordonsville, August 13th, which made manifest to me the position and force of the enemy and their determination to overwhelm the army under my command before it could be reinforced by any portion of the Army of the Potomac. I held on to my position thus far to the front for the purpose of affording all time possible for the arrival of the Army of the Potomac at Aquia Creek and Alexandria, and to embarrass and delay the movements of the enemy as far as practicable. On the 18th of August it became apparent to me that this advanced position, with the small force under my command, was no longer tenable in the face of the overwhelming forces of the enemy. I determined, therefore, to withdraw behind the Rappahannock with all speed.

CHAPTER X

GENERAL LEE promptly advanced his army and crossed the Rapidan River. Longstreet's wing crossed at Raccoon Ford, the brigade of cavalry under General Fitzhugh Lee having preceded it; and Jackson's wing crossed at Somerville Ford, Robertson's brigade of cavalry leading in the advance, accompanied by General Stuart. In the afternoon of the 20th General Fitzhugh Lee had a sharp and successful skirmish with the rear-guard of the enemy, near Kelly's Ford on the Rappahannock, and found the enemy holding the north side of the river in strong force. About the same time General Robertson's brigade of cavalry encountered a large body of the enemy's cavalry near Brandy Station and drove them across the Rappahannock. General Pope's army was now posted along the line of the Rappahannock, with its left at Kelly's Ford and its right about three miles above Rappahannock Station. On the morning of the 21st General Stuart, with a brigade of cavalry and a section of artillery, forced a passage across the river at Beverly Ford, capturing a number of prisoners and arms. Stuart maintained his position for some hours, when General Robertson, who, with his command, had crossed the river above, reported that the enemy was advancing in large force upon the position held by General Stuart, and as General Lee had meanwhile determined not to cross the army at that point, Stuart was directed to withdraw to the south side of the river. The enemy soon appeared in large force upon the opposite bank, and an animated fire was kept up during the rest of the day between his batteries and those of Jackson's leading division.

General Lee determined to seek a more favorable place to cross, higher up the river, so as to gain the enemy's right. General Longstreet was therefore ordered to leave his position at Kelly's Ford and occupy the positions held by General Jackson's troops at Beverly Ford and the Rappahannock bridge. General Jackson, thus relieved, was ordered to move higher up the river. On the 22d Jackson crossed Hazel River at Welford's Mill and proceeded up the Rappahannock. He reached Warrenton Springs ford in the afternoon, and immediately began to cross his troops to the north side of the river, occupying the Springs and the adjacent heights. During the night there was a very heavy storm. The rain came down in torrents, and on the next morning the river was found to be out of its banks. Under these circumstances General Jackson deemed it advisable to withdraw the troops from the north side, and they recrossed on the night of the 23d on a temporary bridge constructed for the purpose.

General Stuart, who had been ordered to move to the enemy's rear and cut his communications, crossed the Rappahannock on the morning of the 22d, some distance above where Jackson crossed—part of his command at Waterloo Bridge and the remainder at Hart's Mill. Proceeding on the road to Warrenton, General Stuart reached that point in the afternoon. He found no force of the enemy there, and ascertained that none had been there for days. He then directed the march of his column to the vicinity of Catlett's Station, which place he reached after dark. Having captured the enemy's pickets, General Stuart was soon in the midst of the

Federal camps, but, as he says in his report, the night was the darkest he ever knew. It rained incessantly, making the progress of artillery very difficult. Guided by a negro who recognized him and offered to lead him to the tents occupied by the staff of General Pope, General Stuart was soon in possession of Pope's headquarters, capturing a large number of prisoners, including many officers, and securing a large amount of public property. Attempts were then made to destroy the railroad bridge over Cedar Run, but owing to the heavy rain this was found to be impossible.

Fearing that the streams in his rear would be rendered impassable by the heavy rainfall, General Stuart determined to retrace his steps at once, and on the morning of the 23d he joined General Jackson's force at Warrenton Springs. In his report General Stuart says:

As day dawned, I found among the great number of prisoners Pope's field-quartermaster, Major Goulding, and ascertained that the chief quartermaster and Pope's aide-de-camp, Colonel L. H. Marshall, narrowly escaped the same fate. The men of the command had secured Pope's uniform, his horses and equipments, money-chests, and a great variety of uniforms and personal baggage; but what was of peculiar value was the despatch-book of General Pope, which contained information of great importance to us, throwing light upon the strength, movements, and designs of the enemy, and disclosing General Pope's own views against his ability to defend the line of the Rappahannock. Over three hundred prisoners, of whom a large number were officers, were marched safely within our lines at Warrenton Springs on August 23d, where General Jackson was found constructing a bridge.

While the movements just recorded had consumed several days, and General Lee's purpose of striking a blow at Pope's army was yet unaccomplished, the delay was not altogether disadvantageous.

There being no longer any doubt about the withdrawal of the army under General McClellan from the Peninsula, the Confederate authorities at Richmond breathed more freely, and General Lee was permitted to carry out his design of reuniting his army.

The divisions of D. H. Hill and McLaws, two brigades under General J. G. Walker, and Hampton's cavalry brigade, that had been left at Richmond, were now ordered to join the army under General Lee. Although none of these troops took part in the operations against Pope's army, the very fact that they were en route and rapidly approaching, as also the fact that they served to protect the communications of General Lee, contributed very materially in strengthening his hands for the work before him. Time did not permit that he should await the arrival of these reinforcements. The army under General Pope was being daily augmented by the arrival of reinforcements from the army of General McClellan. The occasion demanded celerity and audacity.

A defensive campaign by General Lee, along the line of the Rappahannock, with the prospect of being confronted in a very few days by the combined armies of generals McClellan and Pope, one hundred and fifty thousand strong, offered no attractions to the Confederate leader. While General Lee has been criticized by some because of the great risk that he ran in detaching Jackson for the movement against Pope's right and rear, these critics have never told us what better alternative was then offered him; and there could be no more conclusive vindication of the strategy of General Lee than the success that attended his plans in this particular case.

The army under General Pope was massed between the town of Warrenton and Sulphur Springs, and guarded all the fords of the river as far above as

Waterloo. The command of General Jackson lay between Jeffersonton and the Warrenton Springs ford. The lower fords of the river had been made impassable by the heavy rains.

General Longstreet was ordered to ascend the river, with the view of having him within supporting distance of General Jackson, and reached Jeffersonton in the afternoon of August 24th.

In accordance with the plan adopted by General Lee, General Jackson was to cross the river above Waterloo and move well around the enemy's right, so as to strike the railroad in his rear. General Longstreet was meanwhile to divert the enemy's attention by threatening him in front, and to follow Jackson as soon as he was sufficiently advanced.

On the morning of August 25th, at an early hour, the troops that had so often been led to victory by Jackson, in light marching order, crossed the river at Hinson's Mills, about four miles above Waterloo. Jackson was himself again; his men were in their element. Here were no Chickahominy Rivers, no Grapevine Bridges, no White Oak Swamps to embarrass leaders and men, but respectable rivers, with decent bottoms and substantial banks; and as the men emerged from the water and inhaled the inspiriting mountain air of upper Virginia, there was an elasticity in their step and a vigor in their movements that carried joy to the heart of their leader. Every man in that body of troops thought for himself. There was a marked personality in the mode of thought and action of the Southern soldier. He planned campaigns and studied the art of war; but when, as on this occasion, troops were detached from their supports and took up their line of march to the very heart of the territory held by the enemy, such was their supreme confidence in him who led them, there was no hesitation, no reluctant obedience, but an enthusiastic acquiescence in the purpose of their leader, which, though unannounced, was already divined by them.

Swift as an arrow went this column to Orleans, and thence to Salem, near which place it bivouacked for the night. A march of twenty-five miles in one day ! On the next morning General Jackson resumed his march, "continuing his route with his accustomed vigor and celerity," as General Lee records in his report. He passed the Bull Run mountains at Thoroughfare Gap, and proceeding by way of Gainesville, reached the railroad at Bristoe Station after sunset. At Gainesville he was joined by General Stuart, with the brigades of Robertson and Fitzhugh Lee, who continued with him during the rest of his operations, vigilantly and effectually guarding both his flanks. General Jackson was now between the large army of General Pope and the Federal capital. In his movements thus far he had encountered no considerable force of the enemy. On his reaching Bristoe Station the Federal guard at that point withdrew precipitately. Several trains of cars were captured, and a few prisoners were taken. Manassas Junction was distant about four miles, and it was known that the Federals had there a large quantity of supplies. Although it was now nearly dark, and the men were greatly fatigued by their long march from Salem, General Jackson determined to send a force there immediately to capture those supplies. General Trimble volunteered to take command of the infantry assigned to this service. General Stuart accompanied him with a part of his cavalry, by command of General Jackson, and as ranking officer assumed command.

The Federal guard at the Junction was quickly overcome by the two regiments under General Trimble, and the Confederates were soon in possession of the place. More than three hundred prisoners, eight pieces of artillery, one hundred and seventy-five horses, and immense quantities of stores of every kind were captured. Leaving one division at Bristoe Station, early in the morning of the next day General Jackson moved with the rest of his command to Manassas Junction. A small force of Federals, sent from Alexandria by rail, in an attempt to recapture the Junction was quickly overwhelmed and put to flight.

The Confederates, who had started upon this expedition with three days' rations, and who had taken exercise after extraordinary fashion, now had opportunity of regaling themselves upon the stores captured from the Federals, and were not slow in availing themselves of it. The rest of the day was uneventful.

In the afternoon, however, General Ewell, who was at Bristoe Station with three of his brigades to guard against any approach of the enemy from the direction of Warrenton Junction, was attacked by Hooker's division of Heintzelman's corps of McClellan's army. After having successfully resisted two assaults, and developed the fact that the enemy was present in large force, and it having become apparent that the Federal commander had now been made aware of the situation of affairs and had turned upon General Jackson with all his force, General Ewell, in compliance with his instructions, withdrew his command gradually, one brigade at a time, and proceeded to rejoin General Jackson at Manassas Junction, having destroyed the railroad bridge and the captured trains in the morning. The enemy did not press beyond Bristoe Station.

General Jackson now determined to withdraw from Manassas Junction and to take position where he could be more readily joined by Longstreet, whose command was approaching. After the troops had abundantly supplied themselves, the remaining captured stores were destroyed on the night of the 27th. During the same night Taliaferro's division moved to the west side of the turnpike road from Warrenton to Alexandria, and took position near Groveton, where it was joined on the 28th by the divisions of A. P. Hill and Ewell. Thus posted, General Jackson was in excellent position to await the arrival of General Longstreet, who was to come through Thoroughfare Gap, to retire by way of the Gap if occasion should require him to decline battle with a superior force, and to threaten the flank of the enemy moving toward Manassas.

General Pope, meanwhile, having realized that the affair at Manassas Junction was something more than a cavalry raid, and that Jackson's entire command had possession of the railroad in his rear, had given orders, on the night of the 27th, for the concentration of his army next day at and near Manassas Junction. In his order to General McDowell he says:

At daylight to-morrow morning march rapidly on Manassas Junction with your whole force, resting your right on the Manassas Gap Railroad, throwing your left well to the east. Jackson, Ewell, and A. P. Hill are between Gainesville and Manassas Junction. We had a severe fight with them to-day, driving them back several miles along the railroad.* If you will march promptly and rapidly at the earliest dawn of day upon Manassas Junction, we shall bag the whole crowd.

This order to General McDowell included his own corps, that of General Sigel, and Reynolds's division of the First Corps. At the same time General Heintzelman was ordered to move with his corps, and Reno's command of the Ninth Corps, to Greenwich, so as to reach there during the night of the 27th, or early on the morning of the 28th. General Banks was ordered to relieve the command of General Fitz John Porter at Warrenton, and as soon as relieved General Porter

* This refers to Ewell's withdrawal from Bristoe Station.

was ordered to proceed immediately in the direction of Greenwich and Gainesville.

General Banks was ordered to assume the charge of the trains on arriving at Warrenton Junction, and to cover their movement toward Manassas Junction.

BATTLE OF GROVETON

During the afternoon of the 28th, soon after the concentration of his divisions near Groveton, General Jackson learned that a large body of the enemy, approaching from the direction of Warrenton, was moving down the turnpike toward Centreville. This proved to be King's division of McDowell's corps. General Pope had changed his former orders and was now endeavoring to concentrate about Centreville. As the column moved, apparently unconscious of the nearness of Jackson's troops, its flank was exposed, and General Jackson immediately made dispositions to attack. The divisions of Ewell and Taliaferro were advanced through the woods, leaving Groveton on the left; three batteries of artillery were placed in position and began to shell the troops massed upon the turnpike. The Federal troops were promptly deployed and moved in the direction of the Confederate batteries. On the side of the Federals there were four brigades of infantry and four batteries of artillery. The Confederate line had now emerged from the woods and was moving in gallant style through the open field. Meanwhile the leading brigade of the Federal force was moving forward in line of battle toward the Confederate batteries. The conflict that ensued was fierce and sanguinary, attended by heavy losses on both sides. The fighting continued until after dark. Neither side gained any material advantage, and during the night the Federal forces retired.

In his report of this engagement General Jackson says:

This obstinate resistance of the enemy appears to have been for the purpose of protecting the flank of his column until it should pass the position occupied by our troops. Owing to the difficulty of getting artillery through the woods, I did not have as much of that arm as I desired at the opening of the engagement. But this want was met by Major Pelham with the Stuart horse artillery, who dashed forward on my right and opened upon the enemy at a moment when his services were much needed. Although the enemy moved off under cover of the night and left us in quiet possession of the field, he did not long permit us to remain inactive or in doubt as to his intention to renew the conflict. The loss on both sides was heavy, and among our wounded were Major-general Ewell and Brigadier-general Taliaferro.

General Ewell's wound was a very serious one. The bones of one leg were so shattered as to necessitate amputation. He was rendered unfit for service for months, and did not report for active duty in the field until the spring of 1863.

On the morning of the 29th it was ascertained that the enemy had taken a position to interpose his army between General Jackson and Alexandria.

General Jackson, anticipating an attack from the direction of Manassas and Centreville, took up a line of defense in the vicinity of and along the line of the cut of an unfinished railroad, stretching from the Warrenton turnpike in the direction of Sudley Mills. Jackson's division, under Brigadier-general Starke, was on the right, Ewell's division, under Brigadier-general Lawton, in the center, and A. P. Hill's division on the left. This was the general arrangement early in the morning of the 29th, but two brigades of Ewell's division—Early's and Hay's—with a battery of artillery, under command of General Early, were moved some distance to the rear of the right of the line to a position that commanded a view of the turnpike in front, to protect our right flank and rear against a force that had been reported to be advancing on the road from Manassas toward Gainesville.

We shall now follow the movements of General Longstreet's column. General R. H. Anderson reached the position occupied by Longstreet's command, opposite Warrenton Springs, on the 26th of August. General Longstreet, on being relieved, marched at once to join General Jackson. He crossed the river at Hinson's Mill in the afternoon and encamped for the night near Orleans. He reached White Plains the next day, and on the 28th, at about 3 P.M., arrived at Thoroughfare Gap. Here he found the enemy prepared to resist his passage. Dispositions were immediately made to force a way through. This duty was assigned to General D. R. Jones, who quickly advanced two of his brigades, and soon opened the way through the gorge. Longstreet's command passed through, a part that evening and the remainder early the next morning, when the whole command resumed the march, the sound of cannon at Manassas announcing that Jackson was already engaged. The head of the column soon reached Gainesville, and moved down the turnpike toward the right of the line occupied by Jackson's troops. The two brigades under General Early were relieved and proceeded to rejoin their division. The two wings of General Lee's army were now united, and the crucial test of strength between him and General Pope was on.

SECOND MANASSAS

At an early hour on this day, August 29th, General Jackson had ascertained that the force of the enemy attacked by him on the previous evening had abandoned the ground occupied at the close of the engagement and moved toward his left. The Federal army was now being concentrated in Jackson's front, and General Pope entertained high hope of being able to overwhelm him before reinforcements could reach him. He seems to have labored under the delusion that Jackson was retreating, although it was Jackson who attacked in the engagement with McDowell's troops on the evening of the 28th. Indeed, in his report covering the movements of his troops at this time, General Pope says: "I felt sure then, and so stated, that there was no escape for Jackson."

During the morning the Federal artillery opened a brisk fire upon Jackson's right, which was replied to by his batteries. After a while the enemy seemed to change the plan of attack and moved against Jackson's left. The Federal army corps under General Sigel, about ten thousand men, was the first to advance against the Confederate lines. In obedience to orders from General Pope, Sigel was to hold Jackson in check until his army was concentrated. Three divisions of Sigel's corps were hurled against that portion of A. P. Hill's line occupied by the brigades of Gregg and Thomas. The assault, though made with great spirit, was firmly met and repulsed. Reinforced by a portion of Reno's corps that had now reached the field, the assault was repeated, but with no better results. For half of the day there was desultory but severe fighting along Hill's front. Although the Federals were acting on the aggressive, there were several counter-strokes delivered by the Confederates under Gregg and Thomas. The battle was waged with incessant fury and varying success.

On the side of the Federals, up to this time, there had been engaged Sigel's corps, the divisions under Hooker and Kearny, Milroy's brigade, and a portion of Reno's corps. But the end was not yet. Upon the arrival of the fresh troops under Reno and Heintzelman, General Pope having also arrived at the front and being in command, a more determined and concentrated assault was made by the Federals against the line so long and stubbornly held by Hill's brigades.

Once the Federals penetrated the line between the brigades of Gregg and Thomas, but reinforcements were at hand; the Fourteenth South Carolina regiment, hitherto in reserve, and the Forty-ninth Georgia of Thomas's brigade were thrown forward, and the Federals were quickly driven back with great slaughter. The contest was close and obstinate, the men at times delivering their fire at ten paces, and the bayonet was frequently in requisition. The Confederate line remained firm and unbroken. General Hill in his report says:

The enemy prepared for a last and determined attempt. Their serried masses, overwhelming superiority of numbers, and bold bearing made the chances of victory to tremble in the balance; my own division exhausted by seven hours' unremitted fighting, hardly one round (of ammunition) per man remaining, and weakened in all things save its unconquerable spirit. Casting about for help, fortunately it was here reported to me that the brigades of generals Lawton and Early were near-by, and, sending to them, they promptly moved to my front at the most opportune moment, and this last charge met the same disastrous fate that had befallen those preceding.

In speaking of the attack of Early when called to the aid of Gregg's brigade, General Jackson says in his report:

General Early, on reaching his position, found that the enemy had obtained possession of the railroad and a piece of wood in front, there being at this point a deep cut, which furnished a strong defense. Moving through a field, he advanced upon the enemy, drove them from the wood and railroad cut with great slaughter, and followed in pursuit some two hundred yards. The Thirteenth Georgia (of Lawton's brigade) at the same time advanced to the railroad and crossed with Early's brigade.

In these repeated assaults of the Federals, four divisions, numbering at least thirty thousand men, had been thrown against Jackson's front, which remained firm and unbroken. The Federal loss was very heavy. In his report General Pope puts it at from six to eight thousand in killed and wounded.

The Confederate loss cannot be stated accurately. A. P. Hill's division was about ten thousand strong. In his report of the two days' fighting, August 29th and 30th, he puts the loss of his command at 199 killed, 1308 wounded, total 1507, of which Gregg's brigade lost 619. Brigadier-general Field and Colonel Forno, commanding Hay's brigade, were severely, and Brigadier-general Trimble seriously, wounded.

While Jackson was being heavily assailed, the troops of General Longstreet were arriving on the field, and the leading brigades were at once deployed on Jackson's right. Hood's two brigades, with Evans's brigade as a support, were deployed across the turnpike and at right angles to it. In rear of these troops, and within supporting distance, were three brigades under General Wilcox on the left, and three brigades under General Kemper on the right. Jones's division formed the extreme right of the command, but was broken off to the rear, across the Manassas Gap Railroad, to resist a force of the enemy reported by General Stuart to be advancing on Longstreet's right from that direction; but no serious attack was made, and after firing a few shots the enemy withdrew. At twelve o'clock Longstreet reported that his command was formed for battle.

The question will naturally arise, Why did not Longstreet attack, and so relieve the heavy pressure on Jackson? General Longstreet relates how earnestly General Lee desired that he should attack, but says he "did not order." General Lee, in his report, is silent on this point. To one accustomed to his ways it is easy to understand why he did not *order* an attack, in view of General Longstreet's reluctance to make one; and it can be quite as readily appreciated, by those who knew him, why General Lee made no mention of the difference of views between the two in his report. General Longstreet was apprehensive of an advance by the enemy from the direction of Manassas. It really happened that General Pope had ordered General Porter to move with his corps to and around Jackson's right so as to envelop it, but he did this in ignorance of the fact that Longstreet had arrived and taken position on the right of Jackson. Nothing would have suited Longstreet better than to have had Porter assail him. General Porter, however, had encountered the ever vigilant General Stuart, who promptly reported the presence of infantry in force moving on Longstreet's right, when the brigades of Wilcox were sent to the support of D. R. Jones, and, as previously related, the Federal force withdrew after exchanging a few shots. The facts are that General McDowell, whose corps was moving along with Porter's, arrived at Porter's front about noon, and arrested Porter's movement. General Stuart was raising a great dust on the road by dragging brush, so as to create the impression that a large body of troops were moving in that direction. The official report of the Federal board of officers appointed to investigate the case of General Fitz John Porter says: "The dust in Porter's immediate front and extending across toward Groveton, as well as back toward Gainesville, showed that large forces of the enemy, in addition to those reported by Buford, were already on the field." From the same report it appears that General McDowell then said to General Porter, in the hearing of several officers, "Porter, you are too far out; this is no place to fight a battle," or words to that effect. Whether it was Porter or McDowell that was at fault, General Pope always held the former responsible, and he did not hesitate to say so in his report. He was not, however, aware of Longstreet's presence, whereas Porter had reason to think that a large force was in his front, and readily acquiesced with General McDowell, and declined to give battle.

General Longstreet, apprehensive of an attack on his right and rear by the troops that had been withdrawn from that quarter, opposed General Lee's desire for him to attack. He says:

Our Chief now returned to his first plan of attack by his right down the turnpike. Though more than anxious to meet his wishes, and anticipating his orders, I suggested, as the day was far spent, that a reconnaissance in force be made at nightfall to the immediate front of the enemy, and if an opening was found for an entering wedge, that we have all things in readiness at daylight for a good day's work. After a moment's hesitation he assented, and orders were given for the advance at early twilight.

A distinguished military critic,* writing impartially with a view to historical accuracy, has this to say about this matter:

Longstreet, with a complacency it is hard to understand, has related how he opposed the wishes of the commander-in-chief. Three times Lee urged him forward. The first time he rode to the front to reconnoiter, and found that the position, in his own words, was not inviting. Again Lee insisted that the enemy's left might be turned. While the question was under discussion, a heavy force (Porter and McDowell) was reported advancing from Manassas Junction. No attack followed, however, and Lee repeated his instructions. Longstreet was still unwilling. A large portion of the Federal force on the Manassas road now marched northward to join Pope, and Lee, for the last time, bade Longstreet attack toward Groveton.

* "Stonewall Jackson," by Lieutenant-colonel G. F. R. Henderson.

We have seen how General Longstreet hesitated and urged as a substitute for this a reconnaissance in force. Two brigades, Hood's and Evans's, with Wilcox as a support, were ordered to advance. They soon ran into King's division, also advancing to attack. The fight was spirited, but the Federals gave way before the impetuous Texans until Hood's line was a mile and a half advanced. One cannon, a number of flags, and a few prisoners were taken. The reconnaissance was accomplished, the ground was examined, and the troops, after night, were withdrawn to their original positions.

As matters turned out, it was all right. General Jackson had succeeded in holding his lines, so fiercely and continuously assailed. General Longstreet, perhaps, found his justification in the success that crowned the efforts of the Confederates the next day; and yet I know of no good reason to doubt that the same success would have been attained the first day had the same energy been displayed.

On the morning of the 30th the positions of the two armies remained practically as at the close of the day preceding. On the Confederate side the division under General R. H. Anderson had arrived on the field and was held in reserve. General Pope, reinforced by the commands of McDowell and Porter, had his army well in hand. All promised well for the Federal commander. He was still under the impression that his opponent was endeavoring to get away from him. To his mind every indication pointed to the retreat of the enemy from his front. Paroled Federal prisoners, captured the evening previous and allowed to return to his lines, reported the Confederates as retreating during the night along the Warrenton turnpike. They had mistaken the reconnaissance and withdrawal made by Longstreet's brigades for a battle and a retreat. He repelled every suggestion that Longstreet had united with Jackson, and was confirmed in this belief by the report of one of the paroled prisoners that had " heard the rebel officers say that their army was retiring to unite with Longstreet." It was not until after noon, however, that General Pope had made his dispositions to attack. General Lee, anticipating the purpose of his opponent, quietly awaited the assault. Jackson's troops, disposed in the same relative positions as on the previous day, lay on their arms. A number of batteries of artillery, some from Jackson's command and some from the reserve artillery under General S. D. Lee, had been posted upon a commanding eminence on Jackson's right, where his troops joined Longstreet's, and so placed as to command the front of Jackson's line. In the ensuing battle those batteries played a most conspicuous and wonderfully effective part in determining the issue between the contending armies. Indeed, the fighting of the big guns at Second Manassas was the handsomest exhibition of the effectiveness of that branch of the service seen during the war, in my estimation.

As the enemy massed his troops in Jackson's front, it became evident that the assault was to be delivered there. I have always admitted that I cannot recall the exact time of day when any important event took place during the period of active operations when fighting was going on, and have always spoken with reluctance and hesitation when interrogated on this point. As an illustration of the uncertainty of the evidence of eyewitnesses and participants in such a matter, I submit the following conflicting testimony concerning the hour when Pope made his assault on Jackson. General Lee says in his report: " About 3 P.M. the enemy, having massed his troops in front of Jackson, advanced against his position in strong force." General Jackson says: " After some desultory skirmishing and heavy cannonading during the day, the Federal infantry, about four o'clock in the evening, moved from under cover of the wood and advanced in several lines, first engaging the right, but soon extending its attack to the center and left. In a few moments our entire line was engaged in a fierce and sanguinary struggle with the enemy." General A. P. Hill says: "On the 30th, about two o'clock, the enemy again made an attack along our whole line. The attack on my part of the line was gallantly resisted by Archer and Thomas, Gregg still holding the extreme left. This onset was so fierce and in such force that at first some headway was made, but throwing in Pender and Brockenborough, their advance was again checked and eventually repulsed with great loss." General Longstreet says: "About one o'clock in the afternoon General Pope ordered attack against Jackson's front by the corps under General Porter." And General Pope says: "Between twelve and two o'clock in the day I advanced the corps of Porter, supported by King's division of McDowell's corps, to attack the enemy along the Warrenton turnpike."

Porter's corps advanced to the attack with King's division in support; at the same time Heintzelman and Reno, on the right of Porter, were ordered to push forward toward Warrenton turnpike and attack Jackson's left; Ricketts's division was so placed as to support this movement on the Federal right, but was soon recalled and ordered to the Federal left.

The Confederate commanders are agreed in according unstinted praise to the dash and courage of the Federal troops in making this attack, but General Pope states that "the attack of Porter was neither vigorous nor persistent, and his troops soon retired in considerable confusion." As the second and third lines of great strength moved to support the first in the attack on the Confederate left, so impetuous and determined were these assaults as to excite General Jackson's apprehension as to the ability of his troops to continue successfully to maintain their position, and he called on General Lee for reinforcements. Immediate orders were sent to General Longstreet to send a division to General Jackson. General Longstreet had just then reached a point in advance of his lines from which he could observe the assaulting Federals "piling up against Jackson's right, center, and left." He saw at a glance that if batteries of artillery were posted at that point their fire would enfilade the Federal masses and make such havoc in their ranks as to compel them to retire. He concluded that this was the quickest and surest way to relieve the pressure on Jackson. He immediately ordered two batteries to this position, and two others were advanced at the same time by General S. D. Lee. As anticipated by General Longstreet, the fire from these batteries was most destructive, and in a very short time the ranks of the enemy were broken, and the whole force rapidly retired.

Their repeated efforts to rally were unavailing, and Jackson's troops, being thus relieved from the pressure of overwhelming numbers, began to press steadily forward, driving the enemy before them. He retreated in confusion, suffering severely from our artillery, which advanced as he retired. General Longstreet, anticipating the order for a general advance, now threw his whole command against the Federal center and left. Hood's two brigades, closely followed by Evans, led the attack. R. H. Anderson's division came gallantly to the support of Hood, while the three brigades under Wilcox moved forward on his left, and those of Kemper on his right. D. R. Jones advanced on the extreme right, and the whole line swept steadily on, driving the enemy with great carnage from each successive position until 10 P.M., when darkness put an end to the battle and pursuit.*

* General Lee's report.

I recall an impressive incident of this battle, the recollection of which remains very fresh with me, despite the long time that has since elapsed. It occurred after the advance made by Longstreet's troops, when we were driving the enemy from each successive stand made in their sullen retirement. We would drive their batteries from their position, then our pieces would advance, unlimber, and go into action upon the elevation just abandoned, and again the enemy would be forced to retire from their new position by our impetuous assault. In the midst of this pursuit, as I rode with General Lee, my attention was attracted by a Federal officer who lay upon the ground wounded, and whose look was so eager and appealing as to cause me to stop, dismount, and go to him. Before I could speak to him he said: " Is Frank Huger here ? " I replied that Huger was not just at that point. Then he said: "Is Ramseur here ? " Again I replied in the negative, and then I asked: "Why do you ask for Huger and Ramseur ? " " Oh," he replied, " they are old friends of mine and fellow cadets at West Point."

Again how sad it all was! Here was a splendid specimen of manhood stricken down, whose profession was war, which called for self-sacrifice; but alas, whose so-called enemies were the beloved friends of his youth and his former comrades in arms!

Of course all this passed very rapidly. I asked his name, which he gave as Captain Chamberlain,* turned him over at once to a field-surgeon, promised to look him up later, and rode rapidly to overtake General Lee. Poor fellow! His wound was mortal, and when I went

* Lieutenant W. W. Chamberlain, aide-de-camp to General Sykes, who in his official report says: "Lieutenant Chamberlain, sent with an order to Colonel Warren near the close of the day, is among the missing. His fate is not yet determined, but he is believed to be a prisoner, wounded, and in the hands of the enemy."

to look after him at the close of the battle I ascertained that he was dead.

During the night Pope's army retired to the north side of Bull Run, and on the morning of August 31st, when the cavalry was pushed forward at an early hour by General Stuart, it was ascertained that the Federals occupied the heights around Centreville, a strong position about four miles from Bull Run. It had rained very heavily during the night, and the run was well-nigh impassable.

At this time a serious mishap befell General Lee, that made life a trial to him for several weeks, and came near depriving the army of his presence. It happened on the day after Pope's army had retreated, when General Lee halted for conference with General Longstreet. The party had dismounted near a high railroad embankment and culvert. General Lee, surrounded by a number of general and staff officers, held his horse, with the bridle loosely depending from his arm. Suddenly a large number of prisoners, with a guard, swarmed over the embankment and scurried in the direction of General Lee and party. My recollection is that they moved in haste because the fire from the enemy made it unsafe on the embankment. This sudden apparition frightened General Lee's horse, and he quickly threw up his head and jumped backward. General Lee was thrown violently to the ground. and both wrists were seriously sprained and the small bones of one hand broken. He had no use of either hand, and for some days each arm had to be carried in a sling. He could not ride his horse, and for some time thereafter moved in an ambulance. This was a sore trial to the general's patience. The ambulance could not go into many places where a horse would have carried him, and so his movements were greatly hindered: all this in addition to the physical suffering he was experiencing. Napoleon occasionally moved in a carriage; but I am sure General Lee would never have done so from choice.

General Lee directed General Longstreet to remain upon the field to engage the attention of the enemy and to care for the dead and wounded, and ordered General Jackson to proceed in pursuit of the enemy, by Sudley Ford to the Little River turnpike, so as to turn Pope's right and get between his army and Washington. Jackson's troops reached Little River turnpike in the evening, and on the morning of September 1st advanced toward Fairfax Court House. Jackson's movement was now so well developed that General Pope made immediate arrangements to evacuate his position at Centreville, and directed his troops to a new position at Fairfax Court House.

CHANTILLY, OR OX HILL

Jackson's troops encountered the enemy late in the afternoon at Ox Hill, and a serious engagement ensued, during a drenching rainstorm, without decisive results. The Federals lost two of their best generals, Kearny and Stevens. General Kearny, in some way, in the confusion of the fight, had ridden into our lines. He quickly wheeled, and as he rode received a volley from the advancing Confederate skirmishers, and fell dead. Under orders from General Lee I delivered his body at the Federal lines the next day under a flag of truce. It was a sad duty. There was no place for exultation in the contemplation of the death of so gallant a man, and as I accompanied his remains I was conscious of a feeling of deep respect and great admiration for the brave soldier, who, as stated by General Pope, had "died as he would wish to die, and as became his heroic character."

Longstreet's command arrived at the scene of action

late in the evening, and some of his troops were deployed to the relief of Jackson's, but did not become engaged. During the night the Federals withdrew, and it was ascertained the next morning, September 2d, that General Pope was retiring with his army behind the line of fortifications erected for the defense of Alexandria and Washington.

To show the extent of the discomfiture of General Pope and his army, it is only necessary to recite his own language in his despatches to General Halleck at Washington. Said he: "Unless something can be done to restore tone to this army it will melt away before you know it. . . . The enemy is in very heavy force, and must be stopped in some way. These forces under my command are not able to do so in the open field, and if again checked, I fear the force will be useless afterward." He had at that time, according to his own statement, sixty-two thousand men; whereas General Lee's army at no time exceeded fifty thousand, from which should be deducted his losses to arrive at his strength at that date. In summing up the results of his campaign against General Pope, General Lee says: "In the series of engagements on the plains of Manassas more than seven thousand prisoners were taken, in addition to about two thousand wounded left in our hands. Thirty pieces of artillery, upward of twenty thousand stands of small arms, numerous colors, and a large amount of stores, besides those taken by General Jackson at Manassas Junction, were captured."

The Federal loss in these battles was 1733 killed and 10,135 wounded; the Confederate loss was 1090 killed and 6154 wounded.

CHAPTER XI

GENERAL LEE now determined to cross the Potomac River and invade the State of Maryland. His army had been increased by the arrival of the infantry divisions of D. H. Hill, McLaws, and Walker, and by Hampton's cavalry. The spirit of the army was fine, but it was poorly equipped, and deficient in all things that make for bodily comfort. These matters had been fully considered; the advantages and disadvantages of an aggressive campaign into the enemy's country had been well weighed, and with the sanction of the authorities at Richmond and the approval of his own judgment, General Lee gave the order for his army to advance. The cavalry was ordered to follow and harass the retreating Federals, and the infantry was put in motion, with orders to cross the Potomac by the fords east of the mountains. General Jackson led with his command by way of Leesburg, and was followed by General D. H. Hill with his division. Longstreet's command followed Hill. The cavalry served to screen these movements of the infantry. Jackson's men were permitted to have one day's rest, and D. H. Hill's division went to the front. General Lee went to Leesburg, and was entertained by Mr. Henry Harrison, at whose house he spent the night.

Between September 4th and 7th the several columns of the army crossed the Potomac at the fords nearest to Leesburg, and on September 7th the army was concentrated about Frederick, Maryland. This bold move on the part of the Confederates had startled and alarmed the people of the North, and excitement rose to fever heat in some localities. The Governor of Pennsylvania issued a proclamation and called out every able-bodied man in the State to assist in repelling the rebel invaders. General Pope was relieved from the command of the Army of Virginia, and General McClellan was put in command of the combined forces of that army and the Army of the Potomac, as also of all the troops in front of Washington. While the people at the North were much excited over the invasion of their territory, our own people were indulging hopes as to the effect of the presence of General Lee and his army in Maryland that never materialized. In his proclamation to the people of Maryland, General Lee clearly shows that he hoped for some movement of the people to the Confederate standards, with the view of regaining the rights of which they had been despoiled. This view was also held by the authorities at Richmond, and Mr. Davis formed the purpose of going in person to join General Lee.

I think that General Longstreet is in error, however, when he says that it was General Lee's "deliberate and urgent advice to President Davis to join him and be prepared to make a proposal for peace and independence from the head of a conquering army." General Lee was made aware on the 9th of the intention of Mr. Davis to join him; and to prevent an undertaking so fraught with danger, he sent me to meet Mr. Davis with the following letter:

HEADQUARTERS, NEAR FREDERICKTOWN, MD.,
September 9, 1862.

His Excellency President Davis—

Mr. President: I h·· ᵓ just received your letter of the 7th instant from Rapidan informing me of your intention to come on to Leesburg. While I should feel the greatest satisfaction in having an interview with you, and consulting upon all subjects of interest, I cannot but feel great uneasiness for your safety should you undertake to reach me. You will not only encounter the hardships and fatigues of a very disagreeable journey, but also run the risk of capture by the enemy. I send my aide-de-camp Major Taylor back to explain to you the difficulties and dangers of the journey, which I cannot recommend you to undertake.

I am endeavoring to break up the line through Leesburg, which is no longer safe, and turn everything off from Culpeper Court House toward Winchester. I shall move in the direction I originally intended, toward Hagerstown and Chambersburg, for the purpose of opening our line of communication through the valley in order to procure sufficient supplies of flour. I shall not move until to-morrow, or perhaps next day, but when I do move, the line of communication in this direction will be entirely broken up. I must therefore advise that you do not make an attempt that I cannot but regard as hazardous.

I have the honor to be, with high respect, your obedient servant,

R. E. LEE, General.

I was also charged with the duty of seeing after the sick and wounded around and about the scenes of the recent battles, and of arranging for their transportation to Winchester, which place was made a rendezvous for all the men returning from sick or wounded furlough, and for all stragglers who had become separated from their command. In compliance with these orders, I left General Lee on the 9th of September, crossed the Potomac, and rode to Leesburg, at which place I spent another night under the roof of the hospitable Mr. Harrison. The next day I continued my journey to Warrenton, at which point I ascertained that Mr. Davis had abandoned his purpose to join the army and returned to Richmond. The sick and wounded had all been removed, and after reporting by telegraph to the President at Richmond I made all haste to get through the mountains into the Shenandoah Valley, and proceeded directly to Winchester.

On arriving at Winchester I found quite a number of men and officers who were returning to their commands and who were in good condition. There was a much larger number of those who were sick, footsore, and broken down, who had not been able to keep up with their commands; a very large proportion of these were without shoes. A provost guard had charge of the camp and maintained a rigid line beyond which none were to be allowed to go until advices were received from General Lee as to the route by which such of these men and officers as were able should rejoin their commands.

Taking with me Colonel Frank Huger and Colonel John S. Saunders, both of the artillery, I crossed the Potomac and proceeded to Hagerstown. Here we put up for the night at the Hamilton Hotel, and after having seen that our horses were properly cared for, we retired for sleep, hoping we were to have a good night's rest. About one or two o'clock in the morning—that is, on September 15th—we were aroused by a great commotion in the hotel, caused by a number of people who had assembled there and reported a heavy engagement between the forces of Lee and McClellan at Boonsborough Gap, and who also represented that a Federal force was marching on Hagerstown. We saddled our horses without delay, and, although accepting the wild reports with some allowance, we deemed it the part of wisdom to get out of the town. After we had proceeded some distance in the direction of Sharpsburg, to which place it was stated that General Lee was retiring, we went into a field, picketed our horses some distance from the road, and laid ourselves down under the protection of a hayrick to wait for daylight. We heard nothing unusual while there, but in the morning, when we resumed our journey, we ascertained that a large body of Federal cavalry, which proved to be that escaping from Harper's Ferry, had passed along the road, and congratulated ourselves on our narrow escape. I reached General Lee on the morning of the 15th near Sharpsburg, and found him with the commands of Longstreet and D. H. Hill awaiting the advance of McClellan's army.

While General Lee was at Frederick he learned that the Federal forces in the lower valley were concentrating for defense at Harper's Ferry. The combined forces numbered about thirteen or fourteen thousand men. Such a force at Harper's Ferry would have constituted a standing menace to General Lee's new line of communication, and it was necessary to be rid of it. The progress of McClellan's army up to this time had been very slow. Knowing his adversary well, and relying upon a continuation of the cautious tactics he had always pursued, General Lee determined to send a force sufficient for the purpose to insure the capture of the Federal forces at Harper's Ferry, with the expectation that such purpose could be accomplished and his army reunited in time to give battle to General McClellan. General Jackson was to undertake the reduction and capture of Harper's Ferry, in which McLaws and Walker were to coöperate, while Longstreet and D. H. Hill were to hold McClellan in check. The following order of march was issued:

HEADQUARTERS ARMY OF NORTHERN VIRGINIA,
September 9, 1862.
SPECIAL ORDERS, No. 191.

1. The citizens of Fredericktown being unwilling, while overrun by members of this army, to open their stores, in order to give them confidence all officers and men of this army are strictly

prohibited from visiting Fredericktown except on business, in which case they will bear evidence of this in writing from division commanders. The provost marshal in Fredericktown will see that his guard rigidly enforces this order.

2. Major Taylor will proceed to Leesburg, Virginia, and arrange for transportation of the sick and those unable to walk to Winchester, securing the transportation of the country for this purpose.

The route between this and Culpeper Court House east of the mountains being unsafe will no longer be traveled. Those on the way to this army already across the river will move up promptly; all others will proceed to Winchester collectively and under command of officers, at which point, being the general depot of this army, its movements will be known and instructions given by commanding officer regulating further movements.

3. The army will resume its march to-morrow, taking the Hagerstown road. General Jackson's command will form the advance, and after passing Middletown with such portion as he may select, take the route toward Sharpsburg, cross the Potomac at the most convenient point, and by Friday morning take possession of the Baltimore and Ohio Railroad, capture such of the enemy as may be at Martinsburg, and intercept such as may attempt to escape from Harper's Ferry.

4. General Longstreet's command will pursue the main road as far as Boonsborough, where it will halt with reserve, supply, and baggage trains of the army.

5. General McLaws, with his own division and that of General R. H. Anderson, will follow General Longstreet. On reaching Middletown he will take the route to Harper's Ferry, and by Friday morning possess himself of the Maryland Heights and endeavor to capture the enemy at Harper's Ferry and vicinity.

6. General Walker, with his division, after accomplishing the object in which he is now engaged, will cross the Potomac at Check's Ford, ascend its right bank to Lovettsville, take possession of Loudon Heights, if practicable, by Friday morning, Keys's Ford on his left, and the road between the end of the

mountain and the Potomac on his right. He will, as far as practicable, coöperate with generals McLaws and Jackson, and intercept the retreat of the enemy.

7. General D. H. Hill's division will form the rear-guard of the army, pursuing the road taken by the main body. The reserve artillery, ordnance, and supply-trains, etc., will precede General Hill.

8. General Stuart will detach a squadron of cavalry to accompany the commands of generals Longstreet, Jackson, and McLaws, and, with the main body of the cavalry, will cover the route of the army, bringing up all stragglers that may have been left behind.

9. The commands of generals Jackson, McLaws, and Walker, after accomplishing the objects for which they have been detached, will join the main body of the army at Boonsborough or Hagerstown.

10. Each regiment on the march will habitually carry its axes in regimental ordnance wagons, for use of the men at their encampments, to procure wood, etc.

By command of General R. E. Lee.

R. H. CHILTON,
Assistant adjutant-general.

This is the now famous order a copy of which fell into the hands of General McClellan on the 13th of September. What a fatality was there for General Lee! What an advantage to the Federal commander—to be instantly made aware of the division of his adversary's army, the wide separation of his columns, and to have the details of his plan laid bare!

There is no parallel to it in history. A victory for the South at that time meant the recognition by foreign powers of the independence of the Confederate States. Victory that seemed assured for General Lee trembled in the balance, and by this fortuitous incident eluded his grasp. It looks as if the good Lord had ordained

that we should not succeed.   General Lee could manage
General McClellan well enough under normal conditions, but this looks like an interposition of Providence
to thwart his designs.   Some will say that this check to
the wheel of Confederate fortune was not due to the act
of God, but to the carelessness of some one at the headquarters of General D. H. Hill, to whom the copy of the
order was addressed; * to which the fatalist will reply
that it was predetermined and could not have been
otherwise; and this contention will never be settled
until the line is established that marks where Divine
Sovereignty ends and human free-agency begins.

To me it is as if He who controls the destinies of men
and of nations had said: "You, people of the South,
shall be sorely tried, but the blame is not yours, and
therefore to you shall fall the honors—genius, skill,
courage, fortitude, endurance, readiness for self-sacrifice, prowess in battle, and victory against great odds;
but this great experiment to demonstrate man's capacity
for self-government, with its corner-stone of universal
freedom, must continue with undivided front, and therefore I decree to the other side determination, persist-
ence, numbers, unlimited resources, and ultimate success."

BATTLE OF BOONSBOROUGH PASS

Up to this time General McClellan had moved slowly
and cautiously; it took his army four days to march
twenty-four miles.   On the 13th his several commands
made an average of from seven to eight miles only:

* General Hill assured me that he had in his possession, years after the
war had closed, the original of this order addressed to him.   I was sent to
meet Mr. Davis and so did not supervise the promulgation of this order, but
Colonel Venable always contended that two copies were sent to General
D. H. Hill, one from General Lee and a copy from General Jackson, under
whose command he was, temporarily, though his division was unattached;
and that one of these was lost.

the First Corps from New Market to Frederick (eight miles); the Second Corps from Urbana to Frederick (seven miles); the Sixth Corps from Licksville Cross Road to Buckeystown (seven miles); the Ninth Corps from Frederick to Middletown (eight miles); the Twelfth Corps from Ijamsville to Frederick (seven miles); Crouch's division from Barnesville to Licksville (six miles); and Sykes's division from Urbana to Frederick (seven miles). At this rate of progress by McClellan, with no one to dispute his way, it can be readily seen that General Lee would have had ample time for carrying out his plans. But now all is changed. General McClellan is made aware of the division of General Lee's army and of the small force in his front. He sends a despatch to President Lincoln, in which he says:

I think Lee has made a great mistake, and that he will be severely punished for it. The army is in motion as rapidly as possible. I hope for a great success if the plans of the rebels remain unchanged. I have all the plans of the rebels, and will catch them in their own trap, if my men are equal to the emergency.

And he proceeds to "catch the rebels." This sounds like an echo from Pope in his retirement, and seems unnatural as coming from General McClellan, for whom most of the Confederate soldiers had great respect and rather a liking.

Two corps, the First, under Hooker, and the Ninth, under Reno, were sent to the support of Pleasanton, to force a way through the pass on the Frederick and Hagerstown road, near Boonsborough, to which point Pleasanton's cavalry had pressed the Confederates on the evening of the 13th. Franklin's corps was ordered to proceed to Crampton's Gap, so as to cut off the Confederate force under McLaws then at Maryland Heights and coöperating with General Jackson in the reduction of Harper's Ferry.

General Lee on learning of this unexpected energy on the part of the enemy, who was advancing "more rapidly than was convenient," determined to return with Longstreet's command to the Blue Ridge, to strengthen D. H. Hill's and Stuart's commands, engaged in holding the passes of the mountains. Hill became actively engaged and sent to advise General Lee that the enemy was at the main pass, in strong force, pressing him heavily, and asked for reinforcements. Longstreet was rapidly advanced and some of his brigades were soon deployed. The resistance made here by the Confederates was bitter and determined. The brigades of Rodes, Garland, Colquitt, Anderson, and Ripley (the latter, however, was at no time engaged), numbering in the aggregate less than five thousand men, for six or seven hours successfully resisted the repeated assaults of the two corps of the Federal army, fully thirty thousand strong. About 3 P.M. General D. H. Hill was reinforced by the brigades of Drayton and Anderson, numbering nineteen hundred men, and an hour later he was joined by General Longstreet with the brigades of Evans, Pickett, Kemper, Jenkins, Hood, and Whiting; only four of these, however, numbering about three thousand men, became seriously engaged, and they not until dusk. The battle raged until after dark, and all attempts of the enemy to force a passage were successfully resisted.

General Lee having learned late in the evening that Crampton's Gap had been forced by Franklin, and McLaws's rear thus threatened, and anticipating from a report received from General Jackson that Harper's Ferry would be surrendered next morning, determined to withdraw Longstreet and D. H. Hill from their positions and retire to the vicinity of Sharpsburg, where his army could be more readily reunited. Accordingly the troops were withdrawn, without molestation by the enemy, and took position in front of Sharpsburg.

At an early hour on that morning, September 15th, Harper's Ferry capitulated to General Jackson. The surrender involved twelve regiments of infantry, numbering eleven thousand men, three companies of cavalry, and six companies of artillery; with forty-nine pieces of artillery, twenty-four mountain howitzers, seventeen revolving guns, and eleven thousand small arms. The capture of Harper's Ferry also released the Confederates under McLaws threatened by Franklin; they crossed the Potomac at Harper's Ferry and so escaped the trap set for them.

General McClellan did not exhibit much energy in forcing General Lee, nor in following him through the passes of South Mountain, so heroically defended on the 14th. In his report he says that he went into action with about thirty thousand men. He gives his casualties in killed and wounded at 1728; and after stating the positions of the several corps and divisions that reached him after the fight, says: "Thus, on the night of the 14th, the whole army was massed in the vicinity of the field of the battle, in readiness to renew the action the next day, or to move in pursuit of the enemy."

The resistance made by D. H. Hill's troops and Longstreet's few brigades was of such character, however, as not to invite indiscreet haste on the part of the enemy in the pursuit. General Lee says in his report that they did not pass through the Gap until about eight o'clock of the morning after the battle, and that their advance only reached a position in his front at about 2 P.M. on that day.

BATTLE OF SHARPSBURG, OR ANTIETAM

At dawn on the morning of the 15th General Lee, with the troops of Longstreet and D. H. Hill, was aligned for battle along the line of Antietam Creek, near Sharpsburg. Immediately after the surrender of

Harper's Ferry, on the same day, General Jackson proceeded with his divisions to join General Lee. McLaws and Walker were to follow, all moving on the south side of the Potomac. A. P. Hill was left in charge of the surrendered garrison, to parole the prisoners and secure the captured arms and stores.

At two o'clock in the afternoon the advance of the Federal army made its appearance in General Lee's front, having been much retarded by our cavalry under General Fitzhugh Lee. Meanwhile official information was received of the fall of Harper's Ferry and of the approach of Jackson's troops, and as the news of this great victory was conveyed along the lines, it greatly reanimated the courage of the troops and put them in excellent spirits. During the afternoon the leading divisions of McClellan's army were deployed on the opposite side of Antietam. There was some desultory artillery fire, but no effort was made even to feel the strength of the Confederates, or to draw their fire. General Jackson arrived with his troops early on the 16th, and General Walker came up in the afternoon.

General Lee's troops occupied a range of hills between Sharpsburg and the Antietam, nearly parallel to the course of that stream, Longstreet on the right of the road to Boonsborough and D. H. Hill on the left. Two brigades under General Hood had been transferred from the right and posted between D. H. Hill and the Hagerstown road. As Jackson's troops arrived they were directed to take position on Hood's left, and their line extended from the Hagerstown road on their right, with their left extending toward the Potomac River. General Stuart protected this flank with his cavalry and horse artillery. General Walker, as soon as he arrived, with his two brigades, was posted on the right of Longstreet's command, taking the place of Hood's brigades, moved to the left.

Urgent orders had meanwhile been sent to generals McLaws and A. P. Hill to hasten with all despatch to Sharpsburg. General McLaws with his troops reached the scene of action early on the 17th. General A. P. Hill with his brigades, except that under General Thomas left to complete the removal of the captured property, began the march from Harper's Ferry at 7.30 A.M. on the 17th, and the head of his column arrived upon the battle-field at 2.30 P.M., having made a distance of seventeen miles in seven hours. The condition of the several commands after the forced march from Harper's Ferry can be readily understood. There was a continuous line of stragglers from Harper's Ferry to Sharpsburg. Jackson hardly gave the men of his divisions time to contemplate the handsome results of their work in the capture of Harper's Ferry, but hurried them off to join General Lee by a forced march. Walker followed him closely. McLaws, with his own division and that of R. H. Anderson, consumed more time. General McLaws, however, had a more difficult task, as is shown by his report:

The entire command was very much fatigued. The brigades of generals Kershaw and Barksdale had been engaged on Maryland Heights on the 12th, 13th, and 14th, and on the 15th had been marched from the Heights to the line of battle, up the valley, formed to oppose that of the enemy below Crampton's Gap. Those of generals Cobb, Semmes, and Mahone (Colonel Parham) had been engaged and badly crippled at Crampton's Gap, and all the others had been guarding important points under very trying circumstances. A large number had no provisions, and a great portion had not had time or opportunity to cook what they had. All the troops had been without sleep during the previous night, except while waiting in line for the wagon-trains to pass over the pontoon bridge at Harper's Ferry.

All the commands had been subjected to very severe trials. The route from Harper's Ferry was strewn with footsore and weary men, too feeble to keep up with the stronger and more active; and instead of going into battle with full ranks, the brigades were no stronger than regiments, and in some cases numbered no more than a full company. And all this was the result of the lost order and exposure of the plan of the Confederate commander.

On the afternoon of the 16th General McClellan directed an attack by Hooker's corps on the Confederate left. Crossing the Antietam at the bridge near Keedysville, beyond the reach of the Confederate batteries, Hooker's corps advanced against that portion of our line occupied by the two brigades under General Hood, but the attack was gallantly repulsed. After dark Hood's troops were relieved by the brigades of Lawton and Trimble, of Ewell's division, and, after replenishing ammunition, resumed their place on Longstreet's right.

At an early hour on the 17th the Federal batteries opened a vigorous fire upon the Confederate left, under cover of which their infantry advanced to assail the part of the line held by General Jackson. The battle was soon on in earnest, and raged with great fury and varying success during the entire day. The fighting was here heaviest and most continuous. Three distinct assaults by three separate corps were made upon this portion of our line. First Hooker, then Mansfield, and then Sumner essayed to turn this flank, and each corps in turn was driven back; and two of them, shattered, broken, and dispersed, were rendered useless for further aggressive movements. General Sumner, in speaking of the conditions when he was advancing, says:

On going upon the field I found that General Hooker's corps had been dispersed and routed. I passed him some distance in the rear, where he had been carried wounded, but I saw nothing of his corps at all as I was advancing with my command on the field. There were some troops lying down on the left which I took to belong to Mansfield's command. In the meantime General Mansfield had been killed, and a portion of his corps had also been thrown into confusion.

The aggregate strength of the attacking columns at this point reached forty thousand men, not counting the two divisions of Franklin's corps, sent at a late hour in the day to rescue the Federal right from the impending danger of being itself destroyed.

The brunt of these attacks fell upon the men of Jackson's divisions. The lines of the enemy were repeatedly broken and forced to retire, but as fresh troops advanced to the assault, Jackson's men were in turn compelled to fall back, and Jackson's division, with ammunition exhausted and numbers greatly reduced, was relieved by General Hood, with his two brigades, and by General Early, in command of Ewell's division after the wounding of General Lawton, with his brigade. These troops, contending against many times their own numbers, held tenaciously to their ground. The battle became close and fierce. Three brigades of D. H. Hill's division and one of D. R. Jones's division were moved in to the support of General Hood, when the enemy again gave way and his lines were forced back. Fresh numbers of the enemy were thrown in to the support of their wavering line, but the desperate resistance they encountered held them in check until the arrival on the field of McLaws's division from Harper's Ferry, which General Lee ordered to the threatened point, together with the two brigades under General J. G. Walker, moved over from our right to the relief of General Hood. These troops attacked the enemy vigorously, driving him back with great slaughter and reëstablishing our lines.

The enemy next attempted to carry our center, advancing in heavy force against that part of the lines held by a portion of J. G. Walker's command and the two brigades of D. H. Hill's division under generals G. B. Anderson and Rodes. The first assault was repulsed, but owing to some mistake of orders, the brigade of General Rodes was then withdrawn from its position, leaving a gap in our lines, through which the enemy quickly advanced, when G. B. Anderson's brigade was broken and forced to retire, General Anderson being mortally wounded. General Lee thus describes the critical condition of affairs at this time:

The heavy masses of the enemy again moved forward, being opposed only by four pieces of artillery, supported by a few hundred men belonging to different brigades, rallied by General D. H. Hill and other officers, and parts of Walker's and R. H. Anderson's commands, Colonel Cooke, with the Twenty-seventh North Carolina regiment of Walker's brigade, standing boldly in line without a cartridge. The firm front presented by this small force, and the well-directed fire of the artillery, under Captain Miller of the Washington artillery, and Captain Boyce's South Carolina battery, checked the progress of the enemy, and in about an hour and a half he retired.

Meanwhile the enemy had advanced a large force, Burnside's corps, to attempt the passage of the bridge over the Antietam, opposite the right of General Longstreet's position. This bridge was heroically defended by General Toombs's brigade of Georgians, and repeated efforts of the enemy to cross were thwarted. Later in the afternoon the enemy began to extend his line as if to cross the river below the bridge, thus taking Toombs's brigade in reverse, when its brave commander reluctantly ordered it to retire from the position so long and bravely defended.

The enemy then crossed the river in large force and advanced against that part of General Longstreet's line held by the command of General D. R. Jones, who had less than two thousand men in line of battle. After a stout resistance this small force was compelled to give way; but opportunely the division of General A. P. Hill arrived from Harper's Ferry, and was immediately ordered to reinforce General Jones. General Hill promptly advanced his four brigades under generals Archer, Branch, Gregg, and Pender; at the same time several of Hill's batteries of artillery opened with good effect upon the enemy, whose progress was immediately arrested, and as his line began to waver, General Jones ordered Toombs to charge his flank, while Archer, Branch, and Gregg moved upon the front of the Federal line. "The enemy made a brief resistance, then broke and retreated in confusion toward the Antietam, pursued by the troops of Hill and Jones, until he reached the protection of his batteries on the opposite side of the river." *

It was now nearly dark; the enemy had been repulsed at every point and General Lee held his lines intact.

The thirty-five thousand Confederates in line of battle under General Lee on that memorable day constituted the very flower of the Army of Northern Virginia. Never did soldiers render more heroic service; never were troops more skilfully handled. Outnumbered at every point, the right was called upon to go to the rescue of the left; the center was reduced to a mere shell in responding to the demands for assistance from the right and left; and A. P. Hill's division, the last to arrive from Harper's Ferry, reached the field just in time to restore the wavering right. We had no troops in reserve; every man was engaged. At times it appeared as if disaster were inevitable, but succor never failed, and night found General Lee's lines unbroken and his army still defiant.

The field of Sharpsburg, or Antietam, was perhaps

* General Lee's report.

the most fiercely contested and the most sanguinary of all the great battles of the war. Commencing at an early hour in the morning, the fighting was continuous throughout the day, with the advantage first on one side and then the other. The Federal army was fresh and well in hand; it had marched by easy stages for the several days preceding the finding of the lost order, with an abundance of supplies of every kind, and its ranks were full and unbroken. The several columns of the Confederate army, widely separated, were compelled to make forced marches, with scant rations, in order to present a united front to the enemy, and, out of breath from marching, were hurried into battle with empty stomachs and ranks sadly reduced.

General Lee, in his report of this battle, says:

The arduous service in which our troops had been engaged, their great privations of rest and food, and the long marches, without shoes, over mountain roads, had greatly reduced our ranks before the action began. These causes had compelled thousands of brave men to absent themselves, and many more had done so from unworthy motives. This great battle was fought by less than forty thousand men on our side, all of whom had undergone the greatest labors and hardships in the field and on the march. Nothing could surpass the determined valor with which they met the large army of the enemy, fully supplied and equipped, and the result reflects the highest credit on the officers and men engaged.

General McClellan reports that he had 87,164 men of all arms engaged on that day. General Lee's total strength was a fraction over 35,000.

The killed and wounded in this day's fight on the Federal side amounted to 11,657, of which number 2108 were killed.

The total casualties in General Lee's army during the campaign—that is, in the fighting at Boonsborough

Gap, Harper's Ferry, Crampton's Gap, and Sharpsburg—
amounted to something over twelve thousand.

On the 18th General Lee's army maintained the same
position it held at the close of the battle the previous
day. Many of those left behind in the rapid march to
Sharpsburg had rejoined their commands, and so con-
siderably increased their numerical strength; and although too weak to assume the offensive, General Lee
awaited a renewal of the attack by the enemy without
apprehension. Wiser counsels, however, prevailed on
the Federal side. General McClellan in his report thus
states the situation:

The night, however, brought with it grave responsibilities.
Whether to renew the attack on the 18th, or to defer it, even
with the risk of the enemy's retirement, was the question before
me. After a night of anxious deliberation, and a full and careful survey of the situation and condition of our army, the
strength and position of the enemy, I concluded that the success
of an attack on the 18th was not certain. I am aware of the
fact that, under ordinary circumstances, a general is expected
to risk a battle if he has a reasonable prospect of success ; but
at this critical juncture I should have had a narrow view of the
condition of the country had I been willing to hazard another
battle with less than an absolute assurance of success. At that
moment—Virginia lost, Washington menaced, Maryland invaded—the national cause could afford no risks of defeat. One
battle lost and almost all would have been lost. Lee's army
might then have marched, as it pleased, on Washington, Baltimore, Philadelphia, or New York. It could have levied its supplies from a fertile and undevastated country, extorted tribute
from wealthy and populous cities, and nowhere east of the Alle-
ghanies was there another organized force able to arrest its march.

All of which is very true; all of which had been considered by General Lee. What better evidence could
be asked of the sagacity of General Lee in planning the

invasion of Maryland and the campaign as it was to be, and as it would have been but for the "lost order," than this clear-cut, vivid picture of the results of a success to General Lee, presented by the most soldierly and brilliant of all of his opponents?

Among the reasons given by General McClellan why he should not renew the attack, I note the following:

The troops generally were greatly overcome by the fatigue and exhaustion of the severe and continuous fighting on the 17th. They required rest and refreshment. One division of Sumner's and all of Hooker's corps on the right had, after fighting most valiantly for several hours, been overpowered by numbers, driven back in great disorder and much scattered, so that they were for the time somewhat demoralized.

Some of the new troops on the left, although many of them fought well during the battle and are entitled to great credit, were, at the close of the action, driven back and their *morale* impaired.

On the morning of the 18th General Burnside requested that another division be sent to assist him in holding his position on the far side of the Antietam; giving the impression that if he were attacked again that morning he would not be able to make a very vigorous resistance.

The explanation here given by General McClellan for his inaction shows that the Federal army was no more in condition to assume the offensive than was General Lee's. The truth is that both armies were exhausted by the terrible struggle of the previous day. Neither side could claim a victory, although General Lee had repulsed the attacks of the enemy made upon his line, and that is all that can be said of the assault on the third day at Gettysburg by the divisions of Pickett and Pettigrew. It was repulsed. So were Hooker, Mansfield, and Sumner at Antietam. We hear much of one, but little of the other.

CHAPTER XII

DURING the night of the 18th General Lee withdrew his army to the south side of the Potomac, crossing at Shepherdstown, without loss or molestation. On the 20th a body of the Federal troops crossed the river at Shepherdstown, but was met and quickly driven back by General A. P. Hill's division, with great loss.

The army then marched to the Opequon River, near Martinsburg, where it remained some days and then moved to the vicinity of Bunker Hill and Winchester.

No better summary of the results of the campaign thus ended can be given than is found in the congratulatory order issued by General Lee to his army, which reads as follows:

In reviewing the achievements of the army during the present campaign, the commanding general cannot withhold the expression of his admiration of the indomitable courage it has displayed in battle, and its cheerful endurance of privation and hardship on the march. Since your great victories around Richmond you have defeated the enemy at Cedar Mountain, expelled him from the Rappahannock, and, after a conflict of three days, utterly repulsed him on the plains of Manassas, and forced him to take shelter within the fortifications around his capital. Without halting for repose you crossed the Potomac, stormed the heights of Harper's Ferry, made prisoners of more than eleven thousand men, and captured upward of seventy-five pieces of artillery, all their small arms, and other munitions of war. While one corps of the army was thus engaged, the other insured its success by arresting at Boonsborough the combined armies of the enemy, advancing under their favorite general to the relief of their beleaguered comrades.

On the field of Sharpsburg, with less than one third his numbers, you resisted from daylight until dark the whole army of the enemy, and repulsed every attack along his entire front of more than four miles in extent. The whole of the following day you stood prepared to resume the conflict on the same ground, and retired next morning without molestation across the Potomac. Two attempts subsequently made by the enemy to follow you across the river have resulted in his complete discomfiture and being driven back with loss. Achievements such as these demanded much valor and patriotism. History records few examples of greater fortitude and endurance than this army has exhibited, and I am commissioned by the President to thank you in the name of the Confederate States for the undying fame you have won for their arms.

Much as you have done, much more remains to be accomplished. The enemy again threatens with invasion, and to your tried valor and patriotism the country looks with confidence for deliverance and safety. Your past exploits give assurance that this confidence is not misplaced.

The Federal army meanwhile remained in the vicinity of the recent battle-field. On October 8th General Lee ordered General Stuart to cross the Potomac above Williamsport with his command, and endeavor to ascertain the position and purpose of the enemy. Stuart crossed the river at McCoy's Ferry on October 10th, and proceeded at once to Chambersburg, where he spent the night. The next morning he made directly for Gettysburg, thence to Emmitsburg, thence toward Frederick; but before reaching that point, crossing the Monocacy, and thence, fighting his way, to the Potomac, which he crossed at White's Ford, thus making a complete circuit of the Federal army, the main body of which he found posted west of the Blue Ridge range, and stretching from Hagerstown to Rockville, the center resting at Harper's Ferry, with detachments guarding the river.

The Federal authorities at Washington had become impatient about this inactivity of General McClellan. They could not understand why, if the enemy had been "driven across the Potomac," he had not made vigorous pursuit. On the 6th of October he received a telegram from General Halleck in which he was told that the President directed that he should cross the Potomac and give battle to the enemy, or drive him south. The want of clothing for his men and horses for his cavalry constituted General McClellan's reason for delay in complying with this order.

On October 21st he notified General Halleck that he was about supplied with clothing, but still needed horses, and he asked whether the President desired him to move at once on the enemy, in compliance with the order of the 6th, or to await the arrival of the horses. To which General Halleck replied:

The President directs me to say that he has no change to make in his order of the 6th instant. If you have not been, and are not now, in condition to obey it, you will be able to show such want of ability. The President does not expect impossibilities, but he is very anxious that all this good weather should not be wasted in inactivity. Telegraph when you will move, and on what lines you propose to march.

General Halleck, it appears, did not agree with General McClellan in regard to the conditions that rendered a forward movement impracticable or unadvisable. He stated to the Secretary of War that, in his opinion, there had been no such want of supplies in the army under General McClellan as to prevent his compliance with the orders to advance against the enemy.

In the last days of October and the early days of November the different columns of McClellan's army crossed the Potomac, east of the mountains, and advanced southward toward Warrenton, seizing the passes through the Blue Ridge as they were reached. On November 6th the First Corps advanced to Warrenton. As soon as General Lee was made aware of the movement of the Federals toward Warrenton, he moved Longstreet's corps across the Blue Ridge and to Culpeper Court House, which point it reached on November 3d. General Jackson was at the same time ordered to move one of his divisions to the east side of the Blue Ridge.

The enemy gradually concentrated about Warrenton, his cavalry advanced beyond the Rappahannock, in the direction of Culpeper Court House. On November 7th an order was issued from the War Department at Washington relieving General McClellan of the command of the Army of the Potomac, and directing General Burnside to assume command.

About the middle of November General Lee saw unmistakable signs of a purpose on the part of the Federals to move to Fredericksburg. On the 17th McLaws's and Ransom's divisions of infantry, a brigade of cavalry under General W. H. F. Lee, and Lane's battery of artillery, were ordered to proceed to that point. To ascertain more definitely the purpose of General Burnside and the location of his troops, General Stuart was ordered to cross the Rappahannock with his cavalry and feel the enemy. On the morning of the 18th he forced a passage at Warrenton Springs, and after brushing aside the small force that was guarding the ford, he proceeded to Warrenton, which place he reached soon after the last of the Federal army had left. The information then obtained confirmed the reports previously received, and it became evident that the whole of Burnside's army was moving toward Fredericksburg.

On the morning of the 19th General Longstreet was directed to march with the remainder of his corps for that point. The advance of Burnside's army, under General Sumner, reached Falmouth opposite Fredericksburg on the 17th. On the 21st General Sumner sent a communication to the civil authorities of Fredericksburg, in which he made a demand that the city be surrendered at five o'clock that evening; and notice was given that in the event of a refusal of his demand the city would be bombarded at nine o'clock next morning. This threat was subsequently withdrawn in view of certain assurances given by the mayor; the city was not fired into. In reference to this matter General Lee says:

It was impossible to prevent the execution of the threat to shell the city, as it was completely exposed to the batteries on the Stafford hills, which were beyond our reach. The city authorities were informed that while our forces would not use the place for military purposes, its occupation by the enemy would be resisted, and directions were given for the removal of the women and children as rapidly as possible. The threatened bombardment did not take place, but in view of the imminence of a collision between the two armies, the inhabitants were advised to leave the city, and almost the entire population without a murmur abandoned their homes. History presents no instance of a people exhibiting a purer and more unselfish patriotism, or a higher spirit of fortitude and courage, than was evinced by the citizens of Fredericksburg.

General Jackson meanwhile, in pursuance of instructions from General Lee, had crossed the Blue Ridge and moved to the neighborhood of Orange Court House; and about November 26th, as soon as Burnside's purpose was fully developed, he was directed to march to Fredericksburg. The cavalry was stationed so as to guard the upper fords of the Rappahannock, and a portion of it was watching and guarding the river near Port Royal. General Lee's army now occupied a line extending from the river about one and a half miles above Fredericksburg, along the range of hills south and west of the city to Hamilton's Crossing on the Richmond, Frederickburg and Potomac Railroad. The line as thus established was to a great extent commanded by the heights on the opposite side of the river, crowned with the heavy guns of the enemy; but after the construction of earthworks and the placing of our artillery at every point of vantage, it was a very good line for defense, and on the left absolutely safe against an attack in front. The city and the plain between it and the Confederate lines were so completely commanded by the heights on the opposite side that it was deemed unwise to resist in force any attempt that the enemy might make to construct bridges and cross the river. Only a small force, therefore, consisting of Barkdale's brigade of McLaws's division and two regiments from Anderson's division, the Third Georgia and the Eighth Florida, under General Barksdale, was stationed in the city for the purpose of picketing the river-front and impeding as much as possible any attempt that the enemy might make to cross the river.

THE BATTLE OF FREDERICKSBURG

On December 11th, at an early hour, the working parties of the Federals commenced the construction of three bridges at the city, and one lower down near the mouth of Deep Run. Barksdale's men, sheltered by the houses on the river-bank in the city, poured a steady fire on the bridge-builders, making it so hot for them that they were compelled to cease work and seek shelter.

Time and again details for the work gallantly advanced, but as officers and men fell dead or wounded the bridge-builders would again retire and seek shelter from the deadly fire of the Confederate skirmishers. Late in the afternoon, the fog having lifted enough to enable the artillerists to distinguish objects on the opposite side of the river, one hundred and fifty guns of the enemy opened a furious fire upon the city. About the same time the Federals determined to load the pontoons with men, row quickly across the river in the face of the Confederate fire, and so gain a foothold on the southern bank. This daring feat was most gallantly performed. The terrible artillery fire had driven away some of the Confederates, whose fire had slackened considerably, and only a few of the brave men rowing the Federal pontoons were shot down; the shore was reached, the men formed quickly for attack and rushed to the buildings commanding the crossing, when the Confederates retired. Work on the bridges was now resumed, and they were completed about 4 P.M. The resistance at the lower crossing was not so prolonged, and two bridges had been constructed there by noon. Such was the character of the resistance made by Barksdale's men, however, that the whole day was consumed before the way was open for the Federal troops to cross the river. The leading brigades crossed to the south side and occupied the city about daylight on the morning of the 12th. A heavy fog lay upon the river and effectually concealed these movements. During the day the two Grand Divisions under Franklin and Sumner had crossed to the south side and taken position for attack, Sumner on the right and Franklin on the left. Two divisions of Hooker's command were sent on the evening of the 12th to coöperate with Franklin. The remainder of Hooker's Grand Division crossed on the 13th. General Burnside gives the strength of these several commands as follows:

Franklin, 60,000; Sumner, 27,000; and Hooker, 26,000. Total, 113,000.

Longstreet's command constituted the left wing of the Confederates; R. H. Anderson's division rested on the river, and to his right were the divisions of McLaws, Pickett, and Hood; Ransom's division was stationed about Marye's and Willis's hills, in support of the artillery; Cobb's brigade of McLaws's division and the Twenty-fourth North Carolina regiment of Ransom's division constituted the line of battle around the foot of these hills, where they were well protected by a stout stone wall. Jackson's divisions, recalled from their station lower down on the river as soon as Burnside's purpose was fully developed, had now arrived, and were posted on the right of Longstreet. A. P. Hill's division occupied the ground between Hood's right and Hamilton's Crossing; the brigades of Pender, Lane, and Archer made up his first line. Thomas's brigade was posted in the rear of Pender and Lane, and Gregg's brigade was placed in the rear of Lane and Archer. These two brigades and the Forty-seventh Virginia regiment and Twenty-second Virginia battalion of Field's brigade constituted A. P. Hill's reserve. Early's and Taliaferro's divisions made up Jackson's second line, and D. H. Hill's division was in reserve. The Washington artillery under Colonel Walton, the battalion under Colonel E. P. Alexander, together with some of the divisional batteries, were posted on Longstreet's front on the crest of Marye's Hills and the adjacent heights. Lieutenant-colonel Walker with fourteen guns was posted on A. P. Hill's right, supported by two regiments of Field's brigade, commanded by Colonel Brockenborough; Jackson's other batteries were posted at the most favorable positions along his line so as to command the open ground over which the enemy had to advance. General Stuart, with two brigades of cavalry and a few guns, protected Jackson's right, extending to Massaponax Creek. General Lee's total strength on the 10th of December was 78,288.

A heavy fog prevailed on the morning of the 13th, but the noise made by the movement of artillery and the music of the regimental bands could be distinctly heard along the whole line. About nine o'clock the fog lifted and disclosed the Federal army over one hundred thousand strong in martial array moving to attack. Shortly thereafter a large force was seen to be advancing against that part of Jackson's line occupied by A. P. Hill's division. The movement of this body, which proved to be Meade's division of Pennsylvanians, was materially delayed and finally checked by a very brilliant service of Stuart's horse artillery under Major Pelham, operating on Jackson's right. The fire of half a dozen batteries concentrated on Pelham finally compelled him to withdraw. After a considerable interval, during which the Federal batteries continuously shelled the woods protecting Jackson's troops, the Federal advance was resumed and was directed to the piece of woods held by Lieutenant-colonel Walker's artillery. Reserving his fire until the enemy had approached to within about eight hundred yards, Colonel Walker opened upon them with such destructive effect as to cause their line to waver and finally to retire in confusion. After this there was an artillery duel lasting for over an hour, when about one o'clock the Federals were again seen to be advancing against A. P. Hill's front in much greater force, in three compact lines. The Confederate batteries checked them as before, but only temporarily, and gallantly advancing they were soon within range of the infantry, and the contest was close and desperate. The impetus of the Federal advance penetrated the Confederate line between the brigades of Archer and Lane, and suddenly fell upon Gregg's brigade in the second line.

As soon as these facts were reported to General Jackson, he ordered Early and Taliaferro to advance and recover the lost ground. Archer, though his flank had been turned, held on heroically to his line, and the artillery under Walker played havoc in the ranks of the second line of the Federals and checked their advance. The divisions of Early and Taliaferro, in line of battle, now came forward with a rush. The contest was short and decisive; the enemy was driven out with loss, and though reinforced was forced back to the railroad embankment, behind which he found protection. Here he was gallantly charged by two brigades of Early's division, under colonels Atkinson and Hoke, and driven beyond the embankment, across the plain to his batteries. Instructions had been given not to pass beyond the embankment, but the ardor of these troops and their success caused them to continue the pursuit, shooting down the fugitives and taking many prisoners, until they were themselves subjected to a heavy fire of musketry and artillery directed against their front and flank, when they were compelled to fall back to the main body now occupying our original line of battle, with detachments thrown out to the railroad. General Lee says: "The repulse of the enemy on our right was decisive, and the attack was not renewed; but his batteries kept up an active fire at intervals, and sharpshooters skirmished along the front during the rest of the afternoon."

While Franklin was thus endeavoring to turn the Confederate right, Sumner was engaged in the yet more serious effort to force Longstreet's front. Having massed his troops under cover of the houses in the city, General Sumner awaited the order to advance. After a concentrated fire from all his batteries on the heights on the opposite side of the river upon our troops stationed on Marye's and Willis's hills, General Burnside

gave the order for Sumner to attack. In his report he
states:

General Sumner's corps was held in position until after eleven
o'clock, in the hope that Franklin would make such an impression upon the enemy as would enable him (Sumner) to carry the
enemy's line near the Telegraph and Plank roads. Feeling
the importance of haste, I now directed General Sumner to commence his attack. He had already issued his orders, but had,
in accordance with my instructions, directed his troops to be held
in readiness for the attack, but not to move without further
orders from me.

Division after division was hurled against the impregnable position held by the Confederates, only to be torn
to pieces and driven back. The cool, steady veterans of
Lee, under the protection of their extemporized works,
made terrible havoc in the ranks of the assaulting
columns; division after division recoiled from the shock,
shattered, discomfited, and demoralized. Their allotted
task exceeded human endeavor; and no shame to them
that after such courageous and brilliant conduct their
efforts lacked success. In the language of a distinguished soldier: "By those hapless and stout-hearted
soldiers, sacrificed to incompetency, a heroism was displayed which won the praise and the pity of their opponents." Six distinct and separate assaults were made
against Longstreet's front by the divisions of French,
Hancock, Howard, Getty, Sturgis, Griffin, and Humphreys; but each succeeding effort met the fate of the
first, and when night closed in the shattered columns of
the enemy had retired to the city, leaving the ground
covered with dead and wounded. Ah, the pity of it!
The carnage was terrible. How many to this day recall
the cries of agony that came from that sanguinary
field! Not until the 15th was a flag of truce sent to Gen-

eral Jackson's front with the request that there should be a cessation of hostilities between their left and our right wing, for the purpose of removing their wounded from the field. No such request came, at any time, for the relief of the poor fellows lying in front of Marye's Hill; but the Confederates, moved to pity, did all they could to relieve the suffering Federals in their front. Many pathetic stories were told of the efforts of the Southern soldiers to relieve the sufferings of their wounded foes. How light and shadow alternated in fitful fancy in marking the path of the life of the soldier of those days! How colors gay and grave blended in the picture that portrayed the soldier's hopes and trials! How humor and pathos followed close upon each other in his intercourse with his fellows! As illustrating this, I recall an incident of the battle-field at Fredericksburg. A Confederate was moving among the Federal wounded, after dark, for the purpose of affording them such relief as he could, when his attention was drawn to a fine pair of shoes on the feet of a poor fellow, silent and rigid. He was himself badly off in the matter of footwear, and to think was but to act. Those shoes, how useless to one, how necessary to the other! He seized one shoe and began to pull. The supposed corpse feebly raised his head and cast upon his despoiler a reproachful glance that seemed to say, " How could you ?" The Confederate laid the foot gently on the ground, touched his hat, and said: " Beg pardon, sir, I thought you had gone above." The story was told to me and I believed it; but whether true or a fiction, it serves to illustrate my point.

General Lee confidently expected that there would be a renewal of the attack on the 14th, but that day and the next passed without anything more serious than desultory artillery firing and skirmishing by the picket lines. He says in his report:

The attack on the 13th had been so easily repulsed, and by so small a part of our army, that it was not supposed the enemy would limit his efforts to an attempt which, in view of the magnitude of his preparations and the extent of his force, seemed to be comparatively insignificant.   Believing, therefore, that he would attack us, it was not deemed expedient to lose the advantages of our position and expose the troops to the fire of his inaccessible batteries beyond the river, by advancing against him; but we were necessarily ignorant of the extent to which he had suffered, and only became aware of it when, on the morning of the 16th, it was discovered that he had availed himself of the darkness of the night and the prevalence of a violent storm of wind and rain to recross the river.   The town was immediately reoccupied and our position on the river-bank resumed.   In the engagement more than nine hundred prisoners and nine thousand stands of arms were taken.

The losses on the Federal side were 12,653—1284 killed, 9600 wounded, and 1769 missing; and on the side of the Confederates, 5322 killed and wounded.

It was a grand experience to have been at the battle of Fredericksburg.   I have never seen another battle as I saw that one.

It is rarely vouchsafed to any one to witness so grand a tableau as was presented to our gaze on that December morning when the curtain of fog was lifted and the sun lit up the scene with the bright effulgence of its rays. As if by magic, the hosts of the grand Federal army were disclosed in martial array extending from the city down the river as far as the eye could reach.   All was bustle and animation in the ranks of the great blue lines. The bright muskets of the men glistened in the sunlight, and countless flags with the stars and stripes floated with the breeze and marked the direction as the troops were maneuvered into line-of-battle formation to the sound of soul-stirring music.   No doubt every heart of that mighty host beat high with hope in anticipation of the impending struggle.

On the other side of the plain, along the hills that skirted its edge, lay that other army, challenged that morning to a trial of strength, its line not so well and fully defined, because of its neutral tints that mingled and blended with the colors of nature in the soil and forests, but which, though silent, was animated with a no less hopeful spirit as with eager expectancy, and no question of doubt, it awaited the advance of its old-time adversary.

And now the left of the Federal line advances at a quickstep, the troops rapidly traverse the space intervening between the two armies, the big guns belch forth their death-dealing missiles, and the incessant rattle of musketry proclaims the issue joined.

My duties carried me to every part of the field. I was on A. P. Hill's front when Meade's men penetrated our lines, and vividly recall the appearance of General Gregg as he was leading his men in the effort to drive back the enemy just before he was killed. I witnessed the assaults on Marye's Hill from an adjoining height on which General Lee had established his headquarters; and it was here that the general had several narrow escapes, notably when one of our own large guns exploded, around which he and his personal staff were gathered, but no one of us was injured.

In his congratulatory order to his army, issued on December 31, 1862, General Lee says:

The immense army of the enemy completed its preparation for the attack without interruption, and gave battle in its own time and on ground of its own selection. It was encountered by less than twenty thousand of this brave army, and its columns crushed and broken, hurled back at every point with such fearful slaughter that escape from entire destruction became the boast of those who had advanced in full confidence of victory. That this great result was achieved with a loss so small in point of numbers only augments the admiration with which the commanding general regards the prowess of his troops, and increases his gratitude to Him who has given us the victory.

Late in January (1863) General Burnside once more essayed a trial of strength with General Lee. His plan, as arranged after conference with General Halleck, was to cross the Rappahannock at the fords above the city of Fredericksburg and assail General Lee's army on that flank, hoping that by thus turning his left he would defeat General Lee in battle, or compel him to evacuate the position held by his army at Fredericksburg. On the 19th reports were made to headquarters of great activity on the part of the enemy and of a movement in force toward the upper fords; and on the 20th the larger part of Burnside's army was massed in the vicinity of Hartwood Church, and the troops heretofore stationed about Fairfax were advancing toward the Rappahannock. Orders were at once issued by General Lee for the strengthening and reinforcing of our positions at Banks's Ford and United States Ford, where it was evident the enemy would attempt to cross. Late in the evening it commenced to rain heavily, and continued with slight intermissions for two days. This rain interfered very much with the Federal plans. At the appointed hour on the 20th the troops started for their proper positions, but the storm was so severe as to greatly retard their movements. It was almost impossible to move the pontoons and the artillery, and after struggling in the mud for two days, the attempt to cross the river was abandoned. General Burnside ascribes his failure to the elements and the unavoidable delay in getting his troops in position. He says in his report:

It was quite apparent during the forenoon of the 21st that the enemy had discovered our movement, and had commenced their preparations to meet us. Could we have had the pontoons there, ready to have crossed early on the 21st, as was hoped, there is scarcely a doubt but that the crossing could have been effected, and the objects of the movement attained; but the detention was unavoidable. The elements were against us. During the day and night of the 21st I had the positions of the enemy reconnoitered as thoroughly as was possible under the circumstances, and on the receipt of the final report of my chief engineer at 4 A.M. on the 22d, I determined to abandon the attempt to cross the river at that point.

Thus ended what was thereafter known as the "Mud March" of General Burnside. The result was anything but inspiriting to the Federal troops. Open and undisguised sentiments of disgust were manifested by the leading officers of Burnside's army. So pronounced was this feeling, so detrimental to the *esprit de corps* of the army were its manifestations, as to cause General Burnside, on the 23d of January, to issue an order, subject to the approval of President Lincoln, dismissing from the service of the United States generals Hooker, Brooks, Newton, and Cochrane; and relieving from duty with his army generals Franklin, W. F. Smith, and Sturgis. This order failed to meet the approval of President Lincoln, and of course was not effective. On January 25th, by order of the President, General Burnside was relieved of the command of the Army of the Potomac at his own request, and General Hooker was assigned to its command.

On January 27th another storm commenced, and continued until the morning of the 29th. The ground was now covered with snow. Under such conditions the roads were impracticable for active operations, and both armies settled down into winter quarters.

CHAPTER XIII

A SUITABLE spot was selected for the establishment of the headquarters of the army not far from Hamilton's Crossing, and we proceeded to make ourselves as comfortable as possible under canvas. The headquarters camp of General Lee was never of such a character as to proclaim its importance. An unpretentious arrangement of five or six army-tents, one or two wagons for transporting equipage and personal effects, with no display of bunting, and no parade of sentinels or guards, only a few orderlies, was all there was of it. General Lee persistently refused to occupy a house, and was content with an ordinary wall-tent, but little, if any, larger than those about it.

During such a period of inactivity as then ensued, while the movement of any large body of troops was not to be thought of, the men were anything but idle, and the work at headquarters was exceedingly onerous. Put fifty thousand men, who have just passed through an active campaign under the conditions that then prevailed in the Southern army, into winter quarters, and immediately every man gets to work with pen and ink to state his grievance or make known his wants and desires; and the result is the concentration and delivery at army headquarters daily of a mass of correspondence simply appalling.

The winter of 1862-63 was a very trying one to those

charged with the responsibility of maintaining the efficiency and building up the strength of the Army of Northern Virginia. Every corps or independent command of the several arms of the service sent daily to headquarters its package of official papers, involving matters great and small, important and unimportant, from the request for a furlough, or a detail to get a fresh horse, to the notification of some activity in the camp of the enemy, or the submission of some intricate question of the relative rights of the officers of the line and of the staff; and as the lines of the army were quite extended, and some of the commands a considerable distance from headquarters, the couriers who brought these despatches were arriving at all hours of the day and night. Mine was the duty of receiving, examining, and disposing of all such despatches and documents. As we had no stenographers or typewriters in those days, the labor was much heavier than it would be now with the aid of such time- and labor-savers. I became an adept after a while, and could discover at a glance when aroused from sleep whether the communication, to receive which I was awakened, was one of importance, or only a matter of army routine.

General Lee, as can well be understood, constantly had his rest disturbed by reason of the great responsibility resting upon him. The many matters of great import pressing upon his mind caused him to lie awake for hours, and he more than once suggested to me not to arouse him before midnight, unless for a matter of great importance, admitting of no delay, as one hour of sleep before midnight was to him worth more than two hours after midnight. Of course, I refer here to despatches concerning some movement of the enemy, and not to the matters of detail coming from the different commands of our army. For these army communications he had so great a dislike that I endeavored to

spare him as much as possible, and would only submit
for his action such matters as were of a nature to demand the personal consideration and decision of the
commander of the army.

On one occasion when an audience had not been
asked of him for several days, it became necessary to
have one. The few papers requiring his action were
submitted. He was not in a very pleasant mood.
Something irritated him, and he manifested his ill humor by a little nervous twist or jerk of the neck and
head, peculiar to himself, accompanied by some harshness of manner. This was perceived by me, and I hastily concluded that my efforts to save him annoyance
were not appreciated. In disposing of some case of a
vexatious character, matters reached a climax. He
became really worried, and, forgetting what was due
to my superior, I petulantly threw the paper down at
my side and gave evident signs of anger. Then in a
perfectly calm and measured tone of voice he said,
"Colonel Taylor, when I lose my temper, don't you let
it make you angry."

Was there ever a more gentle and considerate and
yet so positive a reproof? General Lee was naturally
of a positive temperament, firm, resolute, occasionally
irascible, but always responsive to the sober second
thought, and ready to make the *amende honorable;*
holding himself in check by the exercise of his will and
conscience. He was not one of those invariably amia-
ble men whose temper is never ruffled; but when we
consider the immense burden which rested upon him,
and the numberless causes for annoyance with which he
had to contend, the occasional cropping out of temper
which we who were constantly near him witnessed
only served to show how great was his habitual self-
command; and it was frequently observed and com-
mented upon that after any such trifling ebullition of

temper he always manifested a marked degree of affability, as if desirous of obliterating all recollection of the unpleasant episode.

The idea prevails with some that General Lee possessed great austerity of manner, rendering him not easy of approach. Such was not the case. Although naturally a man of much dignity, in which he was never deficient when occasion called for the manifestation of that trait, his intercourse with those around him was marked by a suavity of manner that removed all restraint and invited closer fellowship. In our small circle of the personal staff, and indeed with all the members of the staff, there was between General Lee and his military family a degree of *camaraderie* that was perfectly delightful. Our conversation, especially at table, was free from restraint, unreserved as between equals, and often of a bright and jocular vein. He was very fond of a joke, and not infrequently indulged in the pastime of teasing those about him in a mild way. While it would never occur to any one of us to be otherwise than perfectly deferential in our manner toward him, and respectful in our deportment toward each other in his presence, there was an utter absence of the rigid formality and the irksome ceremonial regarded by some as essential features of the military etiquette appertaining to the station of the commander-in-chief of an army.

I have already alluded to his simplicity of taste. This was especially noticeable in the *menage* at army headquarters. All the appointments were of the simplest kind. The table furniture was of tin, and while we never really wanted for food, unless by reason of accidental separation from our camp wagons, we only enjoyed what was allotted to the army generally. Ours was the regular army ration, supplemented by such additions from the country as could be procured by our steward by the use of a little money. General Lee never availed himself of the advantages of his position to obtain dainties for his table or any personal comfort for himself. The use of spirituous liquors, while not forbidden, was never habitual in our camp. There was no general mess-supply, and rarely, if ever, a private nip. I used to think that General Lee would have been better off if he had taken a little stimulant. I recall but one instance of his indulging in this way, and that was at Petersburg, where he received from some admiring friend a few bottles of old wine. When opened, the aroma from this wine filled the camp. We were favored with a taste of it once. It was very fine; it produced a feeling of self-righteousness and inward satisfaction. We never partook of it again, neither did I ever see the general partake of it, and I rather suspect that he sent it to some hospital for the sick, or to some one who, in his judgment, needed it more than he did. He may have used it, however, as I have no doubt that the donor enjoined upon him that it was for his private use; and it certainly was too good for general distribution to indiscriminating guests, whose desire was quite as well appeased by a "whiskey straight" or a bottle of beer.

A respite of three months was allowed the troops in winter quarters about Fredericksburg. In February General Longstreet, with the divisions of Hood and Pickett and two battalions of artillery, was sent to the south side of James River to be in position to resist any movement the enemy might make from that direction, and to relieve the commissary department, as it was hoped that supplies could be had from that section in large quantities, if a sufficient force was there to keep the enemy closely confined to his lines near Suffolk. These troops did not rejoin the army under General Lee until after the battle of Chancellorsville.

On the 17th of March a division of Federal cavalry, under General Averell, crossed the Rappahannock at Kelly's Ford, with orders to attack the Confederate cavalry near Culpeper Court House, under General Fitzhugh Lee, and to rout or destroy it. General Averell's command numbered three thousand men, but as he had to detach nine hundred men to guard his flank and rear, he states that he carried only twenty-one hundred into action. General Fitzhugh Lee's command numbered eight hundred. By a dash across the river the Federals succeeded in capturing the picket of twenty-five men that guarded the ford. The whole of Averell's command then crossed and took position. Meanwhile General Fitzhugh Lee, having been informed of the crossing of the river by the Federals, moved his command in line of battle toward Kelly's Ford. Quite a spirited engagement ensued, with varying success to the combatants, until about 5.30 P.M., when the Federals recrossed the river. In his report General Averell says: "It was 5.30 P.M., and it was necessary to advance my cavalry upon their intrenched position to make a direct and desperate attack, or to withdraw across the river. Either operation would have been attended with imminent hazard. My horses were very much exhausted. We had been successful thus far. I deemed it proper to withdraw."

General Stuart, who was present, but who left the direction of the battle entirely to General Fitzhugh Lee, did not agree with the view expressed by the Federal commander, as he says: "The defeat was decided, and the enemy, broken and demoralized, retired under cover of darkness to his place of refuge, the main army, having abandoned in defeat an expedition undertaken with boasting and vainglorious demonstration." Certainly General Averell did not carry out his orders, which were to "attack and rout or destroy Fitz. Lee." Nevertheless, this was a sad day for the Confederates, for among the fallen was the bold, intrepid, heroic Pelham! Among the Confederate heroes slain in battle, none left a more honorable, a more brilliant record than this young major of the horse-artillery. At the battle of Gainesville special mention was made of his coming into action with his guns by General Jackson, as relieving his right at a most opportune time. Favorable mention was made by both General Lee and General Jackson of the efficient manner in which he served his guns in checking and delaying the attack made by Franklin on Jackson's lines at Fredericksburg. In the language of General Stuart: "Though young in years, a mere stripling in appearance, remarkable for his genuine modesty of deportment, he yet disclosed on the battle-field the conduct of a veteran, and displayed in his handsome person the most imperturbable coolness in danger." Though of slender physique, he was gifted with nerves of steel, the heart of a lion, and the courage of a martyr. He fell mortally wounded in the fight near Kelly's Ford, with "the battle-cry on his lips and the light of victory beaming from his eye."

CHAPTER XIV

THE BATTLE OF CHANCELLORSVILLE

ON April 14th intelligence again reached General Lee of unusual activity on the part of the enemy. On that day the Federal cavalry attempted to make a lodgment on the south side of the Rappahannock River, at the upper fords, but they were successfully resisted and driven back by General Stuart with the brigades of Fitzhugh Lee and W. H. F. Lee. On the 21st bodies of infantry appeared near Kelly's Ford, and a demonstration was made lower down the river opposite Port Royal, where a small body of infantry crossed on the 23d. On the 28th the Confederate pickets on the river-front in the city of Fredericksburg were driven off, and again bridges were constructed just below the city, and quite a large force of the enemy crossed to the south side of the river and took position along its banks. This force manifested no purpose of attacking, and it looked as if the real effort would be made in another quarter. On the 29th General Stuart reported to General Lee that the enemy's infantry had crossed in force near Kelly's Ford on the previous evening, and later in the day he reported the movement of heavy columns in the direction of Germanna and Ely's fords on the Rapidan River. The purpose of the Federal commander was now disclosed; the diversions were over, the real effort had begun, and it was "Fighting Joe" Hooker's turn to wrestle with General Lee. He had devoted three months to the work of raising the standard of efficiency of his army in every way; munitions of war and supplies of every kind had been furnished to the full satisfaction of his requisitions. The depression of the troops consequent upon the results of the senseless sacrifice of life and the defeat at Fredericksburg, and the fiasco of the "mud march" to the upper fords of the Rappahannock, had disappeared and was followed by a certain amount of hopeful anticipation of more creditable results under the leadership of "Fighting Joe," whose soubriquet gave assurance of success. His ranks were full, and with such an army, one hundred and thirty thousand strong, "the finest on the planet," as claimed by him, the promise of victory lured him on, and the authorities at Washington awaited its early coming with anticipations admitting of no doubt.

General Lee had also done all in his power during the period of inactivity toward recuperating and strengthening his army; but supplies of every kind were scarce, and he had been compelled to detach General Longstreet with two divisions of his army to the south side of James River, primarily to obtain food. With the balance of his army, numbering fifty-seven thousand men, embracing Jackson's three divisions and the divisions of McLaws and Anderson of infantry, the cavalry, and reserve artillery, he decided to accept the gage of battle now offered by General Hooker.

The divisions of the Federal army that had crossed the Rapidan River at Germanna and Ely's fords moved toward Chancellorsville, from which point there were several roads leading to the rear of the position occupied by General Lee's army. On the night of the 29th General Lee sent General Anderson with his division toward Chancellorsville with orders so to dispose of his brigades as to cover these roads. On reaching Chancellorsville, General Anderson learned that the enemy that had crossed the Rapidan was approaching that point in strong force; and early on the morning of the 30th he deemed it wisest to retire to the intersection of the Mine and Plank roads, near Tabernacle Church. As Mahone's rear-guard left Chancellorsville it was attacked by the enemy's cavalry, but so effectually were they repulsed no further effort was made to harass the troops in their movement to the chosen position. Here, after having selected a line of defense, General Anderson's command—consisting of three brigades under generals Wright, Posey, and Mahone—proceeded vigorously to intrench itself. Wright and Posey were on the Plank Road, and Mahone on the old turnpike.

On the evening of the 30th the Federal force assembled at Chancellorsville consisted of the Second (except one division with Sedgwick), Fifth, Eleventh, and Twelfth corps, with General Hooker, in person, in command. The Third Corps arrived the evening of next day. The First Corps joined him on the 3d of May, but did not become actively engaged.

The Federal force that had crossed at Fredericksburg continued inactive. The operations of the cavalry, under General Stuart, had revealed the purpose of General Hooker to make his main attack upon our flank and rear. General Lee therefore determined to leave sufficient troops to hold his lines near Fredericksburg, and with his main army to give battle to the approaching columns of the enemy. Leaving Early's division of Jackson's corps and Barksdale's brigade of McLaws's division, with some batteries of the reserve artillery, under General Early, to hold his lines, he ordered generals Jackson and McLaws to move with the rest of their commands toward Chancellorsville. These troops were all in position where Anderson had established his lines early on the morning of May 1st, and about 11 A.M. the order was given to advance. The movement was along the old turnpike and the Plank Road; General McLaws moved on the former with his three brigades, preceded by Mahone's. General Anderson, with the brigades of Wright and Posey, led on the Plank Road, and General Jackson followed with his command. The brigades of Wilcox and Perry, of Anderson's division, coöperated with General McLaws. Colonel Alexander's battalion of artillery accompanied the advance.

The enemy was soon encountered, and heavy skirmishing began. Mahone's brigade, leading on the turnpike, soon became engaged with the United States Regulars, and, after a spirited fight, drove the enemy in the direction of Chancellorsville, capturing many prisoners. About the same time the enemy made a vigorous attack upon McLaws, which was repulsed by Semmes's brigade. One of Alexander's batteries, under Captain Jordan, coöperated in this action and eventually broke the enemy's infantry by the accuracy of its fire. General Anderson had sent General Wright, with his brigade, on April 30th (by way of an unfinished railroad from Fredericksburg to Gordonsville), to a point where he would threaten the enemy's right. General Wright, who was now well on the flank of the enemy, was ordered to advance up the Plank Road, feel for the enemy, and attack him when found. After having proceeded about a mile, Wright's skirmishers became engaged with the enemy's advance, which, finding its flank enveloped, began very soon to give way, when Wright pressed forward with the main body of his brigade. This movement, simultaneous with the repulse of the enemy by Semmes, caused their whole line to retreat rapidly, when our troops pressed forward vigorously until they arrived within from one to one and a half miles of Chancellorsville. Here the enemy was found to be in full force, in a naturally strong position, intrenched, with abatis in front of their line, the approach to which was open and commanded by their artillery. The advancing columns of Confederates were halted, and as soon as the reconnaissance made of the position occupied by the enemy made apparent the inadvisability of an attack in front, line of battle was ordered to be formed, facing toward Chancellorsville, at right angles to the Plank Road, extending to the Mine Road on the right, and in the direction of the Catharine Furnace on the left, where the troops proceeded at once to protect themselves by hastily constructed earthworks.

The day was now far spent, and General Lee's mind was occupied with the problem of how he could best attack the enemy. He and General Jackson conferred together for some time. When they separated and Jackson started to rejoin his troops, the question had been decided. No one can say which of the two first suggested the movement to turn the enemy's right flank; but as such a movement was entirely in accord with General Lee's tactics in giving the counterstroke, and as General Jackson's deference to his superior and confidence in his judgment were such as to justify the belief that he quietly awaited the development of his plan and then gave to it his hearty acquiescence, as being entirely along the line of his own views, it is fair to presume that it was General Lee's own conception of the best method of attack then open to him.

In his report he says:

It was evident that a direct attack upon the enemy would be attended with great difficulty and loss, in view of the strength of his position and his superiority of numbers. It was, therefore, resolved to endeavor to turn his right flank and gain his rear, leaving a force in front to hold him in check and conceal the movement. The execution of this plan was intrusted to Lieutenant-general Jackson, with his three divisions. The command of generals McLaws and Anderson, with the exception of Wilcox's brigade, which during the night had been ordered back to Banks's Ford, remained in front of the enemy.

Surely here was an instance of strategy of the highest order, and an illustration of supreme confidence in the mettle and courage of the troops ! With one third of his army detached, under Longstreet, and with another division at Fredericksburg to protect his rear, confronted by a greatly superior force, General Lee decides to hold fast his lines in front of the powerful army of his adversary with two divisions, and sends his trusted lieutenant with three divisions to gain the enemy's flank and rear by a circuitous route, with the hope of crushing that flank and rolling it up and back, beaten and demoralized, upon the main army, which he would then assail in front.

Bold it certainly was ! Acting on the defensive, he swiftly and vigorously assumes the offensive. Because unexpected, the counterstroke would be so much the more effective. Greatly outnumbered, he offsets this by adopting a plan that infuses dash and enthusiasm into his columns and so adds greatly to the weight of the impact of their blows upon their adversaries.

General Stuart was directed to screen the movement of Jackson's column, which he did effectually with the brigades of Fitzhugh Lee and W. H. F. Lee. General Jackson started early on the morning of the 2d and marched by the Furnace and Brock roads. He reached a point on the old turnpike about three miles in rear of Chancellorsville at 4 P.M., and immediately made disposition for attack. At 5.15 P.M. the order was given to advance, Rodes's division in front, Trimble's division, under Brigadier-general Colston, in the second line, and A. P. Hill's division in the third line. The skirmishers of Rodes's brigades very soon encountered the enemy. The line of battle rapidly closed upon the skirmish line and rushed forward with great impetuosity and vigor. Sweeping everything before them, they forced the enemy to retire precipitately and captured several batteries of artillery. So complete was the surprise to the enemy, and so impetuous was the assault, that there was scarcely any organized resistance after the first volley was fired.

In his report General Rodes says:

They fled in the wildest confusion, leaving the field strewn with arms, accouterments, clothing, caissons, and field-pieces in every direction. The larger portion of his force, as well as intrenchments, were drawn up at right angles to our line, and being thus taken in the flank and rear, they did not wait for the attack. On reaching the ridge at Melzi Chancellor's, which had an extended line of works facing in our direction, an effort was made to check the fleeing columns. For a few moments they held this position, but once more my gallant troops dashed at them with a wild shout, and firing a hasty volley, they continued their headlong flight to Chancellorsville. It was at this point that Trimble's division, which had followed closely on my rear, headed by the brave and accomplished Colston, went over the works with my men, and from this time until the close of the engagement the two divisions were mingled together in inextricable confusion.

The advance continued until arrested by the abatis in front of the enemy's line of works near their central position at Chancellorsville.

The division of General A. P. Hill was then ordered by General Jackson to move to the front and relieve the divisions under generals Rodes and Colston. It was in the dusk of the evening when this exchange of troops was made. General Jackson had gone to the extreme front to reconnoiter, and as he was returning to our lines with his staff and escort the party was mistaken for the enemy and fired upon by some of our troops.

Several of the party were killed and more were wounded, among the latter being General Jackson, who was severely injured and carried from the field.

As next in rank on the field, General A. P. Hill assumed command. Hardly had his division taken position in front when it was vigorously attacked by the artillery and infantry of the enemy. This attack was successfully met and repulsed, but General Hill was then disabled, and General Stuart, who had been all the while coöperating with the infantry in the advance, was sent for that he might take command. As soon as General Stuart arrived the command was turned over to him by General Hill. It was now dark, and any further advance that night was out of the question in that wilderness of forest and tangled undergrowth.

While Jackson's movement upon the enemy's right flank was being executed, General Lee ordered the troops in front of Chancellorsville to engage the enemy actively, to prevent reinforcements from being sent to the force being assailed by Jackson; so that, after notice was received of Jackson's attack, there was fighting all along the line, our troops pressing up to the intrenchments of the enemy, and our artillery doing most efficient service, until night put an end to the conflict.

At an early hour the next morning General Stuart renewed the attack on the enemy's right. Handling his troops with masterful skill, he pushed to a glorious consummation the movement so brilliantly begun by General Jackson.

The line of works occupied by the enemy at the close of the battle of the previous day was quickly carried, as was also a barricade in its rear. The right of the advancing columns, however, now encountered the extensive earthworks behind which the artillery of the enemy was posted. These works were gallantly assaulted by the men of Hill's division, now under General Heth, but being without artillery, and they themselves being subjected to the fire of ten or twelve pieces, their efforts to drive the enemy failed, and these gallant brigades fell back to the line of works from which the enemy had been driven. Reinforcements were soon brought up. About the same time the commanding position of Hazel Grove was gallantly carried by Archer's brigade, and again the order to advance was given. This time the assaulting column had the aid of the artillery under colonels Carter and Jones, which did excellent service, and the enemy then yielded the ground and was driven from his strongly fortified line of defense.

At the same time the troops of Anderson and McLaws, under the immediate supervision of General Lee, were actively engaged with the enemy at Chancellorsville. The orders to General Anderson were to incline to his left so as to form a junction with the troops operating on the flank of the enemy. This junction of forces was soon effected. The troops under General Stuart, driving the enemy before them, were soon in touch with those of Anderson's command. The whole line was ordered forward. The men forced their way through the abatis, mounted the earthworks, and drove the enemy from their fortified positions and forced them back toward the river. By 10 A.M. our troops were in full possession of the field.

Meanwhile there was trouble at Fredericksburg. The orders to General Early were to the effect that if the enemy in his front withdrew from Fredericksburg, he was to proceed without further orders to join the main army under General Lee. These orders were repeated on the 2d, but owing to some misapprehension this last order was so conveyed to General Early as to cause him to commence to withdraw his force from his lines while the Federals, under General Sedgwick, still occupied the south side of the river. The enemy at once gave evidence of a purpose to advance, but the mistake in the transmission of the order to General Early was dis-covered and corrected, and his troops resumed their original position. While this was going on the troops at Chancellorsville were being reformed, having become somewhat scattered and mixed up in the fight, with the view of renewing the attack on the enemy, who had now taken position on a line nearer the river that they had previously fortified. General Lee was considering the propriety of assailing his adversary under these new conditions, when information reached him of the *contretemps* at Fredericksburg. Considerable time then elapsed and nothing more was accomplished that day.

Early on the morning of the 3d the enemy at Fredericksburg advanced in force against the positions held by General Early's troops, and although gallantly re-sisted at the several points of attack, he was enabled finally by sheer force of numbers to drive out the Con-federates, who retired in the direction of Chancellors-ville. General Early rallied his troops and made a successful stand before the Federal column advancing by the Telegraph Road, about two miles from Freder-icksburg. General Wilcox, with his brigade, who had been stationed at Banks's Ford to protect General Lee's rear, on hearing of the disaster to Early moved promptly to his assistance, and arrived in time to check the Federal column that was moving on the Plank Road toward Chancellorsville. General Wilcox retired slowly until he reached Salem Church on the Plank Road, about five miles from Fredericksourg.

BATTLE OF SALEM CHURCH

General Lee, who had been made aware of these movements, had ordered General McLaws, with his three brigades and Mahone's brigade of Anderson's division, to the support of General Wilcox. These troops reached General Wilcox's position early in the afternoon, and were at once deployed in line of battle, the two brigades of Kershaw and Wofford on Wilcox's right, and those of Semmes and Mahone on his left. After a spirited cannonade from the enemy's artillery, their infantry advanced in force against the Confederate line, the assault being delivered directly against that portion held by Wilcox's brigade. This attack was successfully resisted. The first line of the enemy gave way in confusion. Our troops advanced. A second line was soon encountered, but it quickly broke under the close and deadly fire which it received, and the whole Federal mass retired in confusion.

The brigades of Wilcox and Semmes moved forward in pursuit and forced the retreating Federals back fully a mile, when they were halted to reform before encountering the Federal reserve, which now appeared in strong force. It was then nearly dark, and finding himself confronted with so large a force so far in advance of the other troops, General Wilcox deemed it the part of prudence to retire to his original position, leaving his skirmishers far in advance, the enemy not following him.

On the next day General Early advanced along the Telegraph Road and recaptured Marye's Heights and the adjacent hills.

General Lee could not move against the enemy in his fortified position between Chancellorsville and the river with this condition of affairs in his rear. He determined, therefore, to further reinforce the troops opposing General Sedgwick, and, if possible, to drive him across the river. General Anderson, with his remaining three brigades, was ordered to join General McLaws on the 4th, and reached Salem Church about noon. General McLaws, whose troops were disposed as on the previous day, was ordered to hold the enemy in check. General Anderson was directed to move so as to gain the left flank of the enemy and form a junction with General Early, when both would attack. McLaws was ordered to push forward his right brigades as soon as the advance of Anderson and Early should be perceived, so as to connect with them and complete the continuity of our line. There was some delay in getting the troops in position, and it was six o'clock before the advance began. The troops of Anderson and Early then moved rapidly forward and drove the enemy from his positions, meeting with but little resistance. Wright's brigade of Anderson's division advanced with great intrepidity across a wheat-field under a hot fire of grape, and drove one of the enemy's batteries from its position. The enemy retreated toward Banks's Ford, and was followed closely as long as there was light enough to continue the pursuit.

Meanwhile General Early's brigades on Anderson's right had advanced against the enemy,—Gordon on the right, Hays in the center, and Hoke on the left,—all driving the enemy before them. Unfortunately, General McLaws was not made aware of the result of the attack by Anderson and Early until it was quite dark. It was previously reported to him that from the position occupied by Mahone's brigade the noise of the enemy crossing the river on the pontoon bridge at Banks's Ford could be heard, and by his direction Colonel Alexander began to throw shells so as to drop them at the point of crossing. At the same time General McLaws sent General Wilcox with his own brigade and Kershaw's with orders to press the enemy down the road leading to Banks's Ford. After these orders were given, and while they were being carried out, General McLaws learned officially from General Lee of the success of the attack by Anderson and Early, and he was directed to push the enemy and force him across the river that night.   Accordingly General McLaws ordered all of his brigades forward.   Wofford advanced as far as the River Road, driving the enemy before him; Wilcox and Kershaw pushed on, and occupied the redoubts commanding the ford and its approaches.   Colonel Alexander put several batteries in position and opened a vigorous fire upon the ford and the approaches on the opposite side.   It was now too dark to attempt more. "The darkness of the night, ignorance of the country and of the events transpiring on the other end of the line, prevented that coöperation which would have led to a more complete success." *

The next morning it was ascertained that General Sedgwick's whole force had crossed to the north side of the Rappahannock.   General Lee at once ordered General Early to reoccupy his lines near Fredericksburg, and directed generals Anderson and McLaws to return with their commands to Chancellorsville.   A heavy rain now began to fall, interfering very much with the movement of these troops; they reached their destination during the afternoon.   Preparations were made to assail the main army of the enemy in its new position at daylight on the 6th, but when our skirmishers advanced they found the enemy's works deserted.   General Hooker had retired with his army across the river.

Of all the battles fought by the army under General Lee, that of Chancellorsville perhaps adds greatest luster to his fame as a strategist and to the prowess of his troops in battle, under his direction; but glorious as that battle was for the Confederate arms, it was attended with an irreparable and overwhelming loss—it was the last of the many heroic achievements of the bright particular star of the Army of Northern Virginia.   General

* General McLaws's report.

Jackson, severely wounded on the 2d, died on the 10th of May, 1863.

When report was made to General Lee of the fact that it had been found necessary to amputate General Jackson's arm, he directed the officer who conveyed the information to assure General Jackson of his constant thought of him and of his sympathy for him in his suffering and loss; "but," said he, "tell him I am a greater sufferer than he; for whereas he has lost his left arm, I have lost my right."

In his report of the battle, General Lee pays this tribute to his memory:

The movement by which the enemy's position was turned and the fortune of the day decided was conducted by the lamented Lieutenant-general Jackson, who, as has already been stated, was severely wounded near the close of the engagement on Saturday evening. I do not propose here to speak of the character of this illustrious man since removed from the scene of his eminent usefulness by the hand of an inscrutable but all-wise Providence. I nevertheless desire to pay the tribute of my admiration to the matchless energy and skill that marked this last act of his life, forming, as it did, a worthy conclusion of that long series of splendid achievements which won for him the lasting love and gratitude of his country.

I have once stated in these memoirs that, in my belief, the good Lord decided that the South should not succeed in the war between the States; and in the contemplation of the removal of Stonewall Jackson by an all-wise Providence, as stated by General Lee, I am reminded of the story of the good deacon in the South, but of whose name and station I am ignorant, who, when the war was over, accepted the situation in a spirit of Christian resignation, and endeavored to lead his people that way; and who, when his time came to lead in prayer, said: "O Lord, thou who knowest all things, who orderest all things, and who doest all things well, we thank Thee for all Thy mercies, and we ask that we may be resigned to Thy blessed will in all things. Thou hast seen fit to bring distress upon us, and we try to believe that it was for some good purpose that Thou didst permit our enemies to get the better of us; but, O Lord, thou who knowest all things, Thou knowest at the same time that it was necessary for Thee to remove from this world Thy valiant servant Stonewall Jackson before it could be that way."

In these several engagements the Confederates captured 5000 prisoners, exclusive of the wounded, 13 pieces of artillery, 19,500 stands of arms, and 17 colors. The Confederate loss in killed and wounded was 10,281, of which number 1581 were killed and 8700 wounded. The Federal loss was 1575 killed, 9559 wounded, 5711 captured or missing, making a total of 16,845.

I cannot forbear mention of the gallant conduct of two of my friends and fellow townsmen who were killed in the battle of Chancellorsville—Colonel Francis Mallory and Captain W. Carter Williams. Colonel Mallory was a very handsome man, an ex-officer of the United States Army and a thorough soldier. He was in command of the Fifty-fifth Virginia regiment of infantry, Heth's brigade of A. P. Hill's division. I last met him just before the fight; his regiment was then under arms, and we were on the eve of battle. I stopped long enough to exchange a few words with him, and recalled afterward his depression of manner. Every man who goes into battle, before the excitement begins is apt to reflect upon the probabilities of his being killed. Colonel Mallory was in such frame of mind on that occasion; I recall his saying that it would be too bad after having escaped so far to be shot down after all. He was killed in the attack of Rodes's division on the enemy's right, May 2d, while gallantly leading his men against the enemy.

Captain Williams commanded a company of the Sixth Virginia regiment of Mahone's brigade. The courage of this gallant soldier and the manner of his death were reported by his brigade commander in these words:

The advance line of skirmishers of the Sixth Virginia Infantry, under the immediate command of Captain W. Carter Williams, charged over the enemy's abatis near the Plank Road, fired upon him in his rifle-pits, captured three prisoners and the colors and color-bearer of the One Hundred and Seventh Ohio, returning to his position with his handful of men, with the loss of an officer as prisoner. This gallant and successful sortie was made a little after dark, Saturday, May 2d, when General Jackson's fire was heavy, and it was in fighting over the same ground the next morning that the valiant Williams fell, mortally wounded.

I was wonderfully impressed in this fight by the strong personality of the Southern soldier and his independent action in battle, as contrasted with the mechanical movement of the machine soldier. I have nothing to say in disparagement of the soldier of the regular army as we know him in this country, and I recognize fully the great importance of drilling soldiers in the matters of precision, the touch of the elbow, the proper alignment and harmonious movement. All these requirements serve to make "regulars;" but there is a great difference between regulars and veterans. In the early period of the war the regulars were regarded as especially formidable in battle, and great stress was laid upon the fact wherever they were encountered. But let the conditions be such as to render impracticable the precision of movement, the touch of the elbow, and the alignment, and unless the units have in addition strong personality, your machine refuses to work and disaster follows. When the fighting was most severe on the 3d of May, I was present and witnessed the final assault on the fortified position of the enemy. Our troops had advanced close up to the works; felled trees, tangled undergrowth, and abatis made together a very formidable obstacle for the men who were being urged to go forward. First one man went forward, then another, then at intervals two or three; then there would be a wavering and falling back when the fire became hot; then there would be a repetition of this; one or two at a time, encouraging the others, then small parties advanced, the officers waved their swords and called the men "forward," and then with a yell the whole line rushed rapidly forward without precision or order, but irresistibly, sweeping everything before them. I can never forget the scene as the victorious, yelling Confederates pressed forward and passed General Lee near the Chancellor house, which was on fire and burning fiercely. As they caught sight of their general the men rent the air with their cheers of victory, and pushed forward more rapidly, waving their hats on high and calling his name; and as I contemplated their earnest faces, their sparkling eyes, their cheeks in many cases begrimed, their tattered clothing, their bright rifles, I could well understand the emotions awakened in his breast by their manifestations of love and admiration for him, and more especially the feeling of pride he experienced at being in command of them.

A few days later General Lee issued a congratulatory order to his army, from which I make this extract:

Under trying vicissitudes of heat and storm, you attacked the enemy, strongly intrenched in the depths of a tangled wilderness, and again on the hills of Fredericksburg, fifteen miles distant, and, by the valor that has triumphed on so many fields, forced him once more to seek safety beyond the Rappahannock. While this glorious victory entitles you to the praise and gratitude of the nation, we are especially called upon to return our grateful thanks to the only Giver of victory for the signal deliverance He has wrought. It is therefore earnestly recommended that the troops unite on Sunday next in ascribing to the Lord of Hosts the glory due unto His name.

Strange to say, General Hooker on the 6th of May issued a general order to his troops congratulating them on the results of the battle. He said in part:

The major-general commanding tenders to this army his congratulations on its achievements of the last seven days. If it has not accomplished all that was expected, the reasons are well known to the army. It is sufficient to say they were of a character not to be foreseen or prevented by human sagacity or resource. In withdrawing from the south bank of the Rappahannock before delivering a general battle to our adversaries, the army has given renewed evidence of its confidence in itself and its fidelity to the principles it represents. In fighting at a disadvantage we would have been recreant to our trust, to ourselves, our cause, and our country. Profoundly loyal and conscious of its strength, the Army of the Potomac will give or decline battle whenever its interests or honor may demand. It will also be the guardian of its own history and its own fame.

General Hooker was certainly imbued with a most optimistic spirit to have been able to gather up even a few crumbs of comfort in reviewing the operations of his army for the time mentioned; but he could not deceive others, and the true history of the battle was so readily discerned that even at the North his order was read with smiles of derision.

The Federal army returned to its former position on the Stafford heights, and General Lee reoccupied his lines about Fredericksburg.

When General Hooker's movements to assail General Lee were fully developed, orders were sent to General Longstreet to proceed with all possible despatch, with his command, to join General Lee. These troops arrived at Fredericksburg some days after the battle.

CHAPTER XV

GENERAL LEE REORGANIZES HIS ARMY AND AGAIN AS-
SUMES THE OFFENSIVE

THE death of General Jackson, on the 10th of May, was followed by a reorganization of the Army of Northern Virginia into three corps, designated the First, Second, and Third Army Corps. Longstreet, Ewell, and A. P. Hill, each now advanced to the rank of lieutenant-general, were assigned to the command of these corps in the order named. Each of these corps embraced three divisions; one of the divisions of the Second Corps and one of the Third had five brigades; all the others had four brigades.

The artillery was also reorganized. To each corps there were attached two or three battalions of four batteries each, under the command of a chief of artillery for that corps; these three divisions and the reserve artillery were under the command of the chief of artillery of the army. The cavalry remained practically as before.

From the very necessities of the case, the general theory upon which the war was conducted on the part of the South was one of defense. The great superiority of the North in men and material made it indispensable for the South to husband its resources as much as possible, inasmuch as the hope of ultimate success which the latter entertained rested rather upon the dissatisfaction and pecuniary distress which a prolonged war would

entail upon the former—making the people weary of the
struggle—than upon any expectation of attaining peace
by actually subduing so powerful an adversary.

Nevertheless, in the judgment of General Lee, it was
a part of a true defensive policy to take the aggressive
when good opportunity offered; and by delivering an
effective blow to the enemy, not only to inflict upon him
serious loss, but at the same time to thwart his designs
of invasion, derange the plan of campaign contemplated
by him, and thus prolong the conflict.

The Federal army, under General Hooker, had now reoccupied the heights opposite Fredericksburg, where it
could not be attacked except at a disadvantage. Instead
of quietly awaiting the pleasure of the Federal commander in designing and putting into execution some
new plan of campaign, General Lee determined to
maneuver to draw him from his impregnable position,
and, if practicable, to remove the scene of hostilities beyond the Potomac. His design was to free the State of
Virginia, for a time at least, from the presence of the
enemy, to transfer the theater of war to Northern soil,
and by selecting a favorable time and place in which to
receive the attack which his adversary would be compelled to make on him, to take the reasonable chances
of defeating him in a pitched battle; knowing full well
that to obtain such an advantage there would place him
in position to attain far more decisive results than could
be hoped for from a like advantage gained in Virginia.

But even if unable to attain the valuable results which
might be expected to follow a decided advantage gained
over the enemy in Maryland or Pennsylvania, it was
thought that the movement would at least so far disturb
the Federal plan for the summer campaign as to prevent
its execution during the season for active operations.

In pursuance of this design, General Lee commenced
to withdraw his army from the vicinity of Fredericks-

burg on the 3d of June. McLaws's division of the First Corps left Fredericksburg for Culpeper Court House on that day, and Hood's division of the same corps, which was encamped on the Rapidan River, marched to the same place.

On the 4th and 5th the three divisions of the Second Corps, under generals Early, Rodes, and Johnson, followed. The Third Corps, under General A. P. Hill, embracing the divisions under generals Anderson, Heth, and Pender, was left to occupy the lines at Fredericksburg.

On the 6th the enemy constructed a pontoon bridge near Deep Run and crossed a large force to the south side of the Rappahannock; but this force manifested no intention of attacking, and was evidently for purposes of observation, as also to check the movements of General Lee.

General Lee deemed it prudent to halt Ewell's corps that night; but after watching the enemy's operations the next day he became satisfied that A. P. Hill's command could manage the force on the south side. He thereupon sent orders to General Ewell to continue his march, and he left Fredericksburg that evening himself to join the troops in advance.

On the 8th Longstreet and Ewell reached Culpeper Court House, where General Stuart already had his cavalry concentrated. On the 9th a large force of Federal cavalry supported by infantry crossed the Rappahannock and attacked General Stuart. A bitter struggle ensued, lasting the whole day, the advantage being first with one side and then the other. The enemy was finally forced to recross the river with heavy loss, leaving four hundred prisoners, three pieces of artillery, and several colors in our hands.

General Lee now put the Second Corps in advance. General Ewell left Culpeper Court House on the 10th, and crossing the Shenandoah River on the 12th, near Front Royal, he sent General Rodes with his division to Berryville, with instructions to drive off the force of the enemy stationed there, and to cut off communication between Winchester and the Potomac. General Ewell moved with his other two divisions directly upon Winchester, forcing the enemy back into his lines about that town.

On the 14th General Early stormed these works and captured several of the small forts. On the 15th his troops assaulted the main fort and drove the enemy from his lines. The division of General Johnson, which had been sent by General Ewell to the east of the town, intercepted the retreat of the Federals under General Milroy, and after a spirited engagement captured nearly the whole force, numbering about twenty-five hundred. General Milroy, with a small body of cavalry, made his escape to Harper's Ferry. General Rodes on the same day moved with his division to Martinsburg and dispersed the Federal force there, capturing some prisoners, artillery, and stores. These operations cleared the Valley of the enemy, those at Harper's Ferry having crossed the river to the Maryland side. In the several engagements more than 4000 prisoners were captured, together with 29 pieces of artillery, 300 horses, 270 wagons, and a quantity of supplies of all kinds. The Confederate loss was inconsiderable.

Meanwhile, the Federal army, under General Hooker, had withdrawn from its lines opposite Fredericksburg, pursuing the roads near the Potomac, with the purpose, apparently, of covering the approaches to the city of Washington. On the 15th, by direction of General Lee, General Longstreet moved with his whole force, now embracing his three divisions, except one brigade of Pickett's division left at Hanover Junction, and advancing along the east side of the Blue Ridge, occupied Ashby's and Snicker's gaps.   General A. P. Hill at the same time withdrew from the front of Fredericksburg, in accordance with instructions from General Lee, and marched for the Valley in the wake of the Second Corps. General Stuart screened these movements from the enemy operating in front of Longstreet.

Rodes's division of Ewell's corps had already crossed the Potomac, and Jenkins's brigade of cavalry, that accompanied it, had advanced to Chambersburg.   On the 19th Rodes moved to Hagerstown, Johnson crossed the river to Sharpsburg, and Early moved to Shepherdstown, in accordance with orders from General Ewell, who, with his corps thus well in hand, awaited the movements of the other two corps of the army.

Still the Federal army remained in Virginia, but manifested no purpose of attacking Longstreet.   General Lee thereupon ordered the latter to withdraw from his position and move to the west side of the Shenandoah.   General A. P. Hill had already reached the Valley.   General Stuart was left with his cavalry to guard the passes of the mountains and observe the movements of the enemy, whom he was instructed to harass and impede as much as possible, should he attempt to cross the Potomac.   In that event General Stuart was directed to move into Maryland, crossing the Potomac east or west of the Blue Ridge, as in his judgment should be best, and take position on the right of our column as it advanced.   Upon the suggestion of General Stuart that he could damage the enemy and delay his passage of the river by getting in his rear, he was authorized to do so, and it was left to his discretion whether to enter Maryland east or west of the Blue Ridge; but he was instructed to lose no time in placing his command on the right of our column as soon as he should perceive the enemy moving northward.*

* General Lee's report.

On the 21st, in the afternoon, General Ewell received orders from General Lee to advance toward Harrisburg. On the 22d he proceeded with the divisions of Rodes and Johnson, preceded by Jenkins's brigade of cavalry, to Chambersburg, and thence to Carlisle, which place he reached on June 27th. The division of General Early had marched by a parallel route to Greenwood, and thence to York, in accordance with instructions previously given by General Lee to General Ewell.

The two corps under generals Longstreet and A. P. Hill had meanwhile been ordered to cross the Potomac and follow General Ewell, and on the 27th they encamped near Chambersburg. Meanwhile, the Federal Army of the Potomac, now under the command of General Meade, had crossed the Potomac and was concentrated about Frederick, but of this General Lee had received no information whatever.

The cavalry force at this time with the army, consisting of Jenkins's brigade and a battalion under Colonel E. V. White, was operating with the advance of General Ewell's columns. No report had reached General Lee from General Stuart, who was ordered to give notice of the movements of the Federal army should it cross the Potomac; and as nothing had been heard from him, General Lee naturally concluded that the enemy had not yet left Virginia. His confidence in General Stuart, who was so active, so vigilant, so reliable, was such as to reassure him and remove all solicitude concerning the movements of the enemy. Great was his surprise and annoyance, therefore, when on the 28th he received information from one of his scouts to the effect that the Federal army had crossed the Potomac and was approaching South Mountain. How materially different his plans would have been had he been kept informed of the movements of his adversary will never be known. Yet there is no word of censure in his official report, only a simple statement of facts: a striking illustration of his tendency always to suppress all consideration of self and to spare the feelings and reputation of others. His confidence in General Stuart was unlimited, and his admiration for him deservedly great. He realized that he made mistakes himself, and he was tolerant of those of others. His one great aim and endeavor was to secure success for the cause in which he was enlisted; all else was made subordinate to this. No possible good to that cause would result from exposing the errors of judgment of others, or by indulging in useless regrets at what had happened and was beyond recall. The possible effect upon himself of silence in such a case never operated as a motive to cause him to interpose another to shield him from the responsibility that he always assumed for the operations of the army under his command.

In chronological order, and as illustrating the chivalric nature of General Lee, it is well to call attention to the following order issued by him to his troops upon entering the enemy's country. It was issued on the 27th of June at Chambersburg, Pennsylvania, and reads as follows:

General Orders, No. 73.

The commanding general has observed with marked satisfaction the conduct of the troops on the march, and confidently anticipates results commensurate with the high spirit they have manifested.

No troops could have displayed greater fortitude or better performed the arduous marches of the past ten days. Their conduct in other respects has, with few exceptions, been in keeping with their character as soldiers, and entitles them to approbation and praise.

There have, however, been instances of forgetfulness on the part of some that they have in keeping the yet unsullied reputation of the army, and that the duties exacted of us by civilization and Christianity are not less obligatory in the country of the enemy than in our own.

The commanding general considers that no greater disgrace could befall the army, and through it our whole people, than the perpetration of the barbarous outrages upon the unarmed and defenseless, and the wanton destruction of private property, that have marked the course of the enemy in our own country.

Such proceedings not only degrade the perpetrators and all connected with them, but are subversive of the discipline and efficiency of the army, and destructive of the ends of our present movement. It must be remembered that we make war only upon armed men, and that we cannot take vengeance for the wrongs our people have suffered without lowering ourselves in the eyes of all whose abhorrence has been excited by the atrocities of our enemies, and offending against Him to whom vengeance belongeth, without whose favor and support our efforts must all prove in vain. The commanding general, therefore, earnestly exhorts the troops to abstain with most scrupulous care from unnecessary or wanton injury to private property, and he enjoins upon all officers to arrest and bring to summary punishment all who shall in any way offend against the orders on this subject.   R. E. LEE,
                                        General.

CHAPTER XVI

IN the absence of the cavalry it was impossible to ascertain the purpose of the enemy; but to deter him from advancing farther west and intercepting our communication with Virginia, General Lee determined to concentrate his army east of the mountains. General Hill was ordered on June 29th to move to Cashtown, and General Longstreet was directed to follow the next day. On the morning of the 30th General Heth, who had arrived at Cashtown, sent Pettigrew's brigade to Gettysburg to procure supplies, where it encountered the enemy. This was a surprise, and being ignorant of the nature and extent of this force, General Pettigrew retired on the main body of the division.

General Lee reached Cashtown on the morning of July 1st and stopped to confer with General Hill, two of whose divisions were up and the third not far away, who reported to General Lee that the advance of Heth's division had encountered the enemy, presumably cavalry, at Gettysburg.

General Heth had been instructed to ascertain what force was at Gettysburg, and if he found infantry opposed to him, to report the fact immediately, without forcing an engagement. While General Lee and General Hill were conversing, the sound of artillery was heard in the direction of Gettysburg. General Hill hastened to the front, and General Lee followed.

On arriving at the scene of battle, General Lee ascertained that the enemy's infantry and artillery were present in considerable force. Two of Heth's brigades that had been advanced for the purpose of feeling the enemy had encountered a superior force, and had fallen back on the main body. The whole division was now hotly engaged, and it was evident that we had encountered the advance of the Federal Army of the Potomac and serious work was ahead.

Orders had previously been sent to General Ewell to recall his divisions and to concentrate about Cashtown. While en route for that point, on the morning of the 1st of July, General Ewell learned that Hill's corps was moving toward Gettysburg, and on arriving at Middletown he turned the head of his column in that direction. When within a few miles of the town General Rodes, whose division was in advance, was made aware, by the sharp cannonading, of the presence of the enemy in force at Gettysburg, and caused immediate preparations for battle to be made.

On reaching the scene of conflict, General Rodes made his dispositions to assail the force with which Hill's troops were engaged, but no sooner were his lines formed than he perceived fresh troops of the enemy extending their right flank and deploying in his immediate front. With this force he was soon actively engaged.

The contest now became sharp and earnest. Neither side sought or expected a general engagement, and yet, brought thus unexpectedly in the presence of each other, found a conflict unavoidable. The battle continued with varying success until perhaps 3 P.M., when General Early, of Ewell's corps, reached the field with his division, moved in on Rodes's left, and attacked the enemy with his accustomed vigor and impetuosity. This decided the contest. The enemy's right gave way under Early's assault. Pender's division, of Hill's corps, had meanwhile been advanced to relieve that of Heth; and Rodes, observing the effect of Early's attack, ordered his line forward. There resulted a general and irresistible advance of our entire line. The enemy gave way at all points, and were driven in disorder through and beyond the town of Gettysburg, leaving about five thousand prisoners in our hands.

In this action the troops engaged on the Confederate side consisted of the divisions of Heth and Pender, of Hill's corps, except Thomas's brigade of Pender's division, and those of Early and Rodes, of Ewell's corps, except Smith's brigade of Early's division. On the side of the Federals there were the First Corps, embracing the divisions of Wadsworth, Doubleday, and Robinson; the Eleventh Corps, embracing the divisions of Schurz, Barlow, and Steinwehr, except one brigade of Steinwehr's left as a reserve on Cemetery Hill; and the cavalry force under General Buford, consisting of two brigades dismounted and fighting as infantry. The force on each side was about the same, from twenty-two to twenty-four thousand. In his history of the Army of the Potomac Mr. Swinton puts the loss sustained by these two corps at "near ten thousand men."

Viewed by itself, this battle was one of no inconsiderable magnitude. It was a fair, stand-up fight in the open, on equal terms, lasting all day, attended with heavy loss, and there were more troops engaged on each side than were employed by the Confederates in the assault made on the third day by the divisions of Pickett and Pettigrew on the Federal lines on Cemetery Hill. The bitter struggle on the first was as much a part of the battle of Gettysburg as was the ineffectual though heroic charge of the Confederates on the third day; and the results of the battle of the first constituted a far more creditable victory for Confederate arms, when all the conditions are considered, than can be claimed for the Federals, by reason of the failure of the Confederates to carry their works, on the third day. Too many are given to consider the operations of the 3d of July as constituting all there was of the battle of Gettysburg, overlooking the fact that there was quite as important an engagement on each of the two preceding days, in each of which the advantage was all on the side of the Confederates.

General Lee witnessed the flight of the Federals through Gettysburg and up the hills beyond. He then directed me to go to General Ewell and to say to him that, from the position which he occupied, he could see the enemy retreating over those hills, without organization and in great confusion; that it was only necessary to press "those people" in order to secure possession of the heights, and that, if possible, he wished him to do this. In obedience to these instructions, I proceeded immediately to General Ewell and delivered the order of General Lee; and after receiving from him some message in regard to the prisoners captured and the embarrassment of looking after them, I returned to General Lee and reported that his order had been delivered. General Ewell did not express any objection, or indicate the existence of any impediment, to the execution of the order conveyed to him, but left the impression upon my mind that it would be executed. In the exercise of that discretion, however, which General Lee was accustomed to accord to his lieutenants, and probably because of an undue regard for his admonition previously given, not to precipitate a general engagement, General Ewell deemed it unwise to make the pursuit. The troops were not moved forward, and the enemy proceeded to occupy and fortify the position which it was designed that General Ewell should seize.

It is interesting in this connection to read what General Gordon has to say about this in his book "Reminiscences of the Civil War." General Gordon commanded one of the brigades of Early's division. When General Early reached the field and found Rodes's division hotly engaged with the enemy, he immediately ordered his troops into line on Rodes's left, Gordon's brigade being on the right, Hoke's brigade (under Colonel Avery) on the left, Hays's brigade in the center, and Smith's brigade in reserve. Gordon's brigade was at once ordered forward, and as soon as he was engaged the brigades of Hays and Hoke were ordered forward with the artillery in support.

After a short but hot contest Gordon succeeded in routing the force opposed to him, consisting of a division of the Eleventh Corps, commanded by Brigadier-general Barlow, of the Federal army, and drove it back with great slaughter, capturing among a number of prisoners General Barlow himself, who was severely wounded. Gordon advanced across the creek, over the hill on which Barlow had been posted, and across the fields toward the town, until he came to a low ridge, behind which the enemy had another line of battle, extending beyond his left.*

General Early then ordered General Gordon to halt his command.

Now hear what General Gordon says about this check to his victorious advance:

The whole of that portion of the Union army in my front was in inextricable confusion and in flight. They were necessarily in flight, for my troops were upon the flank and rapidly sweeping down the lines. The firing upon my men had almost ceased. Large bodies of the Union troops were throwing down their arms and surrendering, because in disorganized and confused masses they were wholly powerless either to check the movement or return the fire. As far down the lines as my eye could reach the Union troops were in retreat. Those at a distance were still re-

* General Early's report.

sisting, but giving ground, and it was only necessary for me to press forward in order to insure the same results which invariably follow such flank movements. In less than half an hour my troops would have swept up and over those hills, the possession of which was of such momentous consequence. It is not surprising, with a full realization of the consequences of a halt, that I should have refused at first to obey the order. Not until the third or fourth order of the most peremptory character reached me did I obey.

While I have always regarded our failure to push the advantage gained on the first day at Gettysburg and to secure possession of the heights beyond the town as a lost opportunity, constituting one of the pivotal points upon which the fortunes of the Confederacy seemed to turn when hope of success was highest, I feel that it would be unjust to General Ewell and to myself to permit the reader to draw from my report of that incident an unfavorable inference as to the estimation in which I held that gallant soldier and gentleman. No more chivalric spirit, no hardier specimen of American manhood was developed on either side during the war than that of General Richard S. Ewell. He was a thorough soldier, and yet with a heart as tender as a woman's; brave as a lion, he courted the post of danger, always eager for battle, and giving inspiration to his men that contributed greatly to success. Nervous in temperament and at times brusque in manner, he was at heart generous to the unfortunate, gentle to the weak, and sympathetic with those who suffered. His record is a glorious one: doing valiant service in all of the battles of the Army of Northern Virginia, honored with favorable mention time and again by his superiors, he won especial renown in the operations in the Valley of Virginia, where he was an efficient second to General Jackson in the brilliant series of engagements that crowned with glory the standards of the South and caused the name of each of these heroes to be writ high in the Temple of Fame.

Fully five thousand prisoners, exclusive of a large number of wounded, three pieces of artillery, and several colors were captured. Among the prisoners were two brigadier-generals, one of whom was badly wounded. Our own loss was heavy, including a number of officers, among whom were Major-general Heth and Brigadier-general Scales wounded, and Brigadier-general Archer captured.

Our troops bivouacked in the positions occupied at the close of the fight, and the enemy, having retreated to the range of hills south of Gettysburg, proceeded to protect themselves with hastily constructed breastworks, extending their line to the left along Cemetery Hill.

Such was the condition of affairs at the close of the evening of the first day. The prevailing idea with General Lee was to press forward without delay, to follow up promptly and vigorously the advantage already gained. Having failed to reap the full fruit of the victory before night, his mind was occupied with the idea of renewing the assault upon the enemy with the dawn of day on the 2d. The divisions of major-generals Early and Rodes, of Ewell's corps, and Heth and Pender, of Hill's corps, had been heavily engaged and had sustained serious loss, but were still in excellent condition and in the full enjoyment of the prestige of success and a consequent elation of spirit in having so gallantly swept the enemy from their front, through the town of Gettysburg, and compelled him to seek refuge behind the heights beyond. The division of Major-general Edward Johnson, of Ewell's corps, was perfectly fresh, not having been engaged. Major-general Anderson's division of Hill's corps was also now up. With this force General Lee thought that the enemy's position could be assailed with every prospect of success; but after a conference during the night with the corps and division commanders, who represented that, in their judgment, it would be hazardous to attempt to storm the strong position occupied by the enemy, with troops somewhat fagged by the marching and fighting of that day; that the ground in their immediate front furnished greater obstacles to a successful assault than would be encountered on the enemy's left flank; and that it could be reasonably concluded, since they had so severely handled the enemy in their front, that he would concentrate and fortify with special reference to resisting a further advance just there—he yielded to their views and determined to make the main attack on the enemy's left, indulging the hope that Longstreet's corps would be up in time to begin the movement at an early hour on the 2d. He instructed General Ewell to be prepared to co-operate by a simultaneous advance by his corps.

BATTLE OF GETTYSBURG, JULY 2, 1863

As soon as the necessity for the concentration of the army was precipitated by the unexpected encounter on the 1st of July with a large force of the enemy near Gettysburg, General Longstreet was urged to hasten his march. The march of his troops was somewhat delayed on the 1st by Johnson's division of the Second Corps, which came into the road from Shippensburg, making for the same objective point. McLaws's division reached Marsh Creek, four miles from Gettysburg, a little after dark, and Hood's division got within nearly the same distance of the town about twelve o'clock at night. There is a great conflict of testimony regarding the time when General Longstreet's troops reached the scene of action on the 2d of July. The condition of affairs at the close of the battle on the 1st was fully known to General Longstreet, and every consideration should have prompted him to have the divisions of McLaws and Hood at Gettysburg very soon after daylight on the 2d.

In his book " From Manassas to Appomattox" General Longstreet thus refers to his movements at that time:

Colonel Taylor says that General Lee urged that the march of my troops should be hastened and was chafed at their non-appearance. Not one word did he utter to me of their march until he gave his orders at eleven o'clock for the move to his right. Orders for the troops to hasten their march of the 1st were sent without even a suggestion from him, but upon his announcement that he intended to fight the next day, if the enemy was there. That he was excited and off his balance was evident on the afternoon of the 1st, and he labored under that oppression until enough blood was shed to appease him.

How terribly sanguinary this makes General Lee appear! Is it really the utterance of General Longstreet? Then he has greatly changed in his sentiments toward General Lee since I knew him during the war. What a groundless, monstrous charge this is! Think of it, all ye gallant survivors of the Army of Northern Virginia, your old commander depicted to the world as an insatiate, cruel, and bloodthirsty monster! Such a charge as that can do him no permanent harm and will but recoil with crushing force on him who made or approved it.

The war record of General Longstreet was a brilliant one. That he should have made mistakes was but natural and inevitable; but these did not serve to make his case an exception; and such was the story of his heroic achievements they could not mar its brilliancy. It is much to be regretted that in the attempt to prove himself invariably right he should have found it necessary to assail General Lee's motives and defame his character, while claiming for himself qualities as a soldier and leader superior to those possessed by his old commander.

Now, as to the movements of General Longstreet on
the 1st and 2d of July at Gettysburg, to which he refers
in the quotation just made from his book, may we not
ask what more urgent request he could have expected
from General Lee that he should hasten to join him,
than is embraced in his own statement that "orders for
the troops to hasten their march of the 1st were sent without even a suggestion from him [General Lee], but upon
his announcement that he intended to fight the next
day, if the enemy was there"? The greater portion of
the two corps of generals A. P. Hill and Ewell had been
hotly engaged during the 1st of July with an equal
force of the enemy. The result was a great victory for
General Lee's troops, and the enemy had been driven
back some distance through the town of Gettysburg, to
the heights beyond. It was of the first importance to
follow up this success promptly. General Longstreet,
with two of his divisions, camped at a point but four
miles distant on the night of the 1st. He was aware of
what had occurred. He had received orders to hasten
the march of his troops with the "announcement that
General Lee intended to fight the next day, if the enemy
was there." When should he and his two divisions
have reported to General Lee for orders? At what hour
on the morning of the 2d could General Lee have reasonably expected him? At what hour would General Jackson have saluted General Lee and pointed to his divisions just behind him? I have claimed, and still
contend, that General Longstreet was fairly chargeable
with tardiness on that occasion. He was fully aware
of the importance of joining General Lee at the earliest
possible moment. In a letter to me under date of May
31, 1875, he wrote: "An order was given as soon as the
fight of the first day was over for General Ewell to
attack, or rather prepare to attack, at daylight in his
front, but was almost immediately changed so as to

allow time for me to reach the field and make a coöperative attack upon or by our right."

It is useless to discuss here how different the result might have been had General Longstreet moved his two divisions to the front at dawn of day on the 2d. The question is, At what hour did the troops of General Longstreet reach General Lee? For, as will be shown later, there appears to be a contradiction in General Longstreet's own statement about this.

In his book, page 362, General Longstreet says: "The stars were shining brightly on the morning of the 2d when I reported at General Lee's headquarters and asked for orders. After a time generals McLaws and Hood, with their staffs, rode up, and at sunrise their commands filed off the road to the right and rested."

Sunrise in that locality and at that date is about 4.35 A.M. General McLaws, in speaking of the movements of his division on that occasion, says:

My division camped at Willoughby Run, about four miles from Gettysburg, on the night of July 1st. About twelve o'clock, perhaps it was later, while there I received an order to move on at 4 A.M. of the 2d; but that order was countermanded and I was directed to move early. Not long after sunrise I moved forward, and before 8 A.M. the head of my division reached Seminary Ridge, where General Lee was in person.

But I propose to put General Longstreet himself in evidence to contradict the statement just now quoted from his book. I have now in my possession an autograph letter from him, written from New Orleans on the 20th of April, 1875, in which he wrote:

It occurs to me that if General Lee had any such idea as an attack at sunrise, you must surely be advised of it. Right sure am I that such an order was never delivered to me, and it is not possible for me to believe that he ever entertained an idea that

I was to attack at that hour. My two divisions nor myself did not reach General Lee until 8 A.M. on the 2d, and if he had intended to attack at sunrise, he surely would have expressed some surprise or made some allusion to his orders.

The point made by General Longstreet is that he had received no order to attack at sunrise, nor had he such orders; but as the matter is here presented, the defense is purely technical. He had been made to know how necessary to General Lee was the presence of his troops at the front, and he failed to meet the occasion and have his command available in time for the very coöperation with General Ewell, by an early attack by our right, of which he wrote in his letter of May 31, 1875.

In other words, had he placed his troops at General Lee's disposal at the proper time, it was unquestionably the purpose of the latter to have ordered an attack at sunrise, or at the earliest hour practicable. His troops not being in position, of course the attack could not be made. The two statements made by General Longstreet as to the time at which he reported with his divisions cannot be reconciled. In 1875, when he wrote the letter from which I have quoted, he claims that neither he nor his divisions reached General Lee until 8 A.M. In his book, published twenty years later, he claims that he reported at General Lee's headquarters before day— "the stars were shining brightly"—and that his two divisions reached the front "at sunrise," say at 4.35 A.M. The preponderance of contemporaneous evidence goes to prove that General Longstreet accurately described the facts in his letter of April, 1875.

But again there is delay on the part of General Longstreet. He had been made fully aware of General Lee's purpose and of his wishes as to his own movements. He had been told by General Lee that he wished him to move with his command, then up against the enemy's left; and whether his two divisions reached the field at sunrise or at eight o'clock, they should have been moved forward as soon as they did arrive. General Longstreet did not wish to make the attack; his heart was not in the work before him. In speaking of the movements of Law's brigade of Hood's division, which was late in reaching the field, he says: " Previous to his joining, I received instructions from the commanding general to move, with the portion of my command that was up, around to gain the Emmitsburg road, on the enemy's left. . . . Fearing that my force was too weak to venture to make an attack, I delayed until General Law's brigade joined its division. As soon after his arrival as we could make our preparations, the movement was begun."

In the year 1878 General Longstreet published two accounts of the battle of Gettysburg, one supplemental to the other, in one of which he quoted as follows from a letter written to him by General Hood in 1875, concerning the part taken by his division in this battle:

I arrived with my staff in front of the heights of Gettysburg shortly after daybreak on the morning of July 2d. During the early part of the same morning we were both in company with General Lee. . . . General Lee was seemingly anxious you [Longstreet] should attack that morning. You thought it better to await the arrival of Pickett's division—at that time still in rear —in order to make the attack, and you said to me subsequently, " The general is a little nervous this morning; he wishes me to make the attack. I do not wish to do so without Pickett. I never like to go into battle with one boot off." Thus passed the forenoon of that eventful day, when in the afternoon, about three o'clock, it was decided to no longer await Pickett's division, but to proceed to our extreme right and attack up the Emmitsburg road. McLaws moved off, and I followed with my division. In a short time I was ordered to quicken the march of my troops, and to pass to the front of McLaws.

This letter is given in full in General Hood's book " Advance and Retreat," and from it I make the following additional extract:

This movement was accomplished by throwing out an advanced force to tear down fences and clear the way. The instructions I received were to place my division across the Emmitsburg road, form line of battle, and attack. Before reaching this road, however, I had sent forward some of my picked Texas scouts to ascertain the position of the enemy's extreme left flank. They soon reported to me that it rested upon Round Top Mountain; that the country was open, and that I could march through an open woodland pasture around Round Top, and assault the enemy in flank and rear; that their wagon-trains were parked in rear of their line and were badly exposed to our attack in that direction. As soon as I arrived upon the Emmitsburg road I placed one or two batteries in position and opened fire. A reply from the enemy's guns soon developed his lines. His left rested on or near Round Top, with line bending back and again forward, forming as it were a concave line, as approached by the Emmitsburg road. A considerable body of troops was posted in front of their main line between the Emmitsburg road and Round Top Mountain. This force was in line of battle upon an eminence near a peach orchard.

I found that in making the attack according to orders, viz., up the Emmitsburg road, I should have first to encounter and drive off this advanced line of battle; secondly, at the base and along the slope of the mountain, to confront immense boulders of stone, so massed together as to form narrow openings which would break our ranks and cause the men to scatter while climbing up the rocky precipice. I found, moreover, that my division would be exposed to a heavy fire from the main line of the enemy in position on the crest of the high range, of which Round Top was the extreme left, and, by reason of the concavity of the enemy's main line, that we would be subject to a destructive fire in flank and rear as well as in front, and deemed it almost an impossibility to clamber along the boulders up this steep and rugged mountain, and under this number of cross-fires put the enemy to flight. I knew that if the feat was accomplished it must be at a most fearful sacrifice of as brave and gallant soldiers as ever engaged in battle.

The reconnaissance of my Texas scouts and the development of the Federal lines were effected in a very short space of time; in truth, shorter than I have taken to recall and jot down these facts, although the scenes and events of that day are as clear to my mind as if the great battle had been fought yesterday. I was in possession of these important facts so shortly after reaching the Emmitsburg road that I considered it my duty to report to you at once my opinion that it was unwise to attack up the Emmitsburg road as ordered, and to urge that you allow me to turn Round Top and attack the enemy in flank and rear. Accordingly, I despatched a staff-officer bearing to you my request to be allowed to make the proposed movement on account of the above-stated reasons. Your reply was quickly received: "General Lee's orders are to attack up the Emmitsburg road." I sent another officer to say that I feared nothing could be accomplished by such an attack, and renewed my request to turn Round Top. Again your answer was: "General Lee's orders are to attack up the Emmitsburg road." During this interim I had continued the use of the batteries upon the enemy, and had become more and more convinced that the Federal line extended to Round Top, and that I could not reasonably hope to accomplish much by the attack as ordered. In fact, it seemed to me the enemy occupied a position by nature so strong—I may say impregnable—that, independently of their flank fire, they could easily repel our attacks by merely throwing and rolling stones down the mountain-side as we approached.

A third time I despatched one of my staff to explain fully in regard to the situation, and suggested that you had better come and look for yourself. I selected in this instance my adjutant-general, Colonel Harry Sellers, whom you know to be not only an officer of great courage, but also of marked ability. Colonel

Sellers returned with the same message, "General Lee's orders
are to attack up the Emmitsburg road." Almost simultaneously Colonel Fairfax of your staff rode up and repeated the above
orders.

After this urgent protest against entering the battle at Gettysburg, according to instructions—which protest is the first and
only one I ever made during my entire military career—I ordered my line to advance and make the assault.

In the way of comment on this I will only say, General Lee always accorded to his corps commanders great
liberty in the exercise of their discretion as to the manner of the execution of his orders; having made clear
his general plans, he left to them the details of carrying
them out. At Second Manassas General Lee ordered
General Longstreet to send a division of troops to the
relief of General Jackson. General Longstreet thought
he saw a surer and a speedier way of relieving General
Jackson and promptly adopted it, justifying himself by
the plea that "boldness was prudence." The result
proved that he acted wisely. In this case it is to be regretted that the same spirit and motives did not control
his action.

No mention of this letter nor of these incidents is
made in General Longstreet's book. My attention was
called to this by reading a review of the book in
the "Journal of the Royal United Service Institution,
October, 1897," from which I take the following ex-
cerpt:

But there is a mass of evidence which goes to show that General Lee considered Longstreet responsible; and this evidence
the latter has certainly not refuted. In the first place, there can
be no question whatever that he was aware that Lee expected
him to attack as early as practicable on the morning of July 2d.
In the second place, it is certain that Lee explained his wishes,
although he gave no definite orders, soon after sunrise; that he

even pointed out the ground to be taken up by Longstreet's divisions; and that, riding off afterward to the left, he expressed much uneasiness, shortly after nine o'clock, when he found that Longstreet made no move.   In the third place, General Longstreet himself, in a letter which he wrote some years ago to the *Philadelphia Weekly Times,* has cited evidence which shows that he took upon himself to resist the expressed wishes of the commander-in-chief.   Not one of these points is touched upon in the Memoirs.   General Longstreet is content with the assertion that until eleven o'clock he had received no definite order to attack.   But it was never Lee's practice to issue definite orders to his corps commanders.   He was accustomed to explain his general intentions, and to leave the execution in their hands; and if on this occasion he departed from his usual custom, it was because Longstreet declined to move without explicit orders to that effect. . . .   He was aware that Lee was anxious to attack as early as practicable; he was aware that an early attack was essential to success; he was aware how the commander-in-chief desired his divisions should be placed; and yet, until he received a definite order to advance, did absolutely nothing.   He made no attempt to reconnoiter his line of march, to bring his troops into position, or to initiate the attack in accordance with the expressed intentions of his superior.

It was about 4 P.M. on the 2d when Longstreet's two divisions advanced to attack.   Hood's division went in first, on the extreme right.   McLaws followed a little later with his division, supported on the left by four brigades of Anderson's division of the Third Corps, under generals Wilcox, Perry, Wright, and Posey.   The enemy was soon driven from his position on the Emmitsburg road to the cover of the ravine and a line of stone fences at the foot of the ridge in his rear.   He was dislodged from these after a severe struggle, and retired up the ridge, leaving a number of his batteries in our possession.   Wilcox's and Wright's brigades advanced with great gallantry, breaking successive lines of the enemy's infantry, and compelling him to abandon much of his artillery. Wilcox reached the foot and Wright gained the crest of the ridge itself, driving the enemy down the opposite side; but having become separated from McLaws, and gone beyond the other two brigades of the division, they were attacked in front and on both flanks and compelled to retire, being unable to bring off any of the captured artillery.*

Hood's brigades on the right had successfully assailed the enemy's lines and forced them through Devil's Den and back for shelter about Little Round Top. The fighting here was desperate, each side availing itself of the protection of ravines and huge boulders of rock, which gave to the place its euphonious name. We had carried the wheat-field and Devil's Den, and were pressing against Little Round Top. Four pieces of artillery, several hundred prisoners, and two regimental flags were captured.

Early in the morning General Lee had notified General Ewell on our left that it was his intention to make the main attack on the enemy's left, and he was directed as soon as he heard the guns of Longstreet's troops to make a diversion in their favor, to be converted into a real attack if an opportunity offered. General Ewell gives 5 P.M. as the hour when General Longstreet's attack commenced, and he then directed his batteries to open upon the lines of the enemy; but it was sundown, two hours later, before the division of General Johnson advanced to attack the wooded hill in his front. The brigades on the right found the enemy strongly intrenched on the side of a steep hill. The brigades on the left gallantly advanced and took part of the enemy's breastworks, and held them until ordered out about noon of the next day. As soon as General Johnson at-

* General Lee's report.

tacked, General Early, on his right, moved two of his brigades forward against Cemetery Hill. Charging over a hill into a ravine, they broke a line of the enemy's infantry posted behind a stone wall, and advanced up the steep face of another hill, over two lines of breast-works. These brigades captured several batteries of artillery and held them, until, finding that no attack was made on their right, and that heavy masses of the enemy were advancing against their front and flank, they reluctantly fell back, bringing away seventy-five to one hundred prisoners and four stands of captured colors.

While in these operations the lines of the enemy were forced back on each flank,—our lines having been con-siderably advanced as the result of General Longstreet's attack, more advantageous positions for our artillery thereby secured, and several hundred prisoners, four pieces of artillery, and six stands of colors captured,— still there was a lack of accord and coöperation in the assaults of the different columns of attack, and no deci-sive result.

Our losses were very heavy, especially in officers of high rank. Major-general Hood was wounded early in the action. Major-general Pender, brigadier-generals G. F. Anderson, Barksdale, and Semmes, of the First Corps, and J. M. Jones, of the Second Corps, were wounded, Pender, Barksdale, and Semmes mortally so. At the close of the day Longstreet's command was so disposed as to hold the ground gained on the right, with his left withdrawn to the first position from which the enemy had been driven, resting at the peach orchard.

BATTLE OF GETTYSBURG, JULY 3, 1863

General Lee determined to renew the attack upon the enemy's position on the 3d. In his report, in speaking of the operations of the 2d, he says:

The result of this day's operations induced the belief that, with proper concert of action, and with the increased support that the positions gained on the right would enable the artillery to render the assaulting columns, we should ultimately succeed; and it was accordingly determined to continue the attack. Pickett, with three of his brigades, joined Longstreet the following morning, and our batteries were moved forward to the positions gained by him the day before. The general plan of attack was unchanged, except that one division and two brigades of Hill's corps were ordered to support Longstreet. General Ewell was directed to assail the enemy's right at the same time.

But again there is delay. General Lee in his report simply observes, "General Longstreet's dispositions were not completed as early as was expected." General Ewell during the night reinforced General Johnson with three brigades from his other divisions, and prepared him for the early attack ordered for the next day. Knowing of no reason for delay, Johnson's division, at Culp's Hill, on our extreme left, was ordered to assail the enemy's lines and had already become engaged, when General Ewell was apprised of Longstreet's delay; but it was then too late, the fight was on.

After a gallant and prolonged struggle, in which the enemy was forced to abandon part of his intrenchments, General Johnson found himself unable to carry the strongly fortified crest of the hill. The projected attack on the enemy's left not having been made, he was enabled to hold his right with a force largely superior to that of General Johnson, and finally to threaten his flank and rear, rendering it necessary for him to retire to his original position about 1 P.M.*

General Longstreet, whose troops occupied the positions from which they had driven the enemy the previous day, was reinforced by Heth's division, under

* General Lee's report.

General Pettigrew, and by the brigades of Lane and
Scales, of Pender's division of Hill's corps. Wilcox's
brigade of Anderson's division had already been assigned
to the support of Colonel Alexander's artillery, and occupied a line in advance of the Emmitsburg road, and
eventually took part in the assault. About 1 P.M., at
a given signal, our artillery opened fire on the enemy's
lines, and for two hours thereafter there was a terrific
cannonade by the batteries on both sides. General
Longstreet then ordered forward the column of attack,
consisting of Pickett's and Heth's divisions, Pickett on
the right. Wilcox's brigade marched in rear of Pickett's
right to guard that flank, and Heth's (under Pettigrew)
was supported by Lane's and Scale's brigades, under
General Trimble.

The advance was made in very handsome style, all the troops
keeping their line accurately, and taking the fire of the batteries
with great coolness and deliberation. About half-way between
our position and that of the enemy a ravine partially sheltered
our troops from the enemy's fire, where a short halt was made
for rest. The advance was resumed after a moment's pause, all
still in good order. The enemy's batteries soon opened upon
our lines with canister, and the left seemed to stagger under it;
but the advance was resumed, and with some degree of steadi-
ness. Pickett's troops did not appear to be checked by the batteries, and only halted to deliver a fire when close under musket
range. Major-general Anderson's division was ordered forward
to support and assist the wavering columns of Pettigrew and
Trimble. Pickett's troops, after delivering fire, advanced to the
charge and entered the enemy's lines, capturing some of his
batteries, and gained his works. About the same moment the
troops that had before hesitated broke their ranks and fell
back in great disorder, many more falling under the enemy's
fire in retiring than while they were attacking. This gave the
enemy time to throw his entire force upon Pickett, with a strong

prospect of being able to break up his lines or destroy him before Anderson's division could reach him, which would, in its turn, have greatly exposed Anderson. He was therefore ordered to halt. In a few moments the enemy, marching against both flanks and the front of Pickett's division, overpowered it and drove it back, capturing about half of those of it who were not killed or wounded.*

The troops that had taken part in the assault were rallied and reformed, but the enemy manifested no purpose to pursue. Our line of defense was intact, and nothing could have pleased us more than for the enemy to have come out from their intrenched line and to have attacked.

Hood's division was on our right; on its left was McLaws's division, then came Anderson's division and the balance of the Third Corps not in the assault, and then the divisions of Rodes, Early, and Johnson, of the Second Corps, in the order named, constituting our left. The line extended from opposite Little Round Top on the right to Culps Hill on the left, and was continuous and well defended, independently of the troops that had taken part in the assault. This whole line was in readiness for fight, but the troops were quiet spectators of the heroic charge made on Cemetery Hill. It was a battle of two divisions against all the Federal army that could bring them within range; the former charging in the open, the latter resisting behind breastworks.

The critical author of the Review of General Longstreet's book, to whom I have previously referred, has this to say of the operations of the third day:

On the morning of July 3d Lee determined to assault this position in front and flank simultaneously; and according to his chief-of-staff, Longstreet's corps, supported by a division of the

---

* General Longstreet's official report of the battle.

Third Corps, was to make the main attack on the center, while
the Second Corps attacked the right.   But again there was delay, and this time it was fatal.   General Longstreet attempts to
make some capital out of the fact that General Lee in his official
report wrote as follows: "Longstreet, reinforced by Pickett's
three brigades, which arrived on the battle-field during the afternoon of the 2d, was ordered to attack *the next morning.*" "This,"
says Longstreet, "is disingenuous.   He did not give or send the
orders for the morning of the third day, nor did he reinforce me
with Pickett's brigades for morning attack."   And yet a few
lines further on he writes: "He [Lee] rode over after sunrise and
gave his orders.   His plan was to assault the enemy's left center
by a column to be composed of McLaws's and Hood's divisions
reinforced by Pickett's brigades.   I thought it would not do."
Passing by the fact that it was never Lee's plan to assault the
center only, but both center and flank simultaneously, we may
note that, according to Longstreet's own testimony, the order
was given soon after sunrise; and yet, although the Second
Corps attacking the Federal right became engaged at daylight,
it was not until 1 P.M., eight hours later, that the artillery of
the First Corps opened fire, and not until 2 P.M. that the infantry advanced.   Their assault was absolutely isolated.   The Second
Corps had already been beaten back.   The Third Corps, although
a division was ready to move to any point which Longstreet
might indicate, was not called upon by him for assistance.   Two
divisions of his own corps, posted on the right flank, did absolutely nothing; and after a supremely gallant effort, the fifteen
thousand men who were hurled against the front of the Federal
army, and some of whom actually penetrated the position, were
repulsed with fearful slaughter.

The Confederate loss in the assault on the enemy's
line on the third day was very heavy.   Major-general
Trimble and Brigadier-general Pettigrew were wounded,
the former severely.   Of Pickett's division, the three
brigade commanders, generals Armistead, Garnett, and

Kemper, fell on the heights while leading their men; Armistead and Garnett killed, and Kemper dangerously wounded. General Armistead fell at the head of his troops some distance within the enemy's lines, and the place is marked now with a stone " Where Armistead Fell,"—the high-water mark of the Confederate cause, as it is sometimes called.

The total loss on the Confederate side during the three days' fighting at Gettysburg, as compiled from records in the War Department, is as follows: killed, 2592; wounded, 12,709; missing, 5150; total, 20,451. The Federal loss for the three days is given as: killed, 3155; wounded, 14,529; missing, 5365; total, 23,049. General Lee in his report says that 7000 Federals were taken prisoners at Gettysburg, of which number about 1500 were paroled, and the remainder brought to Virginia.

On the 31st of May, 1863, the Army of Northern Virginia numbered: infantry, 59,457; cavalry, 10,292; artillery, 4702; of all arms, 74,451 effective, as appears from the official return of that army on file in the archives of the War Department at Washington. This was immediately before the invasion of Pennsylvania, and may be regarded as representing the maximum strength of General Lee's army in the Gettysburg campaign.

The Monthly Return of the Federal Army of the Potomac of June 30, 1863, shows an effective total of 104,256; this was but a few days before the battle, and therefore should be taken as representing the number of troops engaged.

The Confederate strength at the time of the battle was considerably less than it was on the eve of the campaign, one month previous. The army had marched from Fredericksburg into Maryland; Ewell's corps had lost some men in its engagements with the Federal force in the lower Valley; Stuart's cavalry had made the circuit of the Federal army north of the Potomac and had lost heavily in its constant skirmishing both in Virginia and in its raid to Hanover, and only arrived at Gettysburg on the 3d and 4th of July. I estimate the number of General Lee's army, including all the cavalry, at from sixty-seven to sixty-eight thousand men.*

After the assault on the enemy's works on the 3d of July, there was no serious fighting at Gettysburg. The 4th passed in comparative quiet. Neither army evinced any disposition to assail the other. Notwithstanding the brilliant achievements of Ewell and Hill on the first day, and the decided advantage gained by Longstreet on the second, the failure of the operations of the third day deprived us, in a measure, of the prestige of our previous successes, and gave a shadow of right to our adversary's claim of having gained a victory. Their exultation, however, should be tempered with moderation when it is considered that, after one day of absolute quiet, the Confederates withdrew from their front without serious molestation, and, with bridges swept away and an impassable river in rear, stood in an attitude of defiance until their line of retreat could be rendered practicable, after which they safely recrossed into Virginia. Then, again, so serious was the loss visited upon the Federals in the engagements of the first and second days, and so brilliant was the effort to capture their position on the third day, that they themselves were undecided as to whether they should stand or retreat. General Lee's army was in condition to have justified his moving by either flank to draw the enemy from his impregnable position, and so to have forced a battle on more even terms, with greater promise of success. The spirit of the army was superb; General Lee's confidence in his men was undiminished; and the lack of supplies and of ammunition alone constrained him to abandon the enemy's front and recross the Potomac.

* See note in Appendix.

CHAPTER XVII

THE CONFEDERATES RETURN TO VIRGINIA

ON July 4th the trains were ordered to move to Williamsport, carrying such of the wounded as could bear transportation. During the night the army withdrew from Gettysburg and was put in motion for the Potomac. A very heavy rain set in, and this so delayed the movements of the troops that the rear-guard, a part of Ewell's corps, did not leave Gettysburg until late in the forenoon of the 5th. The enemy offered no serious opposition, and our army reached Hagerstown, a portion in the afternoon of the 6th and the remainder on the morning of the 7th. In consequence of the excessive rains the river was not fordable, and as the only bridge we had laid had been partially destroyed, nothing could be done until the waters subsided or new bridges were constructed. The cavalry under General Stuart performed most valuable service in guarding the flanks of our army during the retrograde movement. It materially aided in the repulse of the enemy in his attack upon our wagon-trains at Williamsport, and, by a bold movement on the 8th in the direction of Boonsborough, checked the advance of the enemy, drove him back to Boonsborough, and so gained more time for General Lee in which to perfect his line of defense. On the 12th the enemy appeared in our front, and a line of defense having been selected, covering the Potomac from Williamsport to Falling Waters, our army took position, ready and anxious for attack. We remained thus for two days, the enemy in front manifesting no disposition to attack, but steadily engaged in throwing up earthworks for defense. We would have remained longer, hoping to be attacked, but food was scarce. The high water had interfered with the working of the mills, sufficient supplies of flour for the troops could not be had, and as our bridge had been reconstructed at Falling Waters, and the river had materially subsided, General Lee reluctantly concluded to abandon his position, and on the night of the 13th the army recrossed into Virginia. Longstreet and Hill crossed on the bridge; Ewell forded the river at Williamsport.

What a night it was! The rain was again coming down in torrents; the mud was frightful, making the movements of the artillery, ammunition-wagons, and ambulances very slow, and so retarding the movements of the troops. Heth's division, constituting the rear-guard, took position about a mile and a half from the bridge to protect the passage of the column. About 11 A.M. the enemy's cavalry appeared in General Heth's front. A small number in advance of the main body was mistaken for our own cavalry retiring, and was suffered to approach our lines. A sharp skirmish ensued, in which most of the party was killed or captured, but the gallant General Pettigrew was mortally wounded in the encounter.

In withdrawing General Heth was attacked by the enemy, but successfully resisted him, and crossed into Virginia about 1 P.M.

Owing to the extent of General Heth's lines, some of his men most remote from the bridge were cut off before they could reach it, but the greater part of those taken by the enemy during the movement (supposed to amount in all to about five hundred) consisted of men from various commands who lingered behind, overcome by previous labors and hardships and the fatigue of a most trying night march. There was no loss of *matériel*, except a few broken wagons and two pieces of artillery, which the horses were unable to draw through the deep mud.*

In all that I have written about this battle my chief aim has been to contribute all I could toward securing a correct history of the events of that date. The vindication of the tactics of General Lee in directing the operations of his army has been with me a secondary consideration and but a corollary of the effort to establish the truth. Knowing how he would scorn any advantage to himself gained at the cost of injustice to another, and how prone he was to take upon himself all blame for any misadventures of his army, I seek no scapegoat for our lack of success at that time. Had he lived, it is my firm belief that he would have assumed the entire responsibility for the battle at Gettysburg,—all three days, —as he did in fact in his report, suppressing all reference to the shortcomings and mistakes of others. When the troops that took part in the assault of the third day were returning to our lines, he rode in their midst, calling upon them to reform, and addressing General Pickett he exclaimed: "Get your men together, general, they did nobly; it is all my fault."

While these lovable traits of character excite our admiration for General Lee as a man, the critical historian of the future will no doubt regard them as incompatible with the attainment of the highest possible success by a military leader in the art of war. Take for example his letter to General Pickett after the battle of Gettysburg. It is much to be regretted that no copy exists of the report forwarded by General Pickett which elicited this letter from General Lee. The report passed through my hands, but was not carefully perused. Not realizing

---

* General Lee's report.

then the extent to which we were making history, I took
no note of the contents of the report; but the inference
is clear from reading General Lee's letter that General
Pickett complained of the lack of support and charged
it home to some one. The letter of General Lee reads:

GENERAL: You and your men have crowned yourselves with
glory; but we have the enemy to fight, and must carefully, at
this critical moment, guard against dissensions which the reflections in your report would create. I will therefore suggest
that you destroy both copy and original, substituting one confined to casualties merely. I hope all will yet be well.

The critic will say that that was all wrong; that in
such a case the facts should not be suppressed; that if
wrong was done or mistakes made, the responsibility
should be placed; that in the art of war, as in nature,
the highest degree of excellence is only to be attained
by a process of evolution and the "survival of the fit-
test." Then, again, the correct measure of the ability of
a great commander can only be obtained when he is
supreme in command. As long as he is subordinate to
others he cannot accomplish the best of which he is capable, but only the best under the circumstances. General Lee commanded the army operating with him in
the field, but not the disposition of all the troops available for the execution of his plans. While he was operating in the field the authorities at Richmond were
nervous and apprehensive about the safety of that city.
Far removed as he was at times, he was handicapped
in his movements by the knowledge that his army was
relied upon to defend the capital from any expedition
the enemy might direct against it. Read what he said
to the Secretary of War, under date of June 13, 1863:

You can realize the difficulty of operating in any offensive
movement with this army if it has to be divided to cover Rich-

mond. It seems to me useless to attempt it with the force against it. You will have seen its effective strength by the last returns. I grieve over the desolation of the country and the distress to innocent women and children, occasioned by spiteful excursions of the enemy, unworthy of a civilized nation. It can only be prevented by local organizations and bold measures. . . . All accounts agree that the Federal forces at Suffolk, Yorktown, Gloucester, etc., have been reduced and General Hooker reinforced.

Again, read what President Davis wrote to General Lee on the 19th of June, 1863:

We have been endeavoring here to organize a force for local defense; but the delays have been vexatious, and, I think, in no small degree the result of misunderstandings, which better management might have prevented. I hope we shall have better progress hereafter, and think, with good outguards,—infantry and cavalry to protect the railroads and give timely notice of an advance of the enemy,—it will be possible to defend the city without drawing from the forces in the field more heavily than may be necessary for the duty of outposts and reconnaissance.

Again, on the 23d of June General Lee wrote to President Davis:

At this distance I can see no benefit to be derived from maintaining a large force on the southern coast during the unhealthy months of the summer and autumn, and I think that a part, at least, of the troops in North Carolina and of those under General Beauregard can be employed at this time to great advantage in Virginia. If an army could be organized under the command of General Beauregard and pushed forward to Culpeper Court House, threatening Washington from that direction, it would not only effect a diversion most favorable for this army, but would, I think, relieve us of any apprehension of an attack upon Richmond during our absence. . . . If success should attend the operations of this army,—and what I now suggest would greatly increase the probability of that result,—we might even hope to compel the recall of some of the enemy's troops from the West. . . . The good effects of beginning to assemble an army at Culpeper Court House would, I think, soon become apparent, and the movement might be increased in importance as the result might appear to justify.

And again, under date of the 25th of June, to President Davis he wrote:

You will see that apprehension for the safety of Washington and their own territory has aroused the Federal government and people to great exertions, and it is incumbent upon us to call forth all our energies. In addition to the one hundred thousand troops called for by President Lincoln to defend the frontier of Pennsylvania, you will see that he is concentrating other organized forces in Maryland. It is stated in the papers that they are all being withdrawn from Suffolk, and according to General Buckner's report, Burnside and his corps are recalled from Kentucky. . . . I think this should liberate the troops in the Carolinas, and enable generals Buckner and Bragg to accomplish something in Ohio. It is plain that if all the Federal army is concentrated upon this it will result in our accomplishing nothing and being compelled to return to Virginia. If the plan that I suggested the other day of organizing an army, even in effigy, under General Beauregard at Culpeper Court House, can be carried into effect, much relief will be afforded. If even the brigades in Virginia and North Carolina, which generals D. H. Hill and Elzey think cannot be spared, were ordered there at once, and General Beauregard were sent there, if he had to return to South Carolina, it would do more to protect both States from marauding expeditions of the enemy than anything else. I have not sufficient troops to maintain my communications and therefore have to abandon them. I think I can throw General Hooker's army across the Potomac and draw troops from the South, embarrassing their plan of campaign in a measure, if I can do nothing more and have to return.

Frederick the Great or Napoleon, instead of suggesting these plans would have ordered that they be carried out. And he who would institute a comparison between General Lee and any of the great captains of history must make a note of the different conditions under which he operated. Perhaps it could not be otherwise under our republican form of government, but it would not be possible to get the full measure of a man's capacity for conducting military operations on a grand scale who was thus trammeled by limitations to his powers.

General Lee allowed his army to rest for some days at Bunker Hill. His purpose was to have moved into Loudon County, but he was prevented by the high water in the Shenandoah. While waiting for that to subside the enemy crossed into Virginia, east of the Blue Ridge, and seized the passes that he would have used. He therefore ordered General Longstreet, on the 19th, to proceed to Culpeper Court House by way of Front Royal. Longstreet, delayed somewhat by high water, reached Culpeper Court House on the 24th. A. P. Hill followed immediately with his corps. Ewell after some skirmishing with the enemy's advance reached Madison Court House on July 29th with the divisions of Rodes and Johnson, leaving Early in the Valley, with orders to move up to New Market. The Federal army was then massed near Warrenton. On July 31st a large force of cavalry and infantry crossed the Rappahannock and advanced toward Brandy Station. General Lee then determined to place his army along the line of the Rapidan River. Longstreet and Hill moved on the 3d of August, leaving the cavalry at Culpeper. Ewell, now rejoined by Early, followed, and by the 14th the army was in position south of the Rapidan, with headquarters established near Orange Court House.

It was at this time that General Lee, whose health was not then at its best, and who had heard of some manifestations of discontent and disappointment at his not having accomplished more in the campaign just closed, placed his resignation as commander of the Army of Northern Virginia in the hands of the President. On the 8th of August, from his camp near Orange Court House, he addressed this letter to Mr. Davis:

MR. PRESIDENT: Your letters of July 28th and August 2d have been received, and I have waited for a leisure hour to reply, but I fear that will never come. I am extremely obliged to you for the attention given to the wants of this army and the efforts made to supply them. Our absentees are returning, and I hope the earnest and beautiful appeal made to the country in your proclamation may stir up the whole people, and that they may see their duty and perform it. Nothing is wanted but that their fortitude should equal their bravery to insure the success of our cause. We must expect reverses, even defeats. They are sent to teach us wisdom and prudence, to call forth greater energies, and to prevent our falling into greater disasters. Our people have only to be true and united, to bear manfully the misfortunes incident to war, and all will come right in the end.

I know how prone we are to censure and how ready to blame others for the non-fulfilment of our expectations. This is unbecoming in a generous people, and I grieve to see its expression. The general remedy for the want of success in a military commander is his removal. This is natural, and in many instances proper. For no matter what may be the ability of the officer, if he loses the confidence of his troops disaster must sooner or later ensue.

I have been prompted by these reflections more than once since my return from Pennsylvania to propose to Your Excellency the propriety of selecting another commander for this army. I have seen and heard of expressions of discontent in the public journals at the result of the expedition. I do not know how far this feeling extends in the army. My brother officers have been too kind to report it, and so far the troops have been too generous to exhibit it. It is fair, however, to suppose that it does exist, and success is so necessary to us that nothing should be risked to secure it. I therefore, in all sincerity, request Your Excellency to take measures to supply my place. I do this with the more earnestness because no one is more aware than myself of my inability for the duties of my position. I cannot even accomplish what I myself desire. How can I fulfil the expectations of others ? In addition, I sensibly feel the growing failure of my bodily strength. I have not yet recovered from the attack I experienced last spring. I am becoming more and more incapable of exertion, and am thus prevented from making the personal supervision of the operations in the field which I feel to be necessary. I am so dull that in making use of the eyes of others I am frequently misled. Everything, therefore, points to the advantages to be derived from a new commander, and I the more anxiously urge the matter upon Your Excellency from my belief that a younger and abler man than myself can readily be obtained. I know that he will have as gallant and brave an army as ever existed to second his efforts, and it would be the happiest day of my life to see at its head a worthy leader, one that would accomplish more than I could perform and all that I have wished. I hope Your Excellency will attribute my request to the true reason, the desire to serve my country and do all in my power to insure the success of her righteous cause.

I have no complaints to make of any one but myself. I have received nothing but kindness from those above me, and the most considerate attention from my comrades and companions in arms. To Your Excellency I am especially indebted for uniform kindness and consideration. You have done everything in your power to aid me in the work committed to my charge, without omitting anything to promote the general welfare. I pray that your efforts may at length be crowned with success, and that you may long live to enjoy the thanks of a grateful people.

With sentiments of great esteem, I am

Very respectfully and truly yours,

R. E. LEE, General.

Mr. Davis declined, as might have been expected, to accept General Lee's suggestion, in a letter familiar to all by reason of its repeated publication in the newspapers and magazines. In regard to the criticisms of his service referred to by General Lee, Mr. Davis wrote:

Expressions of discontent in the public journals furnish but little evidence of the sentiment of an army. . . . Were you capable of stooping to it, you could easily surround yourself with those who would fill the press with your laudations, and seek to exalt you for what you had not done, rather than detract from the achievements which will make you and your army the subject of history and object of the world's admiration for generations to come. . . . But suppose, my dear friend, that I were to admit, with all their implications, the points which you present, where am I to find that new commander who is to possess the greater ability which you believe to be required ? My sight is not sufficiently penetrating to discover such hidden merit, if it exists, and I have but used to you the language of sober earnestness when I have impressed upon you the propriety of avoiding all unnecessary exposure to danger, because I felt our country could not bear to lose you. To ask of me to substitute you by some one in my judgment more fit to command, or who would possess more the confidence of the army, or of the reflecting men of the country, is to demand an impossibility.

Two months of comparative quiet then ensued. Our camp was a comfortable one and our daily life uneventful. General Lee's habit was to rise early, and after breakfast he would ride to some part of the army, accompanied by Colonel Venable or Colonel Marshall, or both. Colonel Chilton would proceed on some tour of inspection, and I would be left to represent the headquarters, receive and answer despatches, and attend to the army communications and other correspondence. Our steward, Bernard Lynch, an original and typical Irishman, familiarly known as " Bryan," would scour the country seeking something to eat more tempting than the regulation bill of fare, and no doubt he advanced the plea of "the gineral's" weakness and need of nourishing food for all that it was worth in his appeals to the country people to spare him something in the matter of edibles. Our table could not boast any great variety, but we had enough to eat; and frequently after a meal the general would rest both hands on the table and say, "Well, Colonel Taylor, we are just as well off as if we had feasted on the best in the land; our hunger is appeased, and I am satisfied."

At this period General Lee made occasional visits to Richmond for the purpose of conferring with the President, sometimes remaining as long as a week. The authorities were being urged to reinforce our army operating in Tennessee, and Mr. Davis was anxious to have General Lee's views in regard to the best method of accomplishing this, and especially to know if he approved of a detachment from his army for this purpose. General Lee when in Richmond the latter part of August wrote to General Longstreet reporting his unexpected detention there by the President, requesting him to use every exertion to prepare the army for offensive operations, and expressing the opinion that nothing better could be done than to endeavor to bring General Meade out in the open field and use our best efforts to crush his army. To which General Longstreet replied:

I do not see that we can reasonably hope to accomplish much by offensive operations, unless you are strong enough to cross the Potomac.* If we advance to meet the enemy on this side, he will, in all probability, go into one of his many fortified positions. These we cannot afford to attack. I know but little of the condition of our affairs in the West, but am inclined to the

---

* This is significant in connection with what General Longstreet has said since.

opinion that our best opportunity for great results is in Tennessee. If we could hold the defensive here with two corps, and send the other to operate in Tennessee with that army, I think that we could accomplish more than by an advance from here.

The result was that early in September orders were issued for General Longstreet to proceed to Tennessee, with the two divisions under McLaws and Hood,—that under Pickett having been already detached for service below Petersburg,—to reinforce the army under General Bragg. We all disliked very much to see this splendid section of our army leave us. No better troops could be found anywhere than those under General Longstreet, and he was so strong in defense,—our " Old War Horse," as he was familiarly called. There was never any doubt about the security of a position that was held by him. Although he realized the necessity for his going, and indeed was anxious to go, and even suggested that he be placed in command of the army in Tennessee, still he felt a certain kind of regret at leaving. On the eve of his departure he wrote to General Lee:

If I did not think our move a necessary one, my regrets at leaving you would be distressing to me, as it seems to be with the officers and men of my command. Believing it to be necessary, I hope to accept it and my other personal inconveniences cheerfully and hopefully. All that we have to be proud of has been accomplished under your eye and under your orders. Our affections for you are stronger, if it is possible for them to be stronger, than our admiration for you.

There were frequent encounters between the cavalry of the two armies during September, generally designed as reconnaissances to ascertain what the other side was doing, and attended with no serious results. Early in October General Lee repeated his flanking movements around his adversary's right, with the view of forcing him to battle. General Meade maneuvered to place his army between General Lee and Washington, and finally took position beyond Bull Run, from which, if turned, he could readily retire to the line of works protecting Washington, where we could not attack with any promise of success. After destroying the railroad as far as practicable, General Lee retired by easy stages to his former position on the Rappahannock, where his army could be more readily supplied.

On November 7th the enemy advanced upon us at Kelly's Ford on the Rappahannock River and at Rappahannock Station, forced a passage at the former point and put down a pontoon bridge, over which a considerable force crossed on that day. During the evening a very large force of the enemy deployed in front of our line on the north side of the river, near Rappahannock bridge, where we had constructed a *tête-du-pont*, massing behind a range of hills parallel to the river and out of reach of our guns. After dark this force advanced and succeeded in overcoming the troops in the rifle-pits, capturing most of the two brigades there stationed and four pieces of artillery.

These successes of the enemy, in gaining a foothold on the south side of the river at Kelly's Ford and control of the north side at the bridge, which controlled the south side of the river, constrained General Lee to withdraw his army to a line between Culpeper Court House and the Rappahannock, where it remained a day. The position not being considered a good one, the army was retired to the south side of the Rapidan the next night, and resumed the position occupied before the advance in October.

CHAPTER XVIII

GENERAL MEADE ADVANCES AND RETIRES

ON November 26th the whole army of General Meade was discovered in motion toward the lower fords of the Rapidan River. By dawn on the 27th General Lee, with his personal staff, was several miles from Orange, on the way to meet General Meade, whose design was supposed to be either to draw General Lee from his position by a flank movement and compel him to give battle, or to advance toward Richmond. General Lee's purpose was to accept the gage of battle offered should events prove the former to be General Meade's object, or to fall upon his flank and rear should he attempt the latter.

The army was withdrawn from its lines during the night of the 26th. The Second Corps, under General Early, General Ewell being ill, was directed to move by the old turnpike and Raccoon Ford Road to Locust Grove. The Third Corps, under General Hill, was ordered to march by the Plank Road. General Stuart, with Hampton's division of cavalry, moved in advance. General Fitzhugh Lee was assigned with his command to the defense of the line on the Rapidan. General Lee's plan was to force General Meade to develop his purpose. During the morning of the 27th Hill's advance met our cavalry slowly retiring before the enemy, about a mile and a half beyond Mine Run. Meanwhile, Early's division, under General Hays, advancing on the old turnpike, had encountered the enemy near Locust Grove, which place was found to be occupied by their infantry in force, and Rodes's division, moving by the Raccoon Ford Road, had become engaged on the left. Sharp skirmishing followed. Some time was occupied in making dispositions of the troops, but at about 4 P.M. General Johnson, whose division had arrived and taken position on Rodes's left, advanced his whole line, and after a sharp engagement the enemy was driven back through the woods occupied by them and pursued into an open field beyond. The character of the country was unfavorable for pursuit, and General Johnson reformed his troops on the edge of the open ground, which position he held until dark.

The cavalry now reported to General Lee that the whole Federal army was moving up the river in the direction of Orange Court House, and during the night our army was withdrawn to the west side of Mine Run, to a more favorable position, which the troops at once proceeded to strengthen by the erection of earthworks. On the next day the Federal army appeared on the opposite side of Mine Run. There was skirmishing along the whole line, but no attack was made on any part of our works. General Lee gave his attention to the whole line, directing important changes and rectifying mistakes readily detected by his educated eye, endeavoring to impress the officers with the importance of success in the impending engagement, and presenting a fine example of untiring energy and zeal. While making one of these tours of inspection along the lines, General Lee, with his staff, accompanied by General Hill and staff, came upon a body of troops engaged in divine worship. It was on Sunday. Observing the devotions of the men, the general promptly halted and listened to the singing of a hymn. He remained quiet until the singing ceased, and then, as the chaplain pronounced the benediction, he uncovered his head, received the blessing, and continued his ride along the lines. It was a striking scene, and I well recall it as one of the soul-stirring tableaux of the war. The troops, with arms in hand, were assembled along the line of hastily constructed works. Here and there, at proper intervals, waved the bullet-scarred battle-flags, and from many embrasures frowned the heavy guns ready for action. It was a picture of war. Men of brave hearts and strong arms were there, ready to do and to die; and yet they invoked the aid of their God, who is the God of peace, so conscious were they of the righteousness of their cause.

On the morning of the 29th a heavy fire of artillery was opened upon our lines, and we confidently expected that an assault by the enemy's infantry would follow; but there was only the usual skirmishing, and the day passed without attack. General Lee could not believe that after all the display of force General Meade would retire without a battle; and so he waited another day, anxious to avail himself of the strength of his position and hoping that Meade would attack; but finding that he hesitated about bringing on an engagement, he determined to take the initiative and move against the enemy the next morning. During the night two divisions were withdrawn from the lines and moved to our right, with the view of making an attack in that quarter. Information received during the night indicated some activity in the enemy's lines, and at dawn of day it was found that he had disappeared from our front and was fast making his way back toward the river. Pursuit was immediately ordered and made; but on arriving near the river it was found that the Federal army had recrossed. General Lee concluded that the withdrawal had begun the previous afternoon, the dense forest, through which ran the roads of retreat, concealing the movement. The same cause prevented the efficient use of the cavalry and made it necessary for the infantry to pursue with caution. We captured about seven hundred prisoners, several hundred mules and horses, and destroyed most of a wagon-train loaded with the ammunition of two corps of the Federal army. Each army then returned to its former position along the line of the Rapidan.

Both armies remained in a state of comparative inaction during the months of January and February (1864), until the 28th of the latter month, when a powerful cavalry expedition, embracing three columns, under Kilpatrick, Dahlgren, and Custer, started from the Federal lines with the avowed purpose of capturing and sacking the city of Richmond. At this time General Lee was at Richmond. The indications of the advance of Custer's column on our left, received by me at army headquarters on the evening of the 28th, were confirmed on the 29th, when the whole movement was developed. The route of this column was to have been via Charlottesville, at which point there was no Confederate force, and the country intervening was filled with our reserve artillery and wagon-camps. Upon the receipt of the first intelligence of this movement, on the evening of the 28th, all trains moving in the direction of the threatened route were diverted. On the 29th a force of infantry was despatched by rail to Charlottesville; but the advance of the enemy operating on this flank was effectually checked before reaching that place by our horse-artillery and dismounted cavalry.

The column which moved upon our right, under Kilpatrick, was more successful. The entire Confederate cavalry picket stationed at Ely's Ford was captured, and this column of the enemy reached the Virginia Central (Chesapeake and Ohio) Railroad before any intelligence was received of its advance. After cutting the road it proceeded toward Richmond. General Lee, having been apprised by wire of these movements, returned to the army on the last train, which passed up but a few hours before the enemy reached this road, and thus barely escaped capture. The fate of this column, and especially of that portion of it commanded by Colonel Dahlgren, is well known. The results were most disastrous to the Federals, including the death of that officer and the capture of his orders, exposing the damaging fact of the intention of the enemy to pillage and burn the city and kill the most prominent Confederate officials.

Early in April General Lee was directed to inquire of General Meade, by flag of truce, if he or his government sanctioned what Colonel Dahlgren had proposed and ordered in his address to his troops. On the 18th of April a reply to his communication was received, to the effect that neither General Meade, General Kilpatrick, nor the authorities at Washington ordered or approved the burning of Richmond, the killing of Mr. Davis and his cabinet, or anything else not rendered necessary by military causes or not legitimate in civilized warfare.

General Kilpatrick stated that the photographic copy of the "address" which had been received through General Lee was a facsimile of an address which Colonel Dahlgren had submitted to him for his approval, and which he had approved in red ink, except that it lacked that approval and contained the objectionable exhortations or orders, which were not in that submitted to him. The disclaimer of General Meade was most candid and emphatic.

It will be seen from what has been written that there was a long period during the winter of 1863–64 when the two armies confronting each other in Virginia were quiet for most of the time, and without any serious engagement. On each side every effort had been made to raise the army to the highest state of efficiency and to add to its numerical strength.

At the North much of the dissension among the people that had prevailed in the early part of 1863 had disappeared, and a more hearty support was being given to the government. There were no longer "draft riots" to plague the authorities, and yet recruits for the army could not be obtained under the volunteer system. In October, 1863, President Lincoln called for three hundred thousand volunteers, and his proclamation stated that such of this number as were not furnished by January, 1864, should be obtained by means of a draft. It is to be presumed that the people manifested no alacrity in volunteering, as on the 1st of February, 1864, President Lincoln ordered a draft to be made on March 10th for five hundred thousand men for the military service of the United States, and this was followed on the 14th of March by a call for two hundred thousand more. All possible means were employed to recruit the ranks of the Federal armies, and especially of the army operating in Virginia. The Ninth Corps was ordered from the neighborhood of Annapolis to reinforce the Army of the Potomac in the latter part of April. General Grant, now advanced to the grade of lieutenant-general and assigned to the command of all the armies in the field, assumed personal command of the Army of the Potomac in the latter part of March. The Federal authorities were marshaling their forces for one supreme effort to overthrow the head and front of the Confederacy, in the person of General Lee, with the well-tried, indomitable army under his command.

The official records show that General Grant had something over one hundred and forty thousand men on the 1st of May, 1864, with which to commence his campaign against General Lee, of which number one hundred and twenty thousand were actually put into battle; while General Lee had, with which to oppose this vast host, less than sixty-five thousand men, including the command under General Longstreet that had now returned to him after the campaign in Tennessee. These figures are not exaggerated in the least. Let him who doubts search the records.* General Lee knew of the odds against which he had to contend, and indeed his men realized the magnitude of the task before them; but with stout hearts and steady nerves, with the touch of the elbow and the thought of home, in a righteous cause, sixty-five thousand men make a formidable force. It is well to bear in mind the great inequality between the two contending armies, in order that one may have a proper appreciation of the difficulties which beset General Lee in the task of thwarting the designs of so formidable an adversary, and realize the extent to which his brilliant genius made amends for paucity of numbers, and proved more than a match for brute force, as illustrated in the hammering policy of General Grant.

* See '' Report of the Secretary of War to the First Session of the Thirty-ninth Congress," Vol. I, 1865–66, pp. 3–5, 55. General Badeau gives the strength of the army opposing General Lee as 119,981.

CHAPTER XIX

THE BATTLE OF THE WILDERNESS

ON the 4th of May General Grant opened his campaign against General Lee. His plan is thus succinctly stated in his official report, written in July, 1865:

From the first I was firm in the conviction that no peace could be had that would be stable and conducive to the happiness of the people, both North and South, until the military power of the rebellion was entirely broken. I therefore determined, first, to use the greatest number of troops practicable against the armed force of the enemy, preventing him from using the same force at different seasons against first one and then another of our armies, and the possibility of repose for refitting and producing necessary supplies for carrying on resistance; second, to hammer continuously against the armed force of the enemy and his resources, until by mere attrition, if in no other way, there should be nothing left to him but an equal submission with the loyal section of our common country to the Constitution and laws of the land.

He premises this announcement of his plans by saying, "The resources of the enemy and his numerical strength were far inferior to ours."

General Grant pursued the line of action indicated, and it eventuated in final success. As it is an axiom in military affairs that "success is the test of merit,"

General Grant earned the title of a great commander; but his is not the brightest name that emerges from the smoke of battle at that eventful period, for higher yet in the Temple of Fame will be found the name of him who, though greatly outnumbered, held his adversary at bay for nearly a year, checked his every move, repulsed his every attack, and only gave up the struggle from a sense of duty to his men, when his army had been reduced to but a shadow of its former self by incessant contact with the enemy, whose losses were constantly recouped, and whose numerical strength was unimpaired.

On the 4th of May General Grant moved his army by Ely's and Germanna fords to the south side of the Rapidan River. General Lee promptly moved two corps of his army to oppose him,—Ewell's by the old turnpike and Hill's by the Plank Road. Longstreet's corps, then near Gordonsville, was ordered to move promptly to the front. On the 5th the Confederates arrived in close proximity to the Federal line of march. The opposing forces were soon in contact. A heavy attack was made on Ewell's corps on our left, which was handsomely repulsed. Many prisoners and four pieces of artillery were captured. A vigorous attack was then made on General Hill's troops—Heth's and Wilcox's divisions receiving the repeated assaults made against them by a stubborn and successful resistance. The enemy was repulsed, but the two divisions that had borne the brunt of the attacks, until darkness put an end to the fight, were exhausted, and they were told that they would be relieved at dawn the next morning by Longstreet's corps, which was approaching. Anticipating to be thus relieved, the divisions of Heth and Wilcox made no preparation for battle, not even replenishing ammunition. Consequently, when the enemy advanced at an early hour on the 6th, before Longstreet's command had reached the scene, these troops gave way and retired in disorder. Matters looked critical indeed. The men were going to the rear in a stream when General Longstreet arrived. General Lee was present as the troops moved into action. The divisions of Kershaw and Field were immediately deployed, Kershaw on the right and Field on the left of the Plank Road. As they advanced General Lee rode as if to lead the Texas brigade, when there was a cry, "General Lee to the rear! General Lee to the rear!" I recall especially one stalwart fellow, of swarthy complexion and earnest expression, who passed by the head of the general's horse as the troops were advancing to line of battle, and cried out, "Go back, General Lee, this is no place for you; go back, we'll settle this." This incident gave spirit and enthusiasm to the men, and very soon the rapid, rattling fire of musketry, receding as it increased in volume, told of the check given to the enemy's advance, and that they were being driven. Finally they were forced back to their intrenched position and our line was reëstablished.

General Longstreet then ordered a reconnaissance of the enemy's left, with the view of assailing their flank and rear. The ground was found to be favorable for such a movement. Anderson's division of the Third Corps had now arrived, and was ordered by General Lee to report to General Longstreet to aid in the contemplated attack; three brigades of the divisions of Field and Kershaw, in reserve, were also available. General Longstreet then ordered Anderson's brigade of Field's division, Mahone's brigade of R. H. Anderson's division, and Wofford's brigade of Kershaw's division, under the direction of Colonel Sorrel, of his staff, to move by the route selected to assail the left of the enemy's line held by Hancock's corps. The attack was made well upon the enemy's left, taking his line in reverse, and as the

Confederates advanced with solid front, the enemy first wavered, and then, seeing how they were enveloped, retreated rapidly toward the Plank Road. Unfortunately the woods were set on fire, and this somewhat interfered with the advance of our troops; but General Mahone, who, as senior brigadier-general, was charged with the immediate direction of the movement, ordered a realignment of his brigade, and the advance went rapidly on. In his report General Mahone says:

The three brigades, in imposing order and with a step that meant to conquer, were now rapidly descending upon the enemy's left. The movement was a success, complete as it was brilliant. The enemy was swept from our front on the Plank Road, where his advantages of position had been already felt by our line, and from which the necessity for his dislodgment had become a matter of much interest. Besides this valuable result, the Plank Road had been gained and the enemy's lines bent back in much disorder; the way was open for greater fruits. His long lines of dead and wounded which lay in the wake of our swoop furnished evidence that he was not allowed time to change front, as well as of the execution of our fire. Among his wounded, Brigadier-general Wadsworth, commanding division, fell into our hands. Lieutenant-colonel Sorrel, of General Longstreet's staff, who was with me in conducting this movement, and Captain Robertson Taylor, assistant adjutant-general of Mahone's brigade, who was wounded in the fight,* specially deserve my earnest commendation for efficiency and conspicuous gallantry on this occasion.

* I doubt if any bullet received in battle was ever for so short a time in the wounded as that received by my brother. I met him as he came from the firing line, where the fighting was fiercest, with his usual smile on his face and a bullet in his leg. I was fortunate in securing the services of a surgeon without loss of time, and there, just in rear of the line of battle, on the ground, with his head resting on me, the wound was probed and the bullet removed. I put him in an ambulance and started him to the rear, on a wounded furlough of indefinite time.

The success of the movement against the enemy's left had cleared the Plank Road and greatly relieved the pressure on General Field, who, with three of his brigades, was fighting strenuously on the left of the road against two divisions—Wadsworth's and Stevenson's—of the enemy. It had also released Kershaw's division by sweeping the enemy from its front. The troops of the enemy thus driven from our front were rallied and reformed behind a line of breastworks that they had previously constructed along the Brock Road.

General Longstreet immediately made dispositions to move again against the enemy's left in his new position. Jenkins's brigade of Kershaw's division, which had been held in reserve, and Kershaw's other brigades now released, and all of Anderson's division not engaged, were available for the movement. The leading brigades had already moved off in the advance, and General Longstreet, accompanied by generals Kershaw and Jenkins, was riding along the Plank Road, when, owing to some misapprehension, there was a volley fired by our own men across the Plank Road just as this body of officers rode along, when General Jenkins was killed and General Longstreet so seriously wounded as to be compelled to leave the field. It required some time to recover from this catastrophe, and in the interval opportunity was given the enemy in which to rally his troops, put in reinforcements, and greatly strengthen that portion of his line, so that, when our troops advanced, although they captured a portion of the intrenched line of the enemy, they were unable to hold it. I have always thought that had General Longstreet not been wounded, he would have rolled back that wing of General Grant's army in such a manner as to have forced the Federals to recross the Rapidan. A strange fatality attended us! Jackson killed in the zenith of his successful career; Longstreet wounded when in the act of striking a blow that would have rivaled Jackson's at Chancellorsville in its results; and in each case the fire was from our own men!   A blunder!   Call it so; the old deacon would say that God willed it thus.

While these movements were being made on our right, General Ewell was several times assaulted on the left, but in each case without difficulty checked the advance of the enemy.   In his report he says that about 9 A.M. he received word from General Gordon, through General Early in person, that his scouts reported the enemy's right exposed, and he urged that he be allowed to lead a movement to turn it; but that this was opposed by General Early, who deemed it unsafe to make the attempt.   General Ewell, however, concluded to examine personally into the feasibility of making the move suggested by General Gordon, and after such examination ordered an attack.   Instead of attacking at 9 A.M., however, it was nearly sunset when the movement began. The attack was led by Gordon's brigade, with Johnson's brigade of Rodes's division as a support, and Hays's brigade partly moved out from our main line so as to connect with Gordon.   The latter attacked with spirit and rolled back the enemy's right flank, driving him from his intrenched position for a mile, and capturing six hundred prisoners of the Sixth Corps, including brigadier-generals Seymour and Shaler.

Darkness put an end to Gordon's most successful assault, and it must ever be a source of regret that the opportunity to inflict a serious blow upon this flank of General Grant's army was not sooner availed of.   These engagements on the left and on the right of the Federal army, counterstrokes in which General Lee took the initiative, and in which the advantage clearly rested with the Confederates, no doubt enlightened General Grant as to the nature of the work before him, and made it apparent to him that it would require all the

men he could command to successfully cope with so
stalwart and aggressive an adversary. From this time
on, in his despatches to the authorities at Washington,
he constantly requests that reinforcements be sent to
him, and during the time covered by this campaign,
from the Wilderness to James River, he received fully
fifty thousand reinforcements, almost as many infantry
as General Lee had at the opening of the campaign.

THE BATTLE OF SPOTTSYLVANIA COURT HOUSE

The 7th passed without any serious encounter between
the two armies. General Lee spent the time in visiting
all parts of his line of battle, seeking to ascertain the
probable design of his adversary. In the evening he
reached the conclusion that General Grant was contem-
plating a flank movement in the direction of Spottsylvania Court House, and he detached a portion of Longstreet's corps, then under the command of General R.
H. Anderson, to move at once, that night, for that point.
This faculty of General Lee, of discovering, as if by intu-
ition, the intention and purpose of his opponent, was a
very remarkable one. I was sent with General Anderson, and with orders to apprise General Stuart, whose
cavalry was at the Court House, of the approach of the
infantry. I remarked to my comrade Venable at the
time that I saw no indication of a movement by Grant's
army in that direction, as they appeared to be present
in heavy force along our entire front; but when I reached
the cavalry I found it hotly engaged with the enemy's
infantry, Warren's corps, and wondered at the unerring
discernment of General Lee.

General Anderson promptly relieved the cavalry
under General Fitzhugh Lee, but not before it had been
forced to retire from the Court House, which was then
occupied by the enemy. He then moved two of his
brigades—Kershaw's and Humphreys's—rapidly to the

left of the road, forming line of battle behind some cover left by the cavalry, and repulsed the advancing enemy with great slaughter. Meanwhile, he had sent two brigades—Wofford's and Bryan's—by a detour to reach the Court House; as this force advanced the enemy retired, leaving the Court House in our possession. These brigades then moved up and joined those of Kershaw and Humphreys. General Grant's movement south commenced at 9 P.M. on the 7th, and in his despatch of the 8th to the authorities at Washington he stated the positions to be occupied by his several corps at the end of the first day's march, in which Warren's corps was placed at Spottsylvania Court House, but General Lee deranged this part of the program. Late in the evening, however, a vigorous effort was made to dispossess us of the coveted place.

The enemy, now reinforced by the Sixth Corps, Wright's, advanced against Anderson's troops. in an endeavor to envelop his right, but opportunely Rodes's division of Ewell's corps arrived just in time to check this movement. Deploying his troops on Kershaw's right, Rodes advanced, driving the enemy for nearly half a mile, when his left, coming upon a fortified line, was checked and he was forced to halt. It was thus that the line of battle was established. Each army formed upon its advance as a nucleus and in such manner as the conditions of the moment dictated. It happened, therefore, that some portions of the line of General Lee's army were weak and defective. There was a very undesirable salient on Ewell's front. On the right of Rodes's division the line bent outward; this left side of the angle was partly occupied by Doles's brigade of that division; on Rodes's right was Johnson's division, which held the rest of this side, the apex and the other side of the angle. General Lee reached the field on the afternoon of the 8th; and the Third Corps, now under

the command of General Early, owing to the temporary
indisposition of General A. P. Hill, arrived and took
position on Ewell's right.

The 9th of May passed without any serious encounter
with the enemy. Each army was engaged in strengthening its own line and in endeavoring to discover the
position of the other. On the 10th there was constant
skirmishing, with artillery fire along the whole line.
Late in the evening a vigorous assault was made against
that portion of the lines held by the First and Second
Corps. The attack against the First was repulsed with
great slaughter, but the enemy succeeded in capturing
a part of Ewell's front, occupied by Doles's brigade of
Rodes's division, with several pieces of artillery. When
report of this was made to General Lee, he started at
once for the point where the lines were broken, with
the intention of personally encouraging the men to recover the lost ground. Those of us who were with him
remonstrated, when he said: "Then you must see to it
that the ground is recovered." I rode at once to the
front, where I found a pandemonium of excitement and
confusion. A second line of breastworks had been constructed at the base of the salient with the view of rectifying this part of the line, but it had not been occupied.
The enemy had possession of a small portion of our line
and were stubbornly holding on to it, while our troops
were endeavoring on the right and on the left of the
break to drive the enemy back. The troops advancing
to this work came to the second line and naturally
availed themselves of the protection thus offered, and it
was a difficult matter to get them beyond it. The enemy,
however, was held to the portion of the line first taken,
and after earnest endeavor, the officers leading, our
troops finally went forward with a rush and recaptured
the works and the pieces of artillery, driving the enemy
back with great loss. Our loss was about six hundred

and fifty, of which number three hundred were captured by the enemy in their assault. At night our lines were intact, and the enemy had nowhere gained any advantage.

General Grant's despatches to Washington at this period contained such sentences as the following:

May 10th. The enemy hold our front in very strong force and evince a strong determination to interpose between us and Richmond to the last. I shall take no backward steps. . . . We can maintain ourselves at least, and in the end beat Lee's army, I believe. Send to Belle Plain all the infantry you can rake and scrape. With present position of the armies, ten thousand men can be spared from the defenses of Washington, besides all the troops that have reached there since Burnside's departure.

And on May 11th:

We have now ended the sixth day of very heavy fighting. The result to this time is much in our favor, but our losses have been heavy, as well as those of the enemy. We have lost to this time eleven general officers, killed, wounded, and missing, and probably twenty thousand men. . . . I am now sending back to Belle Plain all my wagons for a fresh supply of provisions and ammunition, and propose to fight it out on this line if it takes all summer. The arrival of reinforcements here will be very encouraging to the men, and I hope they will be sent as fast as possible, and in as great numbers.

It is easy to read between these lines the realization by General Grant of the fact that he was confronted by a much more serious proposition than he had anticipated in the endeavor to beat Lee's army. He certainly possessed a greater degree of pertinacity and put a lower estimate upon the value of human life than any of his predecessors; and in taking a calm retrospective view of the times, it must be conceded that in the possession of these traits he held the only key to the situation that promised success in any reasonable time.

Toward night on the 11th reports were made to General Lee that seemed to indicate a purpose on the part of General Grant to withdraw and make another move to our right. Orders were given to withdraw the artillery from the salient occupied by Johnson's division to have it available for a countermove to the right. During the night, after the removal of the artillery, General Johnson reported the enemy to be massing in his front, and orders were promptly issued for the artillery to return. General Ewell says that different artillery was sent, and that owing to the darkness and ignorance of the location it was slow in getting into position and only reached the lines in time to be taken. At a very early hour on the 12th the enemy assaulted Johnson's position in great force. Being without artillery, the Confederates were at great disadvantage. The enemy came in on the salient in overpowering numbers, taking possession of the works and of most of Johnson's division, including its brave commander.

Dispositions were immediately made to repair the breach. It was here again that General Lee manifested a purpose of leading his men into battle. A graphic account of this is given by General Gordon in his Reminiscences.

Gordon moved promptly in on the right, and by a strong effort drove back the enemy in his immediate front, regaining a portion of the works on the right of the salient. On the left Rodes had a more difficult task, but he succeeded in retaking a portion of the line, leaving only the apex of the salient in the possession of the enemy. General Ewell in his report thus sums up the operations of the day:

The nature of the struggle will be apparent from the fact that after the loss of Johnson's division, before sunrise, my force barely numbered 8000 men, the reinforcements about 1500 more. General Edward Johnson estimated the enemy's force at this part of the field at over 40,000, and I have every reason to believe this a moderate calculation. The engagement was spoken of in the Northern papers as a general attack by their army. It was met only by my corps and three brigades sent to my aid, and after lasting with unintermitted vigor from 4.30 A.M. till 4 P.M. of May 12th, ceased by degrees, leaving us in possession of two thirds of the works first taken from us, and of four of the captured guns, which the enemy had been unable to haul off.

Ewell's troops were subsequently withdrawn to the new line prepared in rear of the salient and offering much better conditions for defense. No effort was made, however, against this portion of our line until the 18th, when a strong force advanced against it, which was made to retire very quickly by the fire from our artillery. This was the last attempt to force General Lee's line made by General Grant at Spottsylvania. In his official despatch under date of the 12th, he thus characterized the nature of the defense put up by General Lee: " The enemy are obstinate, and seem to have found the last ditch."

On the 19th General Grant wrote to General Halleck: " I shall make a flank movement early in the morning and try to reach Bowling Green and Milford Station." By some telepathic process this purpose of his seems to have been made known to General Lee, who on the same day ordered General Ewell to demonstrate against the enemy in his front, as he believed that Grant was about to move to our right and he wished to force his hand and ascertain his purpose. General Ewell deemed it unwise to make a frontal attack and suggested a movement to the enemy's right, which General Lee approved. General Ewell moved his corps by a detour of several miles through roads impassable for artillery, until he found the enemy in strong force and fortified.

Not feeling strong enough to attack, he was about to withdraw, when the enemy moved to attack him. A spirited engagement ensued, but General Ewell maintained his position until night, when, the force of the enemy having been developed and his object attained, he withdrew and returned to his former position. This, however, only served to delay General Grant's proposed movement, and on the 21st he occupied Milford Station and Bowling Green. General Lee at the same time moved to Hanover Junction.

General Grant at this time seems to have desired that General Butler's force that was on the south side of James River should be sent to him. In his despatch to General Halleck of the 22d of May he wrote:

The force under Butler is not detaining ten thousand men in Richmond, and is not even keeping the roads south of the city cut. Under these circumstances, I think it advisable to have all of it here except enough to keep a foothold at City Point. If they could all be brought at once to Tappahannock or West Point by water, that would be the best way to bring them. They might march across, but if the enemy should fall back of the South Anna, this might become hazardous.

Yes; if General Butler and his command should have gotten within striking distance of General Lee, it would have been very hazardous, and probably disastrous. It was evidently the purpose of General Grant at this period to carry out his original design of "fighting it out on this line if it took all summer." The change of mind to go to the south side of James River only came after Cold Harbor.

There was some maneuvering and some desultory fighting for several days along the North Anna and South Anna rivers. Occasionally the Confederates assumed the offensive. On the 24th of May General Mahone drove three regiments across the river, capturing a stand of colors and a number of prisoners, among them an aide-de-camp of General Ledlie. On the 28th General Fitzhugh Lee's division of cavalry engaged the enemy's cavalry near Haw's Shop and drove them back upon their infantry. We were in constant contact with the enemy, and every day brought its episodes of excitement and struggling at different points of our line. It looks as if these evidences of a defiant and an aggressive spirit furnished material for serious reflection to General Grant. He evidently began to waver in his persistency and to look for some other way of getting to Richmond. On May 25th he informed the authorities at Washington that General Lee was evidently making a determined stand between the two rivers—North Anna and South Anna—and that it would take him two days in which to get in position for a general attack upon Lee's army. On the 26th, after stating the position of the several corps of his army and of those of General Lee, he wrote that to make a direct attack by either wing of his army would cause a slaughter of his men that even success would not justify,—coming from General Grant, that meant a frightful amount of killing,—that any attempt to turn General Lee's right, between the two Annas, would be impossible of execution on account of the swamp upon which his right rested; and that it would be inexpedient to attempt to turn his left, because that would involve the crossing of Little River, New Found River, and South Anna River, all presenting serious obstacles to the movement of an army,—General Lee's knowledge and experience as an engineer served him well in the matter of laying out his lines of defense, —so he had determined to make another movement to his left and to cross the Pamunkey River, into which these small streams united, near Hanover town. In the same despatch, however, General Grant informs General Halleck that "Lee's army is really whipped." It must have afforded General Halleck infinite satisfaction to know that. It was the main thing they were striving for. General Grant then took a position on the south side of the Pamunkey River. General Lee moved on parallel lines, his army still confronting the enemy, and his headquarters established at Atlee's Station.

When near Hanover Court House, General Lee was reinforced by General Breckenridge's command from southwestern Virginia, and by Pickett's division of the First Corps; and at Cold Harbor he was further strengthened by the arrival of Hoke's division from North Carolina. The aggregate strength of these reinforcements was between fourteen and fifteen thousand.

BATTLE OF COLD HARBOR

General Grant's next move was toward Cold Harbor. On June 1st General Fitzhugh Lee, whose cavalry, on our extreme right, occupied Old Cold Harbor, was compelled to retire by the advance of the enemy's infantry in force on that point. It being evident to General Lee that the enemy was moving in that direction, he immediately ordered an extension of his own lines. General Hoke's division was moved well to the right and General Anderson was ordered to take position on his left. The two armies were now on historic ground, and the Confederates took inspiration from the thought of the victory that here crowned their efforts two years before in the Seven Days' Battles around Richmond. On the afternoon of the 1st the enemy attacked in heavy force. Our positions had been hastily taken, and there was an interval between Hoke and Anderson. The enemy succeeded in penetrating this interval, causing the right of Anderson and the left of Hoke to fall back a short distance. General Hoke was reinforced by Hunton's brigade of Pickett's division, and quickly recovered the lost ground in his front. General Kershaw, on Anderson's right, advanced his South Carolina regiments, recovered part of the lost ground, capturing some prisoners and a stand of colors, and assumed a new line connecting with Hoke. The tactics pursued at Spottsylvania were repeated here. Each army formed line of battle on its advance, moving up to the right and left.

On the morning of the 2d General Lee ordered Breckenridge's command and two divisions of Hill's corps to the right of his line, and General Early, with Ewell's corps and Heth's division of Hill's corps, was placed on the left. In the afternoon, by direction of General Lee, General Early moved with a portion of his (Ewell's) corps to endeavor to get upon the enemy's right flank. As soon as proper dispositions were made, Early's troops advanced against the enemy with spirit, driving him from his intrenchments and following him some distance before darkness put an end to the fight. While this attack was being made, Breckenridge's command, reinforced by two brigades from Hill's corps, dislodged the enemy from Turkey Hill, in front of our extreme right.

General Grant now determined to make one supreme effort to crush the army opposed to him. Orders were given for the whole line to attack. General Lee was to be made to feel the tremendous power of the formidable Army of the Potomac, marshaled in compact form, two and three lines deep, and numbering fully one hundred and twenty thousand men. At an early hour on June 3d the battle was opened by a vicious assault upon our right and right center. The attack upon the portion of the right occupied by Hoke's command was readily repulsed with great slaughter; that upon Breckenridge's front was, at first, more successful. The enemy captured a portion of the line and took a number of prisoners; but Finegan's Florida brigade, of Mahone's division, and the Maryland line, of Breckenridge's command, were thrown in the breach and speedily drove the enemy back, recapturing the works and restoring our line.

Later the enemy massed in large force in Kershaw's front on Anderson's right, and attempted to seize the salient, constituting the weak spot in this part of the line, but their every assault was repulsed with terrible slaughter. Time and again the order was given to advance; new troops were moved to the front, and division after division was hurled against the works held by Kershaw and Hoke, where the cool veterans of Lee, with steady nerve and accurate aim, sent death and destruction to the advancing hosts of the enemy.

Similar results attended the assaults upon General Early on the left, who maintained his position of the previous evening. The din and confusion of the battle, that had been incessant and terrific, suddenly ceased on the Federal side; there was a pause along the whole line. We did not understand it then, but later learned that it was the silent verdict of the men that the task was hopeless. "The order was issued through the officers to their subordinate commanders, and from them descended through the wonted channels to advance, but no man stirred, and the immobile lines pronounced a verdict, silent yet emphatic, against further slaughter."

Night found the lines of General Lee intact. The loss of the enemy was frightful to contemplate; the ground in our front was covered with their dead and wounded. The Confederate guns controlled the situation, and it took General Grant two days to make up his mind to ask a truce that he might bury his dead and care for his wounded. And thus the campaign to capture the city of Richmond—from the Wilderness to James River—ended, with Victory perched upon the banner of General Lee.

General Grant now put his army in motion to cross to the south side of James River.

The official reports of the losses sustained by the army

under General Grant during the campaign were as follows:

Battle of Wilderness, May 5th–7th, total.......17,666
Spottsylvania Court House, May 8th–21st......18,399
North Anna, Pamunkey, May 22d–June 1st.... 3,986
Cold Harbor, Bethesda Church, June 2d–15th..12,738
Todd's Tavern, cavalry...................... 625
Trevilian Station, cavalry 1,512
   Aggregate 54,926

During the latter part of May General Lee had experienced a very serious attack of illness that greatly impaired his strength; at one time it looked as if he would have to give up and retire from the field.   After the wounding of General Longstreet, General A. P. Hill became so ill he had to give up, and General Early was placed temporarily in command of his corps.   Hardly had General Hill returned to duty when General Ewell had to relinquish the command of his corps on account of illness, and General Early, as senior officer, was placed in command of it.   All of these causes for trouble weighed heavily upon General Lee, but the most serious and the saddest of all the losses experienced in this campaign was that of the greatest cavalry leader of the war, General J. E. B. Stuart.

While the armies of Lee and Grant were wrestling for the mastery at Spottsylvania Court House, General Sheridan was sent by the latter with his large cavalry corps to attack the city of Richmond. Getting together three brigades of his command, General Stuart moved rapidly to Yellow Tavern, in time to intercept Sheridan, and took position to dispute his further progress. Though greatly outnumbered, General Stuart managed to detain Sheridan so materially that the authorities at Richmond were given time to get together troops sufficient to protect the city from the threatened raid; but in the fight, while encouraging his men, General Stuart received a wound from which he died the next day, May 12th. The loss of this gallant officer was irreparable, and was keenly felt by General Lee, who in General Orders paid the following tribute to his memory:

Among the gallant soldiers who have fallen in this war, General Stuart was second to none in valor, in zeal, and in unfaltering devotion to his country. His achievements form a conspicuous part of the history of this army, with which his name and services will be forever associated. To military capacity of a high order and all the nobler virtues of the soldier he added the brighter graces of a pure life, guided and sustained by the Christian's faith and hope. The mysterious hand of an all-wise God has removed him from the scene of his usefulness and fame. His grateful countrymen will mourn his loss and cherish his memory. To his comrades in arms he has left the proud recollection of his deeds and the inspiring influence of his example.

General Sheridan continued his raid, advancing to the line of fortifications defending the city of Richmond, but after making an examination of the works he found them very strong and gave up all purpose of assaulting them; he then recrossed the Chickahominy and rejoined General Grant.

After the death of General Stuart the three divisions of cavalry serving with the army were made separate commands and reported directly to army headquarters; some months later the organization of the cavalry corps was resumed, and General Hampton was assigned to its command.

On the 8th of June General Hampton reported that General Sheridan with a heavy force of cavalry and artillery had crossed the Pamunkey, moving westwardly. He was directed by General Lee to follow with his division and Fitzhugh Lee's, and to engage the Federals. With his own division General Hampton moved directly toward Charlottesville, which point he believed to be the objective of the enemy; at the same time he ordered General Fitzhugh Lee with his division to follow in the wake of Sheridan's force as rapidly as possible. After two days' march General Hampton succeeded in securing a position in advance of the enemy and across his line of march near Trevilian Station on the Central Railroad. General Fitzhugh Lee encamped the same night, June 10th, near Louisa Court House. General Hampton learned during the night that Sheridan's force had crossed the North Anna River at Carpenter's Ford, and he made preparations to meet the enemy early the next morning. With his small force he was engaged with the enemy for two days, and successfully resisted all attempts to break through his lines; and on the 12th General Sheridan started to retrace his steps to rejoin General Grant. He was followed by General Hampton, who engaged him at every favorable opportunity, punishing him at times and capturing between eight and nine hundred prisoners; but he was too strong for General Hampton to seriously hinder his movements, and he recrossed the Pamunkey River and rejoined the army of General Grant while it was engaged in crossing to the south side of James River.

In taking a retrospective view of the events and conditions of that period, one is impressed by the apparent hopelessness of the cause of the South, and marvels at the persistently courageous spirit exhibited by the leaders and people in their struggle against such overwhelming odds.

General Lee was confronted by an army over twice the size of his own. A Federal column under General Hunter, twenty thousand strong, was moving up the Valley of Virginia, without opposition, devastating that beautiful and fertile section as it advanced, and threatening at Lynchburg the railroad communication from

Richmond to the West, constituting the backbone of the Confederacy. General Butler with thirty thousand troops was near Bermuda Hundred, threatening Petersburg and Richmond.

General Johnston, in the West, was being gradually forced back in the direction of Atlanta by the army under General Sherman, that very soon began its devastating march to the sea. The prospect was gloomy indeed. General Lee had no troops to spare, and yet it was absolutely necessary to resist the movement of General Hunter toward Lynchburg. It was a time, too, for prompt action. General Grant was pushing matters on the south side, with the view of seizing Petersburg before General Lee could get there. To reduce our overtaxed army at such a time was a severe trial, but there was no alternative. The Second Corps, under General Early, was detached and sent to oppose General Hunter, the troops marching to Charlottesville and going thence by rail to Lynchburg.

General Grant's dash to capture Petersburg on the 15th of June was unsuccessful, owing to some delay in the movement of his own troops, but more especially to the heroic defense of the city put up by generals Beauregard and Wise, with the comparatively small force at their command, consisting in great part of Home Guards. The details and incidents of that defense have been fully set forth by those who were participants in the struggle, and the record of their achievements constitutes one of the brightest pages in the history of the war.

On June 16th the advance of General Lee's army entered the lines around the city, and the siege of Petersburg began.

CHAPTER XX

THE SIEGE OF PETERSBURG

ON the 18th of June the headquarters of the army started for Petersburg. On our arrival at that place I selected a spot on the north side of the Appomattox opposite the city, known by the attractive name "Violet Bank," and there established headquarters. The gentleman of the house, Mr. Shippen, kindly offered a room for the use of General Lee, and tents for the staff were pitched in the yard. We were very comfortable, and remained there for three months. Then, as matters became more serious, the general expressed a desire to get nearer the lines. There was another matter which quite reconciled me to a change of location.

The batteries of the enemy firing up the river had gotten the exact range of that yard, whether by accident or from information furnished by spies, I cannot say. One night during a very heavy storm the batteries opened and the shells began to explode around and about our camp. As I lay on my pallet, looking out of my tent door, I caught sight, by the aid of the vivid flashes of lightning, of our two servants, typical darkies, who were wild with excitement and frightened nearly to death. As the shells would explode they would utter unearthly yells and crouch down behind the trees or other objects offering protection, running from one spot to another as the range of the shells seemed to change. The choice was presented to me of going out in the pouring rain or of submitting to the shelling. Fortunately for me the ordeal was not prolonged. After a while the fire ceased, or perhaps I would have sought protection too, as my mind was working pretty rapidly toward the conclusion that safety with a drenching was preferable to the continuing risk of being killed in dry clothes. From that time I was not so much enamored of that particular spot as a camp for the headquarters of the army.

This experience at Violet Bank, however, was not exceptional. The guns of the enemy constantly sent shells and solid shot into the city, and after a time the people got accustomed to such visitations, and treated them quite lightly. One unfortunate feature of this shelling was that it was often heaviest and most continuous at night, and as such cannonading is not conducive to sleep, it required some time to get accustomed to this. The church that we attended, or wished to attend, was quite exposed and in the line of fire, so the rector, Mr. Platt, read the service of the Episcopal Church, and preached under the trees outside of the city, near Violet Bank, with excellent attendance for several Sundays; then all became reassured and services in the church were resumed. Our experience at Petersburg was not entirely one of trial. The intercourse of friends was delightful. We were constantly entertained, and managed to extract a great deal of pleasure out of life, despite the many causes of depression that environed us.

Though the line of circumvallation was being all the time more tightly drawn, repeated sorties were made by our troops, under the orders of General Lee, whenever an opportunity was offered of dealing an effective blow to the enemy.

On June 21st an effort was made by General Grant to extend his left toward the Weldon Railroad. A column of infantry, artillery, and cavalry moving in that direction was attacked with spirit by our troops, and the advance of the infantry was checked; but the cavalry continued by a route farther removed from our lines, threatening the South Side Railroad.

On the 22d the enemy's infantry was attacked on the west side of the Jerusalem Plank Road and driven from its first line of works to its second on that road by General Mahone, with a part of his division. About sixteen hundred prisoners, four pieces of artillery, eight stands of colors, and a large number of small arms were captured.

Again, on the 23d, the enemy made a demonstration with infantry upon the Weldon Railroad. General Mahone promptly moved against him with a portion of his division and drove him back, capturing over six hundred prisoners. The enemy's cavalry that started on the 21st continued its march through Dinwiddie and made for the South Side Railroad, followed by General W. H. F. Lee, who came up with and attacked the Federal column near Blacks and Whites, forcing it to retire in the direction of Keysville. It then moved to attack at Staunton River Bridge, but was repulsed by the small guard stationed there on the afternoon of the 25th, and retired toward Christianville, where it encamped on the night of the 27th. This force was overhauled by General Hampton on the afternoon of the 28th near Sappony Church, and driven beyond that point. The fight continued during the night, and at daylight the next morning General Hampton succeeded in turning the enemy's flank and forcing him to retire. When the Federals reached Reams Station on the Weldon Railroad they found themselves confronted by a portion of Mahone's division that attacked them in front, while their left flank was turned by our cavalry under General Fitzhugh Lee. The enemy then retreated in disorder, leaving in our hands several pieces of artillery and a number of prisoners.

In these several conflicts with the enemy's cavalry in its raids against the railroads, besides dead and wounded left on the field, over one thousand prisoners, thirteen pieces of artillery, thirty wagons and ambulances, a number of small arms, and several hundred negroes taken from the plantations on their route were captured.

There was an ominous quiet on the lines, comparatively speaking, during the month of July. Reports were current that the enemy was at work underground in the construction of mines. The hostile lines were very near each other at certain points. The sharpshooters were very alert and very accurate in their fire. It was certain death to any one who dared expose his person to view. In many cases hats were penetrated and small mirrors shattered that were held up to view just above the earthworks the very instant they were exposed.

Our men in the trenches had heard the noise of the picks and other implements used by the enemy in the construction of their mines. Orders had been given to begin countermining, and the work was being pushed, when on the morning of July 30th, at about 4.45 A.M., there was a terrific explosion at one of the salients on that part of our line occupied by the division of General B. R. Johnson. The Federals had successfully exploded their mine, completely demolishing about two hundred feet of our earthworks, with the annihilation of the troops occupying this space, and making a serious breach in the line, that threatened the integrity and safety of the whole Confederate position.

Colonel Pleasants, of the Forty-eighth Regiment of Pennsylvania Infantry, who had charge of the work, states in his official report that the fuse was first lighted at 3.15 A.M., and that, having waited one hour without any explosion, an officer and sergeant of his regiment volunteered to go into the mine and examine the cause of the delay, and that they found that the fire had stopped where the fuses were spliced. They relighted the fuses, made their exit, and the explosion followed in due time. All honor and praise to the brave men who performed this daring feat!

The same officer thus describes the mine:

The charge consisted of three hundred and twenty kegs of powder, each containing about twenty-five pounds. It was placed in eight magazines connected with each other by troughs half filled with powder. These troughs from the lateral galleries met at the inner end of the main one, and from this point I had three lines of fuses for a distance of ninety-eight feet. Not having fuses as long as required, two pieces had to be spliced together to make the required length of each of the lines.

The immediate effect of the explosion was to paralyze the troops on the right and left of the breach, but this was but momentary, and on either side our troops soon moved up so as to command the crater, and opened a destructive fire on the troops of the enemy that now poured into the excavation, where they were huddled together, white and black, in an utterly disorganized condition. Meanwhile, report of the explosion of the mine had been made to General Lee, whose headquarters were then at Violet Bank, who sent immediate orders to General Mahone to send two of his brigades to the spot, and repaired thither himself with all possible despatch. The story of the brilliant achievement of the troops employed in the recapture of the lines has been too often told to justify its repetition here. Our lines were restored, the enemy had failed to avail themselves of the opportunity that had been offered them of capturing the city of Petersburg, they had suffered the loss of forty-four hundred men, and there resulted an incriminating

controversy among the chief officers, terminating in a
Court of Inquiry, to place the blame for their failure.
General Meade on the 31st of July sent in a flag of truce
asking a suspension of hostilities, to enable him to bury
his dead and gather in the wounded between the lines.
This request was by General Lee referred to General
Beauregard, who agreed to a suspension of hostilities
for the space of four hours. An opportunity was thus
afforded, of which I availed myself, to make an examination of the crater and of the destruction wrought
by the explosion of the mine and the subsequent
fighting.

The earth was torn and rent for a space of about two
hundred feet in length, about fifty feet in width and
twenty-five feet in depth. The sight within the vast
hole, or crater, was gruesome indeed. The force of the
explosion had carried earth, guns, accouterments, and
men some distance skyward, the whole coming down in
an inextricable mass; portions of the bodies of the poor
victims were to be seen protruding from immense blocks
of earth; several of the pieces of artillery that had occupied the fort were thrown high in the air and tumbled
some twenty yards or more to the front of the works, a
mass of junk. Then the troops of the enemy that
charged immediately after the explosion, instead of
maintaining their organization and sweeping beyond
the break made in our lines, sought shelter in the vast
excavation, where the musketry fire from our men could
not reach them, and where pandemonium reigned and
terror not only paralyzed those huddled together, but
utterly disorganized the succeeding lines of troops that
rushed pell-mell into this cavern of death and destruction. The bottom of the pit or crater was covered
with dead, white and black intermingled, a horrible
sight.

As an illustration of the condition of affairs in the

crater, I make the following extract from the report of the commander of one of the Federal brigades engaged in the assault:

Immediately after the explosion of the mine, my brigade advanced rapidly in support of the First Division. . . . The First Division took possession of the crater, and instead of advancing to the front as was expected, turned to the right and came on the ground we were ordered to take—ground covered with pits and traverses, and intrenched lines running in every conceivable direction. At the commencement of the movement nothing could be seen on account of the smoke and dust which had not yet cleared away, and some confusion had ensued in consequence. Finding the First Division not likely to advance from the crater, I ordered my troops forward, but on attempting to advance, they were compelled to pass through the confused ranks of the First Division, and consequently became themselves broken and confused. By this time the enemy had collected troops on the crest and in the ravine in our front, and in the intrenched lines and traverses to our right. Several attempts were made to advance some four hundred yards across an open field and seize the works on the next crest, but the terrible fire of musketry from every direction, with grape and canister from our front, rendered the formation of lines from such confused masses lying in pits an impossibility; and notwithstanding the gallant conduct of both officers and men, every attempt failed. My brigade was, however, pushing gradually but constantly ahead and to the right in the network of pits and traverses, when the Fourth Division came up shouting and yelling, and pouring into the crater and pits already filled with our men, rendering " confusion worse confounded." A few minutes later the enemy made a desperate assault. A panic seized the colored troops, and they went pouring through and over our men, plunging into the pits with fixed bayonets in frightful confusion. My brigade, being principally to the left of the pits at this time, repulsed the enemy handsomely, but the assault being more successful on our right, the colored troops came piling in upon us from that direction, completely paralyzing all our efforts. The rebels returned upon us, and a terrible hand-to-hand struggle ensued.

The loss to the enemy was terrible when they attempted to withdraw. In order to reach their lines they were compelled to retreat across the space intervening between the lines, which was commanded by our artillery posted on the right and left of the crater, and the destruction here by musketry fire and the grape and canister poured into the retreating mass was very heavy.

Of all the columns of the enemy's troops marshaled for the grand attack, there was only one man, so far as my knowledge goes, who fully appreciated the design of his superiors and endeavored faithfully to do his part in carrying out that design. He was a colored soldier of General Ferrero's division of negroes, but of his company and regiment I cannot now speak accurately. He charged with the black contingent, but did not stop at the crater; remembering that his orders were to capture the city of Petersburg, he passed into the Confederate lines and kept right on running for the city, until some one stopped him near Blanford Church, about half a mile in the rear. He was nearly out of breath, but he was doing his best, and but for this accidental check to his advance he would no doubt have entered the city. Upon examination it was ascertained that his piece had not been discharged; he evidently believed in the efficacy of giving your enemy the cold steel when in a tight place. It would be ungracious to question this colored soldier's motives, but he certainly was complying with his orders.

About this time General Grant made a demonstration on the north side of James River threatening the city of Richmond, and General Lee was compelled to send troops there to oppose him. At the same time General Grant moved to extend his left flank so as to take possession of the railroad leading to the South via Weldon. With his limited number of troops, General Lee was thus sorely tried and beset with difficulties. The cry from every quarter was for reinforcements.

On August 15th General Lee went to the north side of James River and established headquarters at Chaffin's Bluff, from which point he directed the operations of his troops.

On August 19th, while Warren's Fifth Corps of the Federal army was extending its left it was attacked by General A. P. Hill, with a part of his corps at Davis's house, about three miles from Petersburg on our right. Success attended this movement. General Hill defeated the force opposed to him, capturing twenty-seven hundred prisoners, including a brigadier-general and several field-officers. On that night, and evidently influenced by this show of life and energy by the Confederates, General Grant issued the order for the withdrawal of his forces from the north side of the James River, sending the Second Corps at once to the support of General Warren. Again, on the 21st, General Hill attacked General Warren's position on the Weldon Railroad, and drove him from his advanced lines to his main intrenchments, from which, however, he failed to dislodge him. Each side reported about the same number of prisoners taken, but neither obtained any material advantage.

On August 25th General A. P. Hill again attacked the enemy in his intrenchments at Reams's Station, on the Weldon Railroad, and carried his entire line. Cooke's and McRae's North Carolina brigades, under General Heth, and Lane's North Carolina brigade of Wilcox's division, under General Conner, with Pegram's artillery, composed the assaulting column. One line of breastworks was carried by the cavalry under General Hampton with great gallantry. Twelve stands of colors, 2150 prisoners, and 9 pieces of artillery were captured.

In these several gallant affairs, scintillations of Confederate spirit, the advantage was on our side; but the ligature was becoming gradually tighter. The enemy still held the Weldon Railroad, and in such force as to render it impossible to dispossess him. The cost to him had been heavy, fully twelve thousand men; but we too had suffered material loss: attrition was doing its work slowly but surely.

General Grant had no difficulty in recouping his losses; he had the whole world to draw from. When patriotism failed soldiers could be bought. At about this time he asked President Lincoln to call for three hundred thousand men to reinforce his armies. By the provisions of the draft the person drawn could put in a substitute; under the system of bounties and substitutes, any number of mercenaries were to be had. How could the South stand up against this? General Lee's losses were permanent.

On September 3d General Lee went to Richmond for a conference with President Davis. General Hood had evacuated Atlanta the day before; matters were as serious as could be in the West. Still, our people were not without hope. At this time we derived some encouragement from the political dissensions at the North. The following extract from notes written by me at the time will serve to show to what extent this sentiment then prevailed. The peace party at the North had attained such proportions as to make us solicitous about everything that was calculated to have any effect upon the approaching election. In speaking of the evacuation and loss of Atlanta I said:

The question is, What effect will it have in the North? Some think it will impede the progress of the peace sentiment and injure the prospects of the McClellanites. It may, however, have the contrary effect. For as Lincoln and Fremont are both out-and-out war men, the other party must be unquestionably a peace party and have a decided peace candidate to secure the support of the element in opposition to the administration and the war. They must declare for peace to make a positive issue with the Republicans. Let them adhere firmly to their intention to propose an armistice and some good may result to us. My idea of the armistice is that the armies will remain as they are now. There will be no disbanding on either side, nor will the Federals withdraw from our territory. We are a very proud and a very exacting people, and I have heard many declare that we could consent to no armistice that did not require the withdrawal of the Federal armies. This is unreasonable; it is not customary. Look, for example, at our armistice in the Mexican War; at that between the Allied Powers and the Russians in the Crimean War; and, more recently, at that in the case of Denmark and the German Powers. In no case were the armies withdrawn. We must not claim what it would be unreasonable to expect; and we must also remember that we are not, and never will be, in a condition to dictate exactly what shall be.

This will show the trend of thought in the South at that time. The hopes and views expressed were but the reflex of those of men high in authority and whose voice controlled in state affairs.

The Democratic convention that met in Chicago on August 29, 1864, and nominated General McClellan as its candidate for the presidency, declared the war a failure. General McClellan in accepting the nomination on September 8th rejected that part of the platform and favored the continuance of hostilities until the Union was restored. In the interval Atlanta fell. From this time on the peace party lost strength.

In March, 1865, General Lee proposed a meeting with General Grant, each being in command of all the armies of his side, for an interchange of views looking toward a convention to arrange terms of peace; but President Lincoln declined to permit such a conference.*

I have always regretted that peace was not attained under some such conditions; for then we would have escaped the heart-burning and bitterness that attended absolute defeat, the humiliating legislation demanded as a condition of our rehabilitation as States of the Union, the wrongs of reconstruction, and the fatal enfranchisement of the negroes. We would have been freemen of coequal States and not quasi-subjects of conquered provinces, and there would have been no solid South.

On September 16th General Hampton attacked the enemy near Sycamore Church. He captured about three hundred prisoners, a number of horses and wagons, and about twenty-five hundred head of cattle, to the great relief of our commissary department. All were safely brought into our lines.

General Grant had it in his power to throw a force upon the north side of James River at any time and with little trouble, and so to compel General Lee to detach troops to oppose the movement, while at the same time an attempt would be made to still further extend his lines to his left, now nearly encircling the doomed city.

On September 28th the Federals advanced in strong force against Fort Harrison, at Chaffin's Farm, on the north side of James River, stormed the works and captured a large portion of the garrison.† Fort Harrison

---

* See Appendix for correspondence.

† My brother, Major R. C. Taylor, second in command, was very badly wounded, and fell into the hands of the enemy. For some days there was uncertainty as to his fate; but through the kind offices of Colonel E. S. Parker, of General Grant's staff, whose aid I had solicited through flag of truce, he was finally found and his actual condition made known.

constituted the left of the line held by General Lee, and its loss occasioned considerable trouble, making it necessary to establish a new line in front of and in opposition to the old, now held by the enemy.

General Longstreet returned to duty in October and was assigned to the command of the troops operating on the north side of the James and including Pickett's division, then holding the line between the James and Appomattox rivers. General Lee spent most of this month on the north side of the river. On the 27th of October the enemy made a determined effort to break through General Longstreet's lines on the Williamsburg and Nine Mile roads, but was repulsed with loss. General Longstreet characterized it as the most determined effort to take the city of Richmond on the north side, and gave the loss of the Federals as eleven stands of colors and about six hundred prisoners. On the same day, and of course by concert of action, a vigorous attempt was made by the enemy on our right at Petersburg to extend their lines. The infantry in General Hill's front crossed Rowanty Creek, below Burgess's Mill, and forced back our cavalry. Later in the day General Heth attacked and at first drove the enemy, but found them so strong that he resumed the defensive. The enemy then attacked, but were repulsed. General Heth's troops captured some colors and prisoners.

It would be uninteresting, and perhaps tiresome, to continue the record of the many brilliant sorties made by our troops during the ensuing four or five months. But a price was exacted for every fight; our numbers were being constantly diminished, and provisions were difficult to obtain.

A conscript law had been passed and a Bureau of Conscription organized for the purpose of compelling every able-bodied man between the age limits to serve in the army, but the number of such was very limited. Conscription was resisted. The decisions in the courts were in many cases adverse to the government, and the results were not encouraging. Such was the need for men that the public mind turned to the negroes with the idea of utilizing them in the struggle for life that was then upon us. There were many ways in which they could be made useful, and many positions filled by white men to which they could be assigned and the whites released for service in the army. The negroes could do duty as cooks, as teamsters, as laborers, and in other like positions; and already some were talking of making soldiers of them. In September, 1864, I wrote:

We are stirring matters up over here and propose to put the whole Bureau of Conscription in the army as the beginning of a great reform; after which we may get some soldiers in the ranks, whereas now too many procure a detail or exemption. We also propose to make the negroes serviceable, and some advocate placing them in the ranks, making soldiers of them, but for this I am not quite ready.

Public sentiment, however, did become reconciled to the enlistment of the negroes as soldiers, and several companies were organized, though, so far as is known to me, they were never put in the field nor under fire.

No doubt, individually, alongside of their masters and encouraged by them, they would have made good soldiers and rendered good service. It should be recorded of the negroes of the South that during those four years of war and its distressing consequences they were universally loyal and their conduct in all respects admirable. Let the fact be noted that while the white men went to the front, the women and children were left at home and on plantations with negroes, without fear or apprehension; and although of the same racial instincts and passions as the negro of to-day, so far as my knowledge and observation enable me to speak, not a single case of assault was ever recorded or ever occurred in the South during that period.   Here is cause for reflection for the philanthropist: The negro under a condition of servitude, acknowledging his subordination to his superiors, is well mannered and contains himself within the bounds of perfect and unfaltering respect for the white race, even when no one is near to make him afraid.   The same negro, with the supposed advantages of freedom and education, after the expenditure of much money and time in the effort to elevate him, becomes a wild beast and a terror, a prey to uncontrollable passion.   How shall this be explained ?   Is it not fairly chargeable to the vicious legislation at the close of the war,—by which it was sought to humiliate the people of the South,—to the unqualified enfranchisement of the blacks and to the corrupt teaching of the meddling and misguided fanatics who came among the negroes and implanted in their minds erroneous and dangerous notions as to their rights and privileges, so that, with vast numbers of them, their conception of freedom is unbridled license, and their tendency to a life of idleness, immorality, and crime is truly sad and disheartening.

CHAPTER XXI

GENERAL LEE'S ARMY ON SHORT RATIONS

THE condition of affairs with the army at this period was most trying and pitiable. In reporting operations in front of Petersburg on the 8th of February, 1865, General Lee wrote to the Secretary of War:

All the disposable force of the right wing of the army has been operating against the enemy beyond Hatcher's Run since Sunday. Yesterday, the most inclement day of the winter, the men had to be retained in line of battle, having been in the same condition the two previous days and nights. I regret to be obliged to state that under these circumstances, heightened by assaults and fire of the enemy, some of the men had been without meat for three days, and all were suffering from reduced rations and scant clothing, exposed to battle, cold, hail, and sleet. I have directed Colonel Cole, chief commissary, who reports that he has not a pound of meat at his disposal, to visit Richmond and see if nothing can be done. If some change is not made and the commissary department reorganized, I apprehend dire results. The physical strength of the men, if their courage survives, must fail under this treatment. Our cavalry has to be dispersed for want of forage. Fitz. Lee's and Lomax's divisions are scattered because supplies cannot be transported where their services are required. I had to bring William H. F. Lee's division forty miles Sunday night to get him in position. Taking these facts in consideration with the paucity of our numbers, you must not be surprised if calamity befalls us.

When this letter was submitted to President Davis for perusal, he indorsed it: "This is too sad to be patiently considered, and cannot have occurred without criminal neglect or gross incapacity. Let supplies be had by purchase, or borrowing, or other possible mode."

As time progressed the enemy continued in the effort to obtain possession of the South Side and the Danville railroads. There was an encounter between the opposing forces almost daily on our right, as the enemy attempted to envelop that flank. With the view of relieving the situation at that point, and anticipating General Grant's purpose to move in heavy force in that direction, for which orders were actually issued on the 24th of March, General Lee directed General Gordon on the 25th to assail the enemy's lines in his front at Fort Stedman, on our left, near the Appomattox River. At the appointed hour, daylight on the 25th, General Gordon moved out of the trenches, assaulted and carried the enemy's works at Hare's Hill, captured nine pieces of artillery, eight mortars, between five and six hundred prisoners, including one brigadier-general and a number of officers of lower grade. The veterans under Gordon swept the enemy's lines for a distance of five hundred yards to the right and left, and repulsed two efforts made to recover the captured works. General Gordon here found himself confronted by an inclosed line in rear, commanding the enemy's main line now held by his troops, which could only be taken at great sacrifice, and he withdrew his troops to their original position.

The attack was gallantly made. All the troops behaved most handsomely, and General Lee especially commended the conduct of the sharp-shooters of Gordon's corps, who led the assault.

But of what avail was it? Our loss was reported as inconsiderable at the time, and so it was in killed and wounded; but many men were left in the enemy's lines,

—General Grant reported nineteen hundred captured,— and this was a severe and irreparable loss. Our lines, already greatly attenuated, were made that much weaker, and the intervals had to be still more prolonged. No doubt the movement caused some delay in the execution of the plans of General Grant, and caused him to be more careful to provide a sufficiently strong force to hold his lines while his flanking movement was in progress of execution; but what did that amount to when the besiegers were to the besieged in the ratio of four to one!

On the 30th of March it was ascertained that a movement in force was being made by the enemy on our right, as if to get possession of the White Oak Road; this continued on the 31st, when two brigades, McGowan's and Gracie's, under General McGowan, were advanced to intercept the enemy, that proved to be Warren's Fifth Army Corps. The hostile forces, each advancing, were soon in close contact, and a fierce engagement ensued. The impetuosity of the Confederates was such as to check the advance of the Federals and drive back their first line upon their supports. The frenzy of battle seemed to have taken possession of the Southerners, and I never took part in nor witnessed a more spirited and successful assault. Two lines of the enemy were forced to give way and retire in confusion, when fresh troops were encountered, and in such force as to prevent our further advance. In his report General Grant says:

General Warren reported favorably as to his ability to get possession of the White Oak Road, and was ordered to do so. To accomplish this he moved with one division instead of his whole corps, which was attacked by the enemy in superior (?) force and was driven back on the Second Division before it had time to form, and it, in turn, was forced back upon the Third Division, when the enemy was checked.

The counterstroke of the Confederates had thus disconcerted the movements of Warren's corps and deranged the Federals' plans; and on the same day the Confederate cavalry, under General Fitzhugh Lee, reinforced by five small brigades of infantry under General Pickett, had forced General Sheridan, who was endeavoring with his corps of cavalry to seize the South Side Railroad, back to Dinwiddie Court House. But these checks to the enemy were but temporary; more troops were moved to the threatened points, and the movement in force to our right continued.

On the 1st of April General Sheridan with his corps of cavalry, now reinforced by Warren's corps of three divisions of infantry, again advanced upon our position at Five Forks, on our extreme right. General Pickett held this portion of our lines with five small brigades of infantry, three of his own division and two of Bushrod Johnson's; on his right was W. H. F. Lee's division of cavalry; one regiment of Munford's command was on his left, uniting with the pickets of General Roberts's command, which filled the gap between this force and the troops at Burgess's Mill; all the cavalry being under the command of General Fitzhugh Lee. Late in the evening the Federals advanced in overwhelming numbers, quickly enveloped the left flank of Pickett's division, rolled it up as a scroll, captured a large portion of it and utterly dispersed the remainder. It was simply a case of extinguishment by an avalanche of overwhelming numbers.

The attenuation of our line had become extreme,—at many points a mere skirmish line,—and it was only a question of where the pressure would be applied, for there the break must certainly result.

On April 2d a general advance was made on our lines in front of Petersburg. The best possible resistance was made, but our brave men were unable to do more than check and delay the advance of the enemy, and it now became evident that unless we abandoned our position, what remained of our army at Petersburg would be captured.

General Lee notified the authorities at Richmond of the condition of affairs and of the necessity for abandoning his lines that night. In a telegram to the Secretary of War he said:

It is absolutely necessary that we should abandon our position to-night, or run the risk of being cut off in the morning. I have given all the orders to officers on both sides of the river, and have taken every precaution that I can to make the movement successful. It will be a difficult operation, but I hope not impracticable. Please give all orders that you find necessary in and about Richmond. The troops will all be directed to Amelia Court House.

I was kept busy, with the aid of a telegraph operator, in issuing the orders necessary to successfully carry out the proposed evacuation of our lines and of the city of Richmond. Our headquarters were then at the house of Mr. William Turnbull on the Cox Road, about two and a half miles from the city of Petersburg. During the day this position became untenable. I held on as long as I could, until the shells of the enemy began to crash through the house. The operator informed me that he could no longer work his instrument, when I directed him to detach it and take it with him, and we left the premises as the enemy's infantry advanced and drove away a battery of our artillery near the house. I mounted my horse and the operator mounted the one I had provided for him, when, in compliance with my instructions, he turned his horse to ride to the rear with the view of getting into Petersburg. He had not proceeded far when a shell took off his horse's legs and sent him sprawling on the ground with his telegraphic instrument; he quickly gathered himself and instrument together, and the last I saw of him he was making very good time for the city. The comfortable dwelling of Mr. Turnbull, occupied by General Lee as his headquarters, and thus hastily evacuated by the rear-guard of his military family, was soon enveloped in flames. It is to be hoped that the fire was accidental; by General Lee it was then thought and feared to have been by design. One of the many arguments always advanced by him why he should not occupy a house was, that in event of its falling into the hands of the enemy, the very fact of its having been occupied by him might possibly cause its destruction; and, as before stated, it was only during the last year of the war, when his health was somewhat impaired, that he consented to occupy a private house.

I soon joined General Lee, whom I found in company with General A. P. Hill, investigating the movements of a body of troops of whose identity they were uncertain. General Hill rode forward to ascertain what troops they were, accompanied only by his trusted courier, Sergeant George W. Tucker. They proceeded to a point where they observed a body of men near the site of the recently vacated headquarters of General Heth, who commanded one of Hill's divisions. Coming suddenly upon two Federal soldiers, Sergeant Tucker put spurs to his horse, ordering them to surrender. They sheltered themselves behind a large tree and raised their muskets. Seeing the imminent danger of his sergeant, General Hill rode forward to his assistance in a chivalrous purpose to save or share the dangers of the brave Tucker, when, as he reached his side, the enemy fired. General Hill fell from his horse, dead, and Sergeant Tucker, catching the riderless horse of his general, rode back into our lines and reported the presence of the enemy and the killing of General Hill.*

Thus terminated the career of one of the most brilliant and successful leaders in the Southern army. From the day he crossed the Chickahominy at Mechanicsville, in June, 1862, and opened the attack on the army under General McClellan, to the day of his death, he was a constant and reliable support to General Lee in the operations of his army. Every chapter in the history of the Army of Northern Virginia is illumined with the story of the gallant and successful conduct of the troops under his command; and the record of the series of brilliant operations on our right in the siege of the city of Petersburg in the spring of 1865, in resisting the extension of the lines of the army under General Grant, may be said to be a diary of the command of A. P. Hill.

It is a singular fact, worthy of record, that in the last moments of both General Jackson and General Lee, when the mind wandered, in the very shadow of death, each should have uttered a command to A. P. Hill, the beloved and trusted lieutenant—ever ready, ever sure and reliable, always prompt to obey and give the desired support. When the strife was fiercest they were wont to call on Hill.

The troops that fired on General Hill were the skirmishers of the Federal line of battle which now advanced. Our line was so thin that it had been penetrated with little opposition and so little excitement that the fact was not made known to either General Lee or General Hill.

The enemy had now cut off those of our forces that were beyond Hatcher's Run, and after a gallant resistance, notably at Fort Gregg and Fort Whitworth, what remained of the army was retired to the interior line of

---

* The Provost Guard of the Third Corps was promptly sent forward and recovered the body of the dead general.

defense around the city of Petersburg prepared for such a contingency. This line was successfully maintained until night.

The deportment of General Lee at that time was such as to excite the admiration of all about him. Self-contained and serene, he acted as one who was conscious of having accomplished all that was possible in the line of duty, and who was undisturbed by the adverse conditions in which he found himself. There was no apparent excitement and no sign of apprehension as he issued his orders for the retreat of his sadly reduced army and the relinquishment of the position so long and successfully held against the greatly superior force opposed to him. As I received his directions for the orders for the evacuation of our lines, I was impressed by the calm demeanor of the man who was the cynosure of the eyes of the people of the South at that critical hour, and who realized more thoroughly than any other the desperate and forlorn character of the work still before him, and yet who neglected nothing in arranging the details for the execution of the delicate operation of removing his little army from the clutches of his powerful antagonist before the dawn of another day.

It was a striking illustration of Christian fortitude, the result of an habitual endeavor to faithfully perform the duties of one's station, and of unquestioning trust in the decree of an all-wise Creator, whose ways are not as man's ways, and in reliance upon whose wisdom and goodness alone one finds strength for every emergency.

The order for the evacuation of our lines and retreat read as follows:

HEADQUARTERS, ARMY OF NORTHERN VIRGINIA,
April 2, 1865.

General Longstreet's corps and General Hill's corps will cross the pontoon bridge at Battersea Factory and take the River

Road, north side of Appomattox, to Bevils's Bridge to-night. General Gordon's corps will cross at Pocahontas and Railroad bridges, his troops taking the Hickory Road, following General Longstreet to Bevils's Bridge, and his wagon-trains taking the Woodpecker Road to Old Colville, endeavoring not to interfere with Mahone's troops from Chesterfield Court House, who will take the same road.

General Mahone's division will take the road to Chesterfield Court House, thence by Old Colville to Goode's Bridge. Mahone's wagons will precede him on the same road, or take some road to his right.

General Ewell's command will cross the James River at and below Richmond, taking the road to Branch Church, via Gregory's, to Genito Road, via Genito Bridge, to Amelia Court House.

The wagons from Richmond will take Manchester Pike and Buckingham Road, via Meadesville, to Amelia Court House.

The movements of all troops will commence at 8 o'clock P.M., the artillery moving out quietly first, infantry following, except the pickets, who will be withdrawn at 3 o'clock A.M. The artillery not required with the troops will be moved by roads prescribed for the wagons, or such other as may be most convenient. Every officer is expected to give his unremitting attention to cause these movements to be made successfully.

After all the infantry and artillery have crossed, Pocahontas and Campbell bridges will be destroyed by the engineers. The pontoon bridge at Battersea Factory and the railroad bridges will be reserved for the pickets. By order of General Lee.

W. H. TAYLOR, A. A. G.

At the close of the day's work, when all was in readiness for the evacuation of our lines under cover of the darkness of night, I asked permission of General Lee to ride over to Richmond and to rejoin him early the next morning, telling him that my mother and sisters were in Richmond and that I would like to say goodby to them, and that my sweetheart was there, and we had arranged, if practicable, to be married that night. He expressed some surprise at my entertaining such a purpose at that time, but when I explained to him that the home of the bride-elect was in the enemy's lines, that she was alone in Richmond and employed in one of the departments of the government, and wished to follow the fortunes of the Confederacy, should our lines be re-established farther South, he promptly gave his assent to my plans. I galloped to the railroad station, then at Dunlops, on the north side of the river, where I found a locomotive and several cars, constituting the "ambulance train," designed to carry to Richmond the last of the wounded of our army requiring hospital treatment. I asked the agent if he had another engine, when, pointing to one rapidly receding in the direction of Richmond, he replied, "Yonder goes the only locomotive we have besides the one attached to this train." Turning my horse over to the courier who accompanied me, with directions to join me in Richmond as soon as he could, I mounted the locomotive in waiting, directed the engineer to detach it from the cars and to proceed to overtake the engine ahead of us. It was what the sailors call a stern chase and a long one. We did not overtake the other locomotive until it had reached Falling Creek, about three fourths of the distance, when I transferred to it and sent the other back to Petersburg. I reached Richmond without further incident, and soon after midnight I was married to Elizabeth Selden Saunders, the daughter of Captain John L. Saunders, who had died in 1860, in the service of his country, a commander in the United States Navy. As will be readily understood, the occasion was not one of great hilarity, though I was very happy; my eyes were the only dry ones in the company. The ceremony was performed by the Rev. Dr. Minnegerode, the rector of St. Paul's Church, in the presence of the members of the two families, then in

Richmond, and a few friends, at the residence of Mr. Lewis D. Crenshaw, on West Main Street.

The people of Richmond were greatly excited and in despair in the contemplation of the abandonment of their beautiful city by our troops. General Lee had for so long a time successfully thwarted the designs of his powerful adversaries for the capture of the city, and seemed so unfailing and resourceful in his efforts to hold them at bay, that the good people found it difficult to realize that he was compelled at last to give way. There was universal gloom and despair at the thought that at the next rising of the sun the detested Federal soldiers would take possession of the city and occupy its streets. The transportation companies were busily engaged in arranging for the removal of the public stores and of the archives of the government. A fire in the lower part of the city was fiercely raging, and added greatly to the excitement.

Somewhere near four o'clock on the morning of the 3d of April I bade farewell to all my dear ones, and in company with my brother-in-law, Colonel John S. Saunders, proceeded toward Mayo's Bridge, which we crossed to the south side of the James in the lurid glare of the fire and within the sound of several heavy explosions that we took to be the final scene in the career of the Confederate navy, then disappearing in smoke on the James River near Rockets.

CHAPTER XXII

THE RETREAT OF THE ARMY UNDER GENERAL LEE

I REJOINED General Lee at an early hour on the morning of the 3d. Our army was then in full retreat, but there was not as much energy displayed by the enemy in the pursuit as the circumstances would lead one to expect, our movements being greatly retarded by the long trains of heavily loaded wagons. Our cavalry, under generals Fitzhugh Lee and W. H. F. Lee, was very active and successful in checking and delaying the advance of the enemy; and it was not until the 6th of April that serious loss was inflicted upon any of our retreating columns.

Our weakness was fully known to the enemy. In a communication to General Sherman, written on the 5th of April, General Grant reported the strength of General Lee's army as "twenty thousand, horse, foot, and dragoons." With the immense force at his command, such a beggarly remnant of an army should have been snuffed out like a candle by an extinguisher.

On the 6th of April General Longstreet's command reached Rice's Station, on the Lynchburg Road. It was followed by the commands of generals R. H. Anderson, Ewell, and Gordon, with orders to close upon it as fast as the progress of the trains would permit, or as they could be diverted on roads farther west. General Anderson, commanding what remained of Pickett's and

Bushrod Johnson's divisions, became disconnected from Mahone's division, forming the rear of Longstreet.*

The cavalry of the enemy, under General Sheridan, penetrated the line of march through the interval thus left and attacked the wagon-train moving toward Farmville, near Sailor's Creek. This caused serious delay in the march of the center and rear of the column, and enabled the Federals, now reinforced by the Sixth Corps of infantry, to mass upon the flank of the disorganized Confederates. After successive attacks Ewell's troops and the small force under R. H. Anderson were completely overwhelmed. Nearly the whole force was captured, including generals Ewell, Kershaw, G. W. C. Lee, and other general officers.

Referring to the operations of this day, General Lee says in his official report:

Gordon, who all the morning, aided by General W. H. F. Lee's cavalry, had checked the advance of the enemy on the road from Amelia Springs and protected the trains, became opposed to his combined assaults, which he bravely resisted and twice repulsed; but the cavalry having been withdrawn to another part of the line of march, the enemy, massing heavily on his front and both flanks, renewed the attack about 6 P.M. and drove him from the field in much confusion. The army continued its march during the night, and every effort was made to reorganize the divisions which had been shattered by the day's operations; but the men being depressed by fatigue and hunger, many threw away their arms, while others followed the wagon-trains and embarrassed their progress.

Several incursions were made by the enemy's cavalry into the line of trains slowly forcing its way along the wretchedly poor roads. During one of these interruptions our headquarters wagons were in danger of being captured. I had caused to be made a light chest with rope

* General Lee's report.

handles, in which were carried the headquarters archives, including order books, letter-copy books, and other valuable documents, and our clerks and guards had been instructed to carry this box off should there be danger of capture of the wagons by the enemy. When the train was raided and cut into near them, the men guarding the valuable books and papers deemed it advisable to destroy them, and the box and contents were burned to prevent their falling into the hands of the enemy. As events proved, a precaution quite unnecessary and occasioning irreparable loss.

It had been a great disappointment to General Lee on reaching Amelia Court House not to find the supplies for his troops that he expected. On the morning of the 7th rations were issued to the troops as they passed Farmville, but even then all were not supplied, as the safety of the supply-wagons required that they be hurried away when the activity of the enemy seemed to endanger them.

The army, now reduced to two corps of infantry, not over ten thousand strong, one under the command of General Longstreet and the other under General Gordon, with the cavalry, continued its march toward Appoamttox Court House, Longstreet's command changed now to rear-guard.

On April 7th General Grant addressed the following to General Lee from Farmville:

GENERAL: The result of the last week must convince you of the hopelessness of further resistance on the part of the Army of Northern Virginia in this struggle. I feel that it is so, and regard it as my duty to shift from myself the responsibility of any further effusion of blood, by asking of you the surrender of that portion of the Confederate States Army known as the Army of Northern Virginia.

U. S. GRANT,
Lieutenant-general.

This reached General Lee, by flag of truce, on the same day. It had then become apparent that we could not hope to save the cumbrous wagon-trains, but it was quite feasible for the small but well-seasoned army then remaining to make good its escape to the mountains of Virginia or North Carolina by abandoning all incumbrances. Such a course, however, promised no permanent advantage and involved the further and useless sacrifice of good men.

In reply General Lee sent the following to General Grant:

April 7, 1865.

GENERAL: I have received your note of this date. Though not entertaining the opinion you express on the hopelessness of further resistance on the part of the Army of Northern Virginia, I reciprocate your desire to avoid useless effusion of blood, and, therefore, before considering your proposition, ask the terms you will offer on condition of its surrender.

R. E. LEE,
General.

On the same day, whether or not previous to this exchange of notes I cannot say, but without any knowledge of it, several of the general officers of our army had a conference, at which it was decided that one of their number should approach General Lee and open up the matter of a surrender of the troops then under his command. The idea seems to have been that further resistance was hopeless, and that by such a procedure on their part General Lee would, in some way, be relieved of responsibility by being forestalled by them in taking the initiative in the matter of surrendering. Their motive was good, no doubt; but from a military point of view their action was quite irregular and open to censure. It is not only correct, but a duty, for one of inferior rank to give his opinion to his superior in even so delicate a matter as this when asked to do so; but it is a very different matter for an inferior, unsolicited, to volunteer his opinion or advice in such a case. General Pendleton, chief of artillery, was designated as spokesman to convey to General Lee the sense of the officers taking part in the conference; and his report of the interview with General Lee shows that the latter accepted the suggestion in the spirit in which it was offered. Neither General Longstreet nor General Gordon took part in the conference, and the former, in his Memoirs, repudiates all connection with the matter and expresses his disapproval in very positive terms.

On the 8th of April General Grant sent the following reply to General Lee's note of the 7th:

GENERAL: Your note of last evening in reply to mine of the same date, asking the condition on which I will accept the surrender of the Army of Northern Virginia, is just received. In reply I would say that peace being my great desire, there is but one condition I would insist upon, namely, that the men and officers surrendered shall be disqualified for taking up arms again against the government of the United States until properly exchanged. I will meet you, or will designate officers to meet any officers you might name for the same purpose, at any point agreeable to you, for the purpose of arranging definitely the terms upon which the surrender of the Army of Northern Virginia will be received.

U. S. GRANT,
Lieutenant-general.

To which General Lee replied at once as follows:

April 8, 1865.

GENERAL: I received at a late hour your note of to-day. In mine of yesterday I did not intend to propose the surrender of the Army of Northern Virginia, but to ask the terms of your proposition. To be frank, I do not think the emergency has arisen to call for the surrender of this army, but as the restora-

tion of peace should be the sole object of all, I desired to know whether your proposals would lead to that end. I cannot, therefore, meet you with a view to surrender of the Army of Northern Virginia, but as far as your proposal may affect the Confederate States forces under my command, and tend to the restoration of peace, I should be pleased to meet you at 10 A.M. to-morrow on the Old Stage Road to Richmond, between the picket lines of the two armies.   R. E. LEE,
                                                    General.

Two months previous to this General Lee had been made general-in-chief of all the armies of the Confederate States. General Grant, in like manner, had been assigned to the command of all the armies of the United States. I have always thought that it was then General Lee's desire to discuss with General Grant the terms upon which all the armies of the Confederate States should lay down their arms. As has been previously stated in this narrative, General Lee entertained a similar purpose when he proposed to meet General Grant at Petersburg. He rightly divined that there would be far greater reason to hope for real peace and the restoration of good feeling between the two sections of the country, under the conditions likely to be agreed upon between the two commanders of the armies in the field, who had learned to respect each other, than could be hoped for if the terms of a restoration of the Union were left to the determination of the politicians of the successful side.

General Lee had given orders that the march should be resumed at 1 A.M. on the 9th. General Fitzhugh Lee, with his cavalry, supported by the infantry under General Gordon, was ordered to drive the enemy from his front, wheel to the left, and cover the passage of the trains, while General Longstreet, whose command then formed the rear-guard, was to close up and hold the position.

Two battalions of artillery and the ammunition-wagons were directed to move with the army; the rest of the artillery and wagons were ordered to move toward Lynchburg. There was considerable activity during the night. Walker's artillery train was attacked near Appomattox Station, but the enemy was repulsed, and a force of Federal cavalry dashed toward the court-house, but the movement was checked by our line of battle. In consequence of indications of a large force being massed on our left and front, General Fitzhugh Lee was directed to ascertain its strength, and to suspend his advance until daylight if necessary. About 5 A.M. on the 9th he moved forward, and soon encountered a heavy force of the enemy opposite Gordon's right and moving in the direction of Appomattox Court House. This force was vigorously assailed by General Fitzhugh Lee's cavalry on its left flank, and by the troops of General Gordon in front. The enemy was driven back by the impetuosity of this attack. Very soon, however, a large force of infantry advanced upon General Gordon's right and rear, and at the same time a body of the enemy's cavalry appeared on the hills on his left, threatening to interpose between his command and that of General Longstreet. General Gordon thereupon withdrew across the Appomattox River, with Roberts's cavalry brigade of General W. H. F. Lee's division on his right; but not before the brave men of that command had charged upon a Federal battery and captured three guns and moved them safely within our lines, where they were turned over by General E. P. Alexander, chief of artillery of Longstreet's corps, to the men of Captain James N. Lamkin's battery, who had served mortars in our lines about Petersburg, but who had been anxious to secure field-guns since the evacuation of that place.

The rest of the cavalry, under General Fitzhugh Lee,

advanced on the Lynchburg Road and became separated from the army.

In his official report General Fitzhugh Lee says:

Upon hearing that the Army of Northern Virginia had surrendered, the men were generally dispersed and rode off to their homes, subject to reassembling for a continuation of the struggle. I rode out in person with a portion of W. H. F. Lee's division, the nearest to me at the time, and previous to the negotiations between the commanders of the two armies. It will be recalled that my action was in accordance with the views I had expressed in the council the night before—that if a surrender was compelled the next day, I would try to extricate the cavalry, provided it could be done without compromising the action of the commanding general, but that I would not avail myself of a cessation of hostilities pending the existence of a flag of truce. I had an understanding with General Gordon that he should communicate to you the information of the presence of the enemy's infantry upon the road in our front. Apart from the fond though forlorn hope that future operations were still in store for the cavalry, I was desirous that they should not be included in the capitulations, because the ownership of their horses was vested in themselves, and I deemed it doubtful that terms would be offered allowing such ownership to continue.

CHAPTER XXIII

APPOMATTOX

ON learning of the condition of affairs at the front, General Lee concluded that the time had arrived for him to seek General Grant with a view to surrender.

I had been sent by General Lee on the evening of the 8th to take charge of the long wagon-trains that so embarrassed us, to do what was possible to expedite their movements and to see that they were parked safely for the night. The night was spent in this endeavor, and my experience in the performance of this duty caused me to realize that if we persisted in the effort to save the wagons, the end was very near.

I did not rejoin General Lee until the next morning.

After making my report the general said to me, "Well, colonel, what are we to do?"

In reply, a fear was expressed that it would be necessary to abandon the trains, which had already occasioned us such great embarrassment; and the hope was indulged that, relieved of this burden, the army could make good its escape.

"Yes," said the general, "perhaps we could; but I have had a conference with these gentlemen around me, and they agree that the time has come for capitulation."

"Well, sir," I said, "I can only speak for myself; to me any other fate is preferable."

"Such is my individual way of thinking," interrupted the general.

"But," I immediately added, "of course, general, it is different with you. You have to think of these brave men and decide not only for yourself, but for them."

"Yes," he replied, "it would be useless and therefore cruel to provoke the further effusion of blood, and I have arranged to meet General Grant with a view to surrender, and wish you to accompany me."

Shortly after this, General Lee, accompanied by Colonel Marshall and myself, with a courier carrying a flag of truce, started by the Old Stage Road to meet General Grant between the lines of the two armies, as proposed by General Lee in his communication of the previous day. We passed our picket line in the rear and were soon met by Colonel Whittier, of General Humphreys's staff, who delivered to General Lee a communication from General Grant reading as follows:

April 9, 1865.

GENERAL: Your note of yesterday is received. I have no authority to treat on the subject of peace; the meeting proposed for 10 A.M. to-day could lead to no good. I will state, however, general, that I am equally anxious for peace with yourself; and the whole North entertains the same feeling. The terms upon which peace can be had are well understood. By the South laying down their arms, they will hasten that most desirable event, save thousands of human lives, and hundreds of millions of property not yet destroyed. Seriously hoping that all our difficulties may be settled without the loss of another life, I subscribe myself, etc.,

U. S. GRANT,
Lieutenant-general.

To which General Lee sent the following reply:

April 9, 1865.

LIEUTENANT-GENERAL U. S. GRANT—

GENERAL: I received your note of this morning on the picket line, whither I had come to meet you and ascertain definitely what terms were embraced in your proposal of yesterday with reference to the surrender of this army. I now ask an interview in accordance with the offer contained in your letter of yesterday for that purpose.

R. E. LEE,
General.

General Lee was informed by Colonel Whittier that General Grant had gone to join General Sheridan on the Appomattox front, and that it would take some time to communicate with him. Some hesitancy was manifested on the part of the commanding officers of the Federal advance in the matter of suspending operations pending the receipt of orders from General Grant; this was soon adjusted, however, when the character of General Lee's last note to General Grant was made known. General Lee, accompanied by Colonel Marshall and myself, then returned to our lines, and proceeded to the rear of the position held by the troops of General Gordon, when General Lee dismounted at an apple orchard and took a seat under one of the trees.

Meanwhile, an informal truce had been called between the two opposing forces, and it was pretty generally known by the troops that negotiations for surrender were pending. At this juncture, General Forsyth of General Sheridan's staff, accompanied by a staff-officer of General Gordon, rode up to General Lee and reported that he had come by order of General Sheridan to say that as he had doubt as to his authority to recognize the informal truce which had been agreed upon between General Gordon and himself, he desired to communicate with General Meade on the subject, and wished permission for General Forsyth to pass through our lines as the shortest route. I was assigned to the duty of escorting General Forsyth through our lines. I proceeded as far as the Federal outposts, where I met General Miles and staff, while General Forsyth went within the lines in search of General Meade. His mission was soon accomplished, and together we returned to our point of starting, when he crossed through our lines to those of the enemy.

Soon after this, General Babcock of General Grant's staff, accompanied by a Confederate staff-officer, rode to where General Lee was, dismounted, saluted, and announced that he was sent by General Grant to escort General Lee to some point convenient for the proposed interview, at the same time handing to General Lee a communication from General Grant, which read as follows:

April 9, 1865.

GENERAL R. E. LEE, COMMANDING:

Your note of this date is but this moment (11.30 A.M.) received, in consequence of my having passed from the Richmond and Lynchburg road to the Farmville and Lynchburg road. I am at this writing about four miles west of Walker's Church, and will push forward to the front for the purpose of meeting you. Notice sent to me on this road where you wish the interview to take place will meet me.

Very respectfully, your obedient servant,

U. S. GRANT,

Lieutenant-general.

General Lee at once mounted his horse, and, accompanied by Colonel Marshall, rode with General Babcock to Appomattox Court House. He was soon joined by General Grant, and after a short conference in the house of Mr. Wilmer McLean, the two agreed upon the terms of surrender as set forth in the following correspondence:

APPOMATTOX COURT HOUSE, VA.,

April 9, 1865.

GENERAL R. E. LEE—

GENERAL: In accordance with the substance of my letter to you of the 8th instant, I propose to receive the surrender of the

Army of Northern Virginia on the following terms, to wit: Rolls of all the officers and men to be made in duplicate, one copy to be given to an officer to be designated by me, the other to be retained by such officer or officers as you may designate. The officers to give their individual paroles not to take up arms against the government of the United States until properly exchanged; and each company or regimental commander sign a like parole for the men of their commands.

The arms, artillery, and public property to be parked and stacked, and turned over to the officers appointed by me to receive them.

This will not embrace the side-arms of the officers, nor their private horses or baggage. This done, each officer and man will be allowed to return to his home, not to be disturbed by United States authority as long as they observe their paroles and the laws in force where they may reside.

U. S. GRANT,

Lieutenant-general.

To which General Lee made reply as follows:

HEADQUARTERS ARMY OF NORTHERN VIRGINIA,

April 9, 1865.

LIEUTENANT-GENERAL U. S. GRANT—

GENERAL: I have received your letter of this date containing the terms of surrender of the Army of Northern Virginia as proposed by you. As they are substantially the same as those expressed in your letter of the 8th instant, they are accepted.

I will proceed to designate the proper officers to carry the stipulations into effect.

R. E. LEE,

General.

General Lee thus states the result of the conference in his official report:

In the interview which occurred with General Grant in compliance with my request, terms having been agreed on, I surren-

dered that portion of the Army of Northern Virginia which was
on the field, with its arms, artillery, and wagon-trains, the officers and men to be paroled retaining their side-arms and private
effects.

I deemed this course the best under all the circumstances by
which we were surrounded. On the morning of the 9th, according to the reports of the ordnance officers, there were 7892
organized infantry with arms, with an average of seventy-five
rounds of ammunition per man. The artillery, though reduced
to sixty-three pieces, with ninety-three rounds of ammunition,
was sufficient. These comprised all the supplies of ordnance
that could be relied on in the State of Virginia. I have no
accurate report of the cavalry, but believe it did not exceed
2100 effective men. The enemy were more than five times our
numbers.

If we could have forced our way one day longer, it would
have been at a great sacrifice of life, and at its end I did not see
how a surrender could have been avoided. We had no subsis-
tence for man or horse, and it could not be gathered in the
country. The supplies ordered to Pamplin's Station from
Lynchburg could not reach us, and the men, deprived of food
and sleep for many days, were worn out and exhausted.

Attrition had done its work—the career of the Army
of Northern Virginia was closed and its banners furled;
but the record of its achievements glows with undiminished splendor and constrains the admiration of the
world,

CHAPTER XXIV

GENERAL LEE'S FAREWELL ADDRESS TO HIS ARMY

THE next day General Lee issued the following farewell address to his army:

HEADQUARTERS ARMY OF NORTHERN VIRGINIA,
April 10, 1865.

GENERAL ORDER NO. 9.

After four years of arduous service marked by unsurpassed courage and fortitude, the Army of Northern Virginia has been compelled to yield to overwhelming numbers and resources.

I need not tell the survivors of so many hard-fought battles who have remained steadfast to the last that I have consented to this result from no distrust of them; but feeling that valor and devotion could accomplish nothing that would compensate for the loss that must have attended the continuance of the contest, I determined to avoid the useless sacrifice of those whose past service have endeared them to their countrymen. By the terms of the agreement, officers and men can return to their homes and remain until exchanged.

You may take with you the satisfaction that proceeds from the consciousness of duty faithfully performed, and I earnestly pray that a merciful God will extend to you His blessing and protection.

With an unceasing admiration of your constancy and devotion to your country, and a grateful remembrance of your kind and generous consideration of myself, I bid you all an affectionate farewell.

R. E. LEE,
General.

Rations were at once issued to the Confederate troops by order of General Grant and hunger was appeased.

The following agreement was entered into by the officers designated by the commanders of the two armies to arrange the details of the surrender:

APPOMATTOX COURT HOUSE, VA.,

April 10, 1865.

Agreement entered into this day in regard to the surrender of the Army of Northern Virginia to the United States authorities:

1. The troops shall march by brigades and detachments to a designated point, stack their arms, deposit their flags, sabers, pistols, etc., and thence march to their homes, under charge of their officers, superintended by their respective division and corps commanders, officers retaining their side-arms and the authorized number of private horses.

2. All public horses, and public property of all kinds, to be turned over to staff-officers to be designated by the United States authorities.

3. Such transportation as may be agreed upon as necessary for the transportation of the private baggage of officers will be allowed to accompany the officers, to be turned over, at the end of the trip, to the nearest United States quartermaster, receipts being taken for the same.

4. Couriers and mounted men of the artillery and cavalry, whose horses are their own private property, will be allowed to retain them.

5. The surrender of the Army of Northern Virginia shall be construed to include all the forces operating with that army on the 8th instant, the date of the commencement of the negotiations for surrender, except such bodies of cavalry as actually made their escape previous to the surrender, and except, also, such pieces of artillery as were more than twenty miles from

Appomattox Court House at the time of the surrender on the 9th instant.

(Signed)   JOHN GIBBON, Maj.-gen. U. S. Vol.

CHARLES GRIFFIN, Brevet Maj.-gen.U.S.Vol.

W. MERRITT, Brevet Maj.-gen. U. S. A.

J. LONGSTREET, Lieut.-gen. C. S. A.

J. B. GORDON, Maj.-gen. C. S. A.

W. N. PENDLETON,

Brig.-gen. and Chief of Artillery, C. S. A.

On April 10th the work of paroling the army was begun and consumed several days.

The following parole was signed by General Lee and the members of his staff:

We, the undersigned prisoners of war belonging to the Army of Northern Virginia, having been this day surrendered by General R. E. Lee, commanding said army, to Lieutenant-general Grant, commanding the armies of the United States, do hereby give our solemn parole of honor that we will not hereafter serve the armies of the Confederate States, or in any military capacity whatever against the United States of America, or render aid to the enemies of the latter, until properly exchanged in such manner as shall be mutually approved by the relative authorities.

R. E. LEE, General.

W. H. TAYLOR, Lieut.-col. and A. A. G.

CHARLES S. VENABLE,

Lieut.-col. and A. A. G. (serving as aide)

CHARLES MARSHALL,

Lieut.-col. and A. A. G. (serving as aide)

H. E. PEYTON,

Lieut.-col. and A. A. & I. Gen.

GILES B. COOKE,

Major and A. A. & I. Gen.

H. E. YOUNG, Major and A. A. & I. Gen.

Done at Appomattox Court House, Va., the ninth (9th) day of April, 1865.

The parole was countersigned as follows:

The above-named officers will not be disturbed by United States authorities as long as they observe their parole and the laws in force where they may reside.

GEORGE H. SHARPE,
General and Assistant Provost Marshal.

In addition to the officers whose names are signed above, the following were serving on the staff of General Lee and were paroled at Appomattox:

General W. N. PENDLETON, Chief of Artillery.
Lieut.-col. JAS. L. CORLEY, Chief Quartermaster.
Lieut.-col. R. G. COLE, Chief Commissary.
Lieut.-col. B. G. BALDWIN, Chief of Ordnance.
Surgeon LAFAYETTE GUILD, Chief Surgeon.

Each officer and soldier was furnished for his protection from arrest or annoyance with a slip of paper containing his parole, signed by his commander and countersigned by an officer of the Federal army.

I signed these paroles for all members of the staff, and when my own case was reached I requested General Lee to sign mine, which I have retained to the present time. It reads as follows:

APPOMATTOX COURT HOUSE, VA.,
April 10, 1865.

THE BEARER, Lieut.-col. W. H. Taylor, A. A. General of A. N. Va., a paroled prisoner of the Army of Northern Virginia, has permission to go to his home, and there remain undisturbed.

R. E. LEE,
General.

It is countersigned by George H. Sharpe, Asst. Provost Marshal General, U. S. A.

On April the 12th, I think it was, General Lee started on his journey to Richmond, accompanied by colonels Venable and Marshall and myself. Colonel Venable soon left us and went to rejoin his family in Prince Edward County.

We had one headquarters wagon containing our personal effects; also the general's ambulance, driven by the trustworthy Butt, and our mess was still looked after by our steward "Bryan" Lynch.

We pitched our tent and went into camp for the night as usual, while making the journey. Though in a sense a memorable trip, it was attended with no unwonted incident; the conversation was free and of a general character. We had about exhausted the subject of the surrender and its consequences at Appomattox; and the mind of each of the party was no doubt filled with thoughts of the future. General Lee in his intercourse then with those around him, and in his letters written later, counseled all to go home, to take up such work as offered, and to accept the conditions necessary to enable them to take part in the government. It was not a time for useless repining.

On the route General Lee stopped for the night near the residence of his brother, Mr. Carter Lee, in Powhatan County; and although importuned by his brother to pass the night under his roof, the general persisted in pitching his tent by the side of the road and going into camp as usual. This continued self-denial can only be explained upon the hypothesis that he desired to have his men know that he shared their privations to the very last.

We reached the city of Richmond on the 15th of April, and the general quietly proceeded to the house on Franklin Street then occupied by his family.

The city was occupied by Federal troops, but all was quiet and no demonstration attended General Lee's return. I have always considered it a magnanimous thing on the part of General Grant that he did not even go to Richmond at that time. There was no triumphal march led by the victorious general, nor any attempt or act on his part to humiliate or wound the feelings of the supporters of the lost cause.

In June of the same year a United States grand jury at Norfolk indicted Mr. Davis and General Lee for treason. I immediately informed General Lee of the fact, and at the same time expressed a regret that some of our young men were discouraged at not being able to obtain employment, and many, in consequence, talked of migrating to other countries. He replied as follows:

RICHMOND, VA., June 17, 1865.

MY DEAR COLONEL: I am very much obliged to you for your letter of the 13th. I had heard of the indictment by the grand jury at Norfolk, and made up my mind to let the authorities take their course. I have no wish to avoid any trial the government may order, and cannot flee. I hope others may be un-molested, and that you at least may be undisturbed.

I am sorry to hear that our returned soldiers cannot obtain employment. Tell them they must all set to work, and if they cannot do what they prefer, do what they can. Virginia wants all their aid, all their support, and the presence of all her sons to sustain and recuperate her. They must therefore put them-selves in a position to take part in her government, and not be deterred by obstacles in their way. There is much to be done which they only can do.

Very truly yours,

R. E. LEE.

COLONEL W. H. TAYLOR.

But two months had elapsed since the surrender at Appomattox—not a sufficient time for the subsidence of the passion engendered by war and the healing of the wounds occasioned by defeat; the hearts of the people of the South were yet filled with resentment and bitter hatred toward their Northern adversaries—and yet he, their greatest captain, counseled a prompt and ready acquiescence in the inevitable, urging his countrymen not to be deterred by seeming obstacles from resuming their citizenship with all its obligations—that is, not to flinch from a compliance with distasteful requirements, but to conform to all legal enactments to enable them to resume the reins of the government of their State, and thus save her from adventurous aliens, and consequent spoliation and ruin.

As soon as the indictment against General Lee was made known, General Grant, as was understood in the South, notified the Federal authorities at Washington that under the terms of the surrender of the Army of Northern Virginia, as agreed to by him, General Lee could not be disturbed or interfered with so long as he observed the laws of his State, and this effectually estopped all court proceedings so far as they concerned General Lee.

In the case of Mr. Davis the authorities deliberated, delayed, and finally refused to push the proceedings. Mr. Davis would have welcomed a trial, for he well knew that the argument was all on the side of the South, and a recognition of this fact deterred those in power who were best acquainted with the constitutional questions involved from any real attempt to prove treason.

APPENDIX

[COPY]

THE FORCES AT GETTYSBURG

(A supplementary note from Colonel Taylor correcting some disputed figures.)

To the Editor of "The Times" (Philadelphia):

As my account of the battle of Gettysburg was first given to the public in your columns, I respectfully ask space therein sufficient to make the following explanation and correction of the statement then made of the strength of the Confederate army in that campaign.

I would premise with the mention of the fact that two kinds of returns of the strength of the army were required to be made to the department during the war: the one a "field return," made twice a month—on the 10th and 20th—and the other a "monthly return," made on the last day of each month. In the field returns there was a column for the "officers present for duty" and one for "enlisted men present for duty;" the sum of the two would give the "effective total," as generally understood —that is, the fighting strength.

THE MONTHLY REPORTS

In the monthly reports the arrangement was different; there was a column for each grade of officers, both of the line and staff, and also a column for sergeants, one for corporals and one for privates—enlisted men. There was then a column headed

" effective total," which embraced only the enlisted men present for duty—that is, the non-commissioned staff, sergeants, corporals, and privates, there being no column for the aggregate of the commissioned officers present for duty.

There are many methods of comparing the strength of opposing armies. The one adopted by me was to take the "effective total," or the sum of the officers and enlisted men present for duty, excluding all consideration of the special or extra duty men, those sick and those in arrest. As this manner of estimating was applied to both armies, it seemed to me the most equitable and satisfactory. In taking notes from the returns on file in the archive office at Washington, I aimed to arrive at the effective total. This, in the "field returns," was readily determined by adding together the officers and enlisted men present for duty; but in the case of the "monthly reports" it was a very natural error for one to take the addition of the column headed "effective total" as representing the effective strength. Now it so happened that the basis of my estimate of the strength of General Lee's army at Gettysburg was the *monthly report* of the 31st of May, 1863, and not a *field return*. I therefore took the total amount of the column headed "effective total," viz., 68,352, as representing what is generally understood by that term, and under the impression that the extensions under that column embraced the officers and men present for duty. I was the more naturally led into this error as Mr. Swinton, whose figures I had before me, had done precisely the same thing. Lieutenant-general Early, having directed my attention on the 9th instant to the discrepancy between certain figures given by General Humphreys from the same return to the Count de Paris and my own, and having expressed his apprehension that I took the figures from the column headed "effective total," inasmuch as, excluding the cavalry, the strength of the army as taken from the field return of the 20th of May, 1863, was greater than that taken from the monthly report of the 31st of May, 1863, I began to suspect that the officers were not included in the estimate given. I at once made application to the War Department for the information necessary to settle the matter, and having been kindly favored with a prompt reply to my request, I have been enabled to review my figures, and find that the estimate of strength on the 31st of May, 1863, does not include the officers present for duty.

LEE'S EFFECTIVE STRENGTH

At that date the effective strength of General Lee's army was as follows: Longstreet's command, 29,171; A. P. Hill's command, 30,286; cavalry, 10,292; artillery, 4702; total effective of all arms, 74,451. And carrying out the same reasoning as that originally pursued, I would say that General Lee had at Gettysburg, including all the cavalry, 67,000 men—that is to say, 53,500 infantry, 9000 cavalry, and 4500 artillery.

Of course this number was not available to him at any one time, as I have previously explained, but I prefer to adopt the greatest number as shown by the *official reports;* and in like manner I would persist in estimating the strength of the Federal army by the statement of General Hooker to General Halleck made on the 27th day of June, to the effect that his whole force of *enlisted men* present for duty would not exceed 105,000.

As General Hooker thus gave only his enlisted men present for duty, perhaps the figures originally given by me as the strength of General Lee's army, viz., 68,352 on the 31st of May, 1863, and 62,000 at Gettysburg, should be employed in the comparison, as they represent also his enlisted men present for duty. For if we add to the 105,000 enlisted men of the Federal army the same proportion of officers as that found in the Confederate army, it would raise the effective strength of the former to fully 115,000 on the 27th of June, four days previous to the battle. View these figures as one will, the disparity in numerical strength is very apparent. Historical accuracy being my aim in all that I have to say upon this subject, I hasten to correct the error into which I have inadvertently fallen along with Mr. Swinton.

Very respectfully,

WALTER H. TAYLOR.

NORFOLK, VA., February 18, 1878.

PRESIDENT PIERCE'S MESSAGE IN 1856

The language of President Pierce, in his message to Congress of December 20, 1856, referred to by General Lee, is so much to the point and so prophetic, that I cannot forbear making the following extract: "Perfect liberty of association for political objects and the widest scope of discussion are the received and ordinary conditions of government in our country. Our institutions, framed in the spirit of confidence in the intelligence and integrity of the people, do not forbid citizens, either individually or associated together, to attack by writing, speech, or any other methods short of physical force, the Constitution and the very existence of the Union. Under the shelter of this great liberty, and protected by the laws and usages of the government they assail, associations have been formed in some of the States of individuals who, pretending to seek only to prevent the spread of the institution of slavery into the present or future inchoate States of the Union, are really inflamed with desire to change the domestic institutions of existing States. To accomplish their objects, they dedicate themselves to the odious task of depreciating the government organization which stands in their way, and of calumniating with indiscriminate invective not only the citizens of particular States with whose laws they find fault, but all others of their fellow citizens throughout the country who do not participate with them in their assaults upon the Constitution, framed and adopted by our fathers, and claiming for the privileges it has secured and the blessings it has conferred the steady support and grateful reverence of their children. They seek an object which they well know to be a revolutionary one. They are perfectly aware that the change in the relative condition of the white and black races in the slave-holding States which they would promote is beyond their lawful authority; that to them it is a foreign object; that it cannot be effected by any peaceful instrumentality of theirs; that for them and the States of which they are citizens the only path to its accomplishment is through burning cities and ravaged fields and slaughtered populations, and all there is most terrible in foreign, complicated with civil and servile, war; and that the first step in the attempt is the forcible disruption of a country embracing in its broad bosom a degree of liberty and an amount of individual and public prosperity to which there is no parallel in history, and substituting in its place hostile governments, driven at once and inevitably into mutual devastation and fratricidal carnage, transforming the now peaceful and felicitous brotherhood into a vast permanent camp of armed men like the rival monarchies of Europe and Asia. Well knowing that such, and such only, are the means and the consequences of their plans and purposes, they endeavor to prepare the people of the United States for civil war by doing everything in their power to deprive the Constitution and the laws of moral authority and to undermine the fabric of the Union by appeals to passion and sectional prejudice, by indoctrinating its people with reciprocal hatred, and by educating them to stand face to face as enemies, rather than shoulder to shoulder as friends. It is by the agency of such unwarrantable interference, foreign and domestic, that the minds of many otherwise good citizens have been so imflamed into the passionate condemnation of the domestic institutions of the Southern States as at length to pass insensibly to almost equally passionate hostility toward their fellow citizens of those States, and thus fall into temporary fellowship with the avowed and active enemies of the Constitution. Ardently attached to liberty in the abstract, they do not stop to consider practically how the objects they would attain can be accomplished, nor to reflect that, even if the evil were as great as they deem it, they have no remedy to apply, and that it can be only aggravated by their violence and unconstitutional action.

" A question which is one of the most difficult of all problems of social institution, political economy, and statesmanship, they treat with unreasoning intemperance of thought and language. Extremes beget extremes. Violent attack from the North finds its inevitable consequence in the growth of a spirit of angry defiance at the South. Thus, in the progress of events, we had reached that consummation, which the voice of the people has now so pointedly rebuked, of the attempt of a portion of the States, by a sectional organization and movement, to usurp the control of the government of the United States."

CORRESPONDENCE CONCERNING A CONVENTION PROPOSED BY GENERAL LEE TO GENERAL GRANT, WITH THE VIEW OF PUTTING AN END TO HOSTILITIES, IN MARCH, 1865

[COPY]

HEADQUARTERS C. S. ARMIES,
March 2, 1865.

LIEUT.-GEN. U. S. GRANT,
Commanding U. S. Armies:

GENERAL: Lieutenant-general Longstreet has informed me that in a recent conversation between himself and Major-general Ord as to the possibility of arriving at a satisfactory adjustment of the present unhappy difficulties by means of a military convention, General Ord stated that if I desired an interview with you on the subject you would not decline, provided I had authority to act. Sincerely desiring to leave nothing untried which may put an end to the calamities of war, I propose to meet you at such convenient time and place as you may designate, with the hope that upon an interchange of views it may be found practicable to submit the subjects of controversy between the belligerents to a convention of the kind mentioned. In such event I am authorized to do whatever the result of the proposed interview may render necessary or advisable. Should you accede to this proposition, I would suggest that, if agreeable to you, we meet at the place selected by generals Ord and Longstreet for their interview at 11 A.M. on Monday next.

Very respectfully, your obedient servant,
R. E. LEE,
General.

CITY POINT, VA., March 3, 1865, 6 P.M.

HON. E. M. STANTON,

Secretary of War, Washington:

The following communication has just been received from General Lee:

[*Here follows General Lee's letter.*]

General Ord met General Longstreet a few days since, at the request of the latter, to arrange for the exchange of citizen prisoners and prisoners of war improperly captured. He had my authority to do so, and to arrange it definitely for such as were confined in his department; arrangements for all others to be submitted for approval. A general conversation ensued on the subject of the war, and has induced the above letter. I have not returned any reply, but promised to do so at 12 M. to-morrow. I respectfully request instructions.

U. S. GRANT,
Lieutenant-general.

WAR DEPARTMENT, March 3, 1865, 12 P.M.

LIEUTENANT-GENERAL GRANT:

The President directs me to say to you that he wishes you to have no conference with General Lee, unless it be for the capitulation of General Lee's army or on some minor and purely military matter. He instructs me to say that you are not to decide, discuss, or confer upon any political question. Such questions the President holds in his own hands, and will submit them to no military conferences or conventions. Meantime you are to press to the utmost your military advantages.

EDWIN M. STANTON,
Secretary of War.

WAR DEPARTMENT, March 3, 1865, 12 P.M.

LIEUTENANT-GENERAL GRANT:

I send you a telegram written by the President himself in answer to yours of this evening, which I have signed by his order. I will add that General Ord's conduct in holding intercourse with General Longstreet upon political questions not committed to his charge is not approved. The same thing was done in one instance by Major Key, when the army was commanded by General McClellan, and he was sent to meet Howell Cobb on the subject of exchanges, and it was in that instance, as in this, disapproved. You will please in future instruct officers appointed to meet rebel officers to confine themselves to the matters specially committed to them.

EDWIN M. STANTON,
Secretary of War.

CITY POINT, VA., March 4, 1865.

GENERAL R. E. LEE,
Commanding C. S. Army:

Your two letters of the 2d inst. were received yesterday. In regard to any apprehended misunderstanding in reference to the exchange of political prisoners, I think there need be none.

In regard to meeting you on the 6th instant, I would state that I have no authority to accede to your proposition for a conference on the subject proposed. Such authority is vested in the President of the United States alone. General Ord could only have meant that I would not refuse an interview on any subject on which I have a right to act, which, of course, would be such as are purely of a military character, and on the subject of exchanges which has been intrusted to me.

U. S. GRANT,
Lieutenant-general.

A FEW PERSONAL LETTERS FROM GENERAL LEE TO THE AUTHOR. GENERAL LEE'S PURPOSE TO WRITE A HISTORY OF THE ARMY OF NORTHERN VIRGINIA

[COPY]

NEAR CARTERSVILLE, July 31, 1865.

MY DEAR COLONEL :

I am desirous that the bravery and devotion of the Army of Northern Virginia shall be correctly transmitted to posterity. This is the only tribute that can now be paid to the worth of its noble officers and soldiers; and I am anxious to collect the necessary data for the history of the campaigns in Virginia from the commencement of its organization to its final surrender. I am particularly anxious that its actual strength in the different battles it has fought be correctly stated. You know all its official returns, records, etc., from the time of my connection with it have been lost or destroyed.

As you prepared the tri-monthly returns for so long, and tested their accuracy, I have thought its gradual changes may have been impressed upon your memory, and that you might state with some confidence its effective strength at each of the great battles it has fought, in infantry, cavalry, and artillery. You may also have some memoranda within your reach that would assist your memory. Please give me at least the benefit of your recollection.

I have been greatly pleased at hearing that you have been elected to the office of registrar of your native city, which has been stated to me to be one of importance and profit. I know you will fill it worthily and satisfactorily.

Please present my kindest regards to your mother, wife, and sisters and brothers, in which I know I would be joined by all the members of my family did they know I was writing.

Very truly yours,

R. E. LEE.

COL. WALTER H. TAYLOR.

LEXINGTON, VA., 25th May, 1866.

MY DEAR COLONEL:

I am very glad to learn by your letter of the 21st that you had seen Mrs. Davis, and to know that you think favorably of her health and spirits. I cannot tell you how much I have suffered and still suffer on account of Mr. Davis and herself. I hope now that attention has been drawn to the subject that greater consideration will be given him, kinder feelings entertained, and the shadow of magnanimity at least be shown him.

I shall be very much obliged to you if you can obtain from Mr. Burton Harrison copies of my correspondence with Mr. Davis, including my letters to him and his to me, if possible. It will be of great use to me and enable me to speak more fully of movements and their results. I hear occasionally of you through Marshall and other friends, and am glad to learn that you are doing well.

Remember me most kindly to your mother, brothers, and sisters, and though you would never show me your wife, tell her I bear toward her the love I feel for you, which I hope she will not refuse.

We are tolerably well. Mrs. Lee, I think, has less pain this spring than the last, but her powers of locomotion are no greater.

Fitzhugh came up with Agnes and is still with us, though he will leave us for the Pamunkey on Monday.

All unite with me in kind regards.

Very truly yours,

R. E. LEE.

COL. WALTER H. TAYLOR.

LEXINGTON, VA., 28th Dec., 1866.

MY DEAR COLONEL:

I received this morning your letter of the 24th accompanying the package of letters given you in New York, for which I am much obliged.

I hope you and yours are well, and that many happy New Years are in store for you.

Our family circle has been enlivened by the addition of the company of my son Robert, and the expectation of seeing Fitzhugh in a few days.

All unite in kindest regards to you, Mrs. Taylor, your mother and sisters.

I fear that Mr. Burton Harrison cannot fulfill his promise of giving me copies of the letters you mentioned, as he says nothing about them.

Yours truly,

R. E. LEE.

COL. WALTER H. TAYLOR.

LEXINGTON, VA., 26th March, 1868.

MY DEAR COLONEL:

The inclosed is a sample of many letters I receive from all the Southern States. You can readily imagine my inability to respond to them in the way the writers desire, and this occurs in so many cases that are known to me, that I am the less able to meet the wants of those who are not.

Mr. and Mrs.——— are unknown to me, but I have thought that if they were deserving, some employment might be obtained for the husband if his condition was known; at any rate, being able to do nothing else, I have determined to refer it to you, in the hope that something may be devised in Norfolk, their present place of refuge.

I hope Mrs. Taylor and your little girl are well.

Please remember me to your mother and sisters, and believe me,

Very truly yours,

R. E. LEE.

COL. WALTER H. TAYLOR.

LEXINGTON, VA., 13th April, 1868.

MY DEAR COLONEL:

The barrel of oysters which you were so kind as to send me by Bryan on the 8th arrived on the night of the 10th, and have converted our Easter celebration into a feast. Besides being excellent in themselves, they were in fine condition, and the oyster-knife, tell Bryan, proved invaluable. Mrs. Lee sends her personal thanks, and our neighbors unite in acknowledgments for the pleasing knowledge you have given them of so excellent a shell-fish.

I am very sorry to hear that you have been sick. Perhaps the attack was produced by a desire to form the immediate acquaintance of that "splendid baby." Give my congratulations to Mrs. T. Tell her I hope that when her fancy for girls is satisfied (mine is exorbitant) she will begin upon the boys. We must have somebody to work for them.

You will have to bring Mrs. Taylor and the babies up to Lexington to see us. I fear I shall never be able to get to Norfolk to see you.

We are all pretty well. Mary and Agnes have been in Baltimore the past winter and are now in Maryland. Mildred has taken care of us and thinks she has a hard time in regulating her brother Custis and three of my brother's children, who are living with us.

Custis looked very knowing when I delivered your message, but did not divulge his plans.

Remember me most kindly to your mother and sisters, your wife, Mrs. Saunders, and all friends, and believe me,

Very truly,

R. E. LEE.

COL. W. H. TAYLOR.

LEXINGTON, VA., 2d Dec., 1869.

MY DEAR COLONEL:

Smith's Island has been bought by my sons Fitzhugh and Robert. They will sell it, but I do not know whether they will lease it. Fitzhugh's P. O. is Tunstal's Station, New Kent Co., Va. I will send him your letter.

I am glad that the oysters are opening well, but you must not trouble yourself to send us any. We live so far up in the mountains that they do not flourish here.

Keep them for those nice little girls at your house, who I know will make sweet wives for some good Virginians. You know I always bespeak the youngest of the flock for my son Custis. Ask Mrs. Taylor to please have one on hand. I am glad to receive the girls if I can get no boys. You must bring them all up to see me in the summer.

Mrs. Lee and my daughters all unite with me in kindest regards to you and yours.

Always yours,

R. E. LEE.

COL. WALTER H. TAYLOR.

LEXINGTON, VA., 16th Dec., 1869.

MY DEAR COL. TAYLOR:

I must wish you, first, a merry Xmas and many happy New Years for yourself, your wife, and all your little children; and may each revolving year shower upon you more blessings than the preceding. Secondly, I must ask your kind offices to procure me some good oysters for New Year's day. Please ask some reliable oysterman to put me up eight gallons of good Hampton or York River oysters and send them by express so as to reach here the 30th or 31st inst. The express freight comes from Staunton every day, and the packet from Lynchburg leaves there every Monday, Wednesday, and Friday afternoons, after the arrival of the Orange train. The latter is the easier route, but the former the more certain, if the agent at Staunton will forward promptly. The canal sometimes freezes inopportunely, and he had better make it certain. Ask him also to send me his bill for oysters and kegs and I will remit him the money.

I like my friends to taste some good oysters in the course of the year, and hence my troubling you.

All send love, and I remain,

Yours most truly,

R. E. LEE.

COL. WALTER H. TAYLOR.

LEXINGTON, VA., 3d Jan., 1870.

MY DEAR COLONEL:

The oysters arrived in the packet-boat on the 30th ulto. all right and in due time and have been much enjoyed. They were finely flavored and as plump as eggs, and this time we had enough for everybody, which is a great thing. I send you with many thanks my check on the Bank of Lexington for $15.50 to your order in payment of Mr. Dobbs's account.

And now I must thank you for your cordial invitation in your letter of the 22d Dec. to Mrs. Lee and myself to visit you. I need not assure you that it would give me great pleasure to do so, for we should both like to see you and Mrs. Taylor and our other friends in Norfolk, but fear it is out of the question, and must repeat that you will have to come and see us and bring Mrs. Taylor with you and the babies too.

Mrs. Lee joins me in kind regards to yourself, wife, mother, and sisters, in which Custis and my daughters unite, and I remain,

Very truly yours,

R. E. LEE.

COL. WALTER H. TAYLOR.